Teachers play a central role in educating our youth but also serve as mentors and supporters. They are uniquely positioned to recognize children who are struggling emotionally. This excellent book provides a priceless resource in helping them to do this effectively and successfully. Every teacher needs to read and study this book.

—*Victor Schwartz, MD, Former CMO of The JED Foundation, Founder of MindStrategies Advisors, Clinical Assoc. Professor, Dept. of Psychiatry, NYU School of Medicine*

Rogers and O'Brien have created a book that brings out the heart and soul of suicide prevention. Reading *Emotionally Naked* is like having a conversation with the smartest person you know. Policy makers, administrators, educators, and parents will walk away hopeful, inspired, and better equipped to address suicide in schools

—*Jonathan B. Singer, PhD, LCSW, President, American Association of Suicidology, Associate Professor, Loyola University Chicago, School of Social Work*

Students of teachers who read this book are fortunate. It is filled with creative and feasible ways teachers can nurture the mental wellness of students and provides concrete and doable suggestions for asking directly about suicide, responding meaningfully, and shepherding classes compassionately after the death of a peer. It is an amazingly practical, accessible, and thoughtful resource.

—*Julie Goldstein Grumet, PhD, Director, Zero Suicide Institute, Education Development Center*

As suicide is the second leading cause of death for our young people, *Emotionally Naked* is a must-read for all who care for the well-being of our children. Sound information, practical advice, superb collection of resources, and written with compassion. We all have a role in suicide prevention and this book focusing on our youth is as informative as it gets.

—*Jerry Reed, PhD, MSW, Senior Vice President for Practice Leadership, Education Development Center*

EMOTIONALLY NAKED

*A Teacher's Guide
to Preventing Suicide and
Recognizing Students at Risk*

ANNE MOSS ROGERS
AND KIMBERLY H. MCMANAMA
O'BRIEN PhD, LICSW

JB JOSSEY-BASS™

A Wiley Brand

Published by Jossey-Bass
A Wiley Brand
111 River Street, Hoboken NJ 07030
www.josseybass.com

Jossey-Bass books and products are available through most bookstores. To contact Jossey-Bass directly call our Customer Care Department within the U.S. at 800-956-7739, outside the U.S. at 317-572-3986, or fax 317-572-4002.

Wiley also publishes its books in a variety of electronic formats and by print-on-demand. Some material included with standard print versions of this book may not be included in e-books or in print-on-demand. For more information about Wiley products, visit www.wiley.com.

Library of Congress Cataloging-in-Publication Data is Available:

ISBN 9781119758303 (Paperback)
ISBN 9781119758297 (ePDF)
ISBN 9781119764823 (ePub)

Cover Design: Paul McCarthy
Cover Art: © Getty Images | A. Martin UW Photography

SKY10028146_071421

Anne Moss Rogers: To Randy, Richard, and my Emotionally Naked tribe, whose love and support helped keep that pilot light of hope burning after my youngest son Charles's suicide.

Kim O'Brien: To the loves of my life—Kevin, Taylor, Mac, Kelly, and Doug. You are the reason my life is full of purpose, love, and happiness.

Contents

About the Authors   xv
Acknowledgments   xvii
Companion Website   xxi
Preface   xxiii
Introduction   xxxi

Chapter 1: Why Are We Seeing More Mental Health Problems with Students?   1
The Rise in Teen Mental
  Health Problems   2
  The Impact of Increased Screen
    Time   8
Mental Health Disorders   9
  Major Depressive Disorder
    (Depression)   10
  Conduct Disorder   10
  Bipolar Disorder   11
  Substance Use Disorder   11
  Eating Disorder   12
  Schizophrenia   12
  Generalized Anxiety Disorder 13
  Post-Traumatic Stress
    Disorder (PTSD)   14
Notes   14

Chapter 2: Adolescent Suicide: Risk Factors, Protective Factors, and Warning Signs   19
Risk Factors   22
At-Risk Student Populations   23
  Gender and Suicide Risk   24
  Sexual and/or Gender
    Minorities   25

Race and Ethnicity   26
Demographic Region   28
Psychological Factors,
  Including Prior Suicide
  Attempt   29
Access to Firearms   29
Family History of Suicide   30
Non-Suicidal Self-Injury   30
Trauma   31
Teens with Challenging
  Family Dynamics   32
Chronic Illness or Disabilities   33
Youth Living with Autism   34
Precipitating Events   34
Life Transitions   35
School and Extracurricular
  Stress   36
Suicide Contagion   37
Social Media, Texting, Teens,
  and Suicide   38
Protective Factors   44
Suicide Warning Signs   45
What Do Students Say When
  They Are Thinking of Suicide? 48
Notes   51

Chapter 3: Debunking Myths About Student Suicide   57
Myth: Talking About Suicide
  Can Give Them the Idea   58
Myth: Teens Who Say They
  Are Thinking of Suicide Are
  Just Trying to Get Attention 58
Myth: Suicide Is Selfish   59

Myth: You Should Use a "No-
Suicide Contract" with Teens 59
Myth: Once a Teen Gets Past
a Suicide Attempt, They've
Learned Their Lesson 60
Myth: Teens Who Self-Injure
Are Trying to Kill Themselves 60
Myth: There Is No Need to Screen
Kids for Suicide Because
They Won't Tell Anyway 62
Myth: If Someone Is Set on Taking
Their Own Life, Nothing Can
Be Done to Stop Them 64
Myth: The Parent Is Always the
Best Person to Tell When a
Student Is Thinking of Suicide 65
Myth: If They Don't Have a Plan,
They Are Not at Risk for
Suicide 65
Myth: The Holidays Are Peak
Times for Teen Suicide 66
Myth: Most Students Who Die
by Suicide Have Been Bullied 66
Notes 67

**Chapter 4: Suicide-
Related School
Policies** **69**
Prepare School Crisis Plan 70
School Policy for Suicide
Prevention 71
School Policy for Commemoration
and Memorialization 72
Confidentiality Policy 79
Notes 80

**Chapter 5: Prevention:
The Educator's Role
in Creating a Culture
for Suicide Prevention** **83**
Creating a Culture of
Connectedness and
Belonging 85
Collaboration Is the Key to
Success 92
Create a Safe Digital Learning
Environment 93
Choosing the Right Program
or Training 94
Educator/Gatekeeper Training 96
Universal School-Based Suicide
Prevention Programs 100
SOS Signs of Suicide 101
SOS Signs of Suicide
Second ACT 103
Sources of Strength 103
Lifelines: Prevention 106
Hope Squad 107
JED High School 107
CAST, Coping and
Support Training 108
American Indian
Life Skills (AILS) 108
PREPaRE Crisis Training 109
Mental Health Training
Programs 110
Youth Mental Health
First Aid (YMHFA) 110
Teen Mental Health
First Aid (TMHFA) 110
More Than Sad 110

Programs That Bolster Protective
   Factors for Students   111
   CASEL   112
   DBT STEPS-A   112
   The Emerson Model   114
Customizing/Adapting Suicide
   Prevention Programs   115
Screening for Suicide Risk   117
Getting Leadership Buy-in for
   Suicide Prevention Education   119
Notes   125

**Chapter 6: Suicide
Prevention Activities
for Schools   127**
Simple Ideas/Concepts Anyone
   Can Integrate   129
Creative Activities for Bolstering
   Protective Factors   135
   Advice Column Activity   136
   Social Justice Movie   136
   Dia de los Muertos   137
   Hope and Care Video   138
   Mental Health Monday   138
   Connect/Disconnect   140
   Hope Versus Fear   141
   Mental Health Presentations
      by Students   142
   License Plate Project   144
   Podcasts   146
   Tammy's Mental Health   146
Affinity Groups   147
Student-Led Mental Wellness
   Clubs   147
   Initiatives and Ideas for
      Student Wellness Clubs   150

Nobles Heads Together   151
NHT Video Project   152
Fishbowl   153
Rock Painting   154
Middle School Visit   155
No Eagle Left Behind   155
Active Minds   157
Organizations Supporting
   School Mental Wellness
   Club Initiatives   158
Framework and
   Guidelines for Speaking,
   Panel Events, Videos,
   and News   160
Funding for Your Mental
   Wellness Club   166
Notes   168

**Chapter 7: Intervention:
They've Told You They're
Thinking of Suicide.
What Now?   169**
Kids Want to Tell   173
Removing Means   181
What to Say, What to Do   182
Assessing Suicide Risk   190
Safety Planning   191
Notes   195

**Chapter 8: Reintegrating
a Student into School
After a Suicide
Attempt or
Family Loss   197**
Transition from the Hospital
   Setting   199

Key Aspects of Reentry
 Meeting 200
Peer Connections and
 Support 201
Returning to School After
 Suicide Loss 202
What Does the Teen Want
 to Say? 205
Notes 207

Chapter 9: Postvention: After a Student or Teacher Suicide 209

Communication with the
 Impacted Family 215
Protocol and Maintaining
 Structure 221
Educator Talking Points with
 Students After Suicide 227
What Teachers Shouldn't
 Do or Say 231
Scripts on How to Facilitate
 Conversation with Your
 Class 233
 Sharing Stories About
  the Deceased Script 234
 Feelings Check-in Script 235
 Working Through Our
  Grief Script 236
 Responding to Grieving
  Adolescents 237
Memorial Activities and
 Support After a Student
 Suicide 238

The Empty Desk Syndrome
 and Taking Care of You 241
Notes 246

Chapter 10: How Students Move Forward After a Suicidal Crisis 247

How Did These Teens Move
 Out of a Self-Defeating
 Cycle? 249
Note 254

Chapter 11: Resources 255

Comprehensive Suicide-Related
 School-Based Models
 and Toolkits 255
Suicide-Related Fact Sheets 257
Best Practices for Storytelling
 and Reporting on Suicide 257
Recommended
 Websites 258
Educator/Gatekeeper Training
 Programs Mentioned in
 the Book 262
Universal School-Based Suicide
 Prevention Programs
 Mentioned in the Book 263
Crisis and Mental Health
 Training Programs
 Mentioned in the Book 264
Programs that Bolster
 Protective Factors for
 At-Risk Youth 264

Nonprofits and Government Agencies 265

Recommended Suicide-Related Books for Schools 267

Chapter 12: Quizzes, Worksheets, Handouts, Guides, and Scripts **269**

Worksheet 1: How to Tell Someone You Are Thinking of Suicide 269

Worksheet 2: Creating a Safe Digital Learning Environment 272

Worksheet 3: Student Wellness Surveys 273

Worksheet 4: True or False Suicide Prevention Quiz 275

Worksheet 5: True or False Suicide Prevention Quiz: Answer Key 276

Worksheet 6: Sample Confidentiality Policy for Students 278

Worksheet 7: How Educators Can Help Youth Bereaved by Suicide 279

Worksheet 8: Managing a Loss by Suicide for Middle and High School Students 283

Worksheet 9: The Coping Strategies and Resilience Building Game 287

Worksheet 10: Coping Skills Worksheet 292

Worksheet 11: What Is Your Passion? 294

Worksheet 12: Sample Schedule of Student Mental Wellness Events/Ideas 295

Worksheet 13: Script for Responding to Students Who Think Information Is Being Withheld 297

Worksheet 14: Script for Asking Parents' Permission to Disclose a Suicide Death 298

Worksheet 15: Guidelines for Telling Your Story 300

Seuss-like Scripts: A Serious Message in an Engaging Format 301

Worksheet 16: Bullies Aren't the Boss of You! 302

Worksheet 17: Toodle-oo to Taboo 303

Worksheet 18: Ears for Your Peers 304

Worksheet 19: I'm Rooting for You! 306

Worksheet 20: Don't Balk, Do Talk 307

Notes 308

Glossary **309**

Index **317**

Trigger Warning

This book tackles a tough topic and contains some emotional content. Most chapters that mention suicide method have a "trigger warning." Teachers and other educators suffer from mental illness and have thoughts of suicide, too. So if you are struggling with mental illness and/or thoughts of suicide and if this is triggering, please stop or take breaks. There are a few instances where method is mentioned briefly in a story but there are no graphic details.

Your life is important. If you do experience thoughts of suicide, reach out to the prevention lifeline, a crisis text line, a trusted adult friend, a counselor, or find a support group.

There is only one you. If you left us, we'd be robbed of your potential, all your gifts, and what you could contribute to suicide prevention.

Crisis Hotlines

If you are experiencing thoughts of suicide, please reach out.

US National Suicide Prevention Lifeline: 1-800-273-8255 (By July 26, 2022, it will be simplified to the 3-digit crisis number 988.)

US and Canada Crisis Text Line: Text "help" to 741-741

US Trevor Project Crisis line for LGBTQ Youth: 1-866-488-7386

US Trevor Project Crisis text line for LGBTQ Youth 678-678

US Trans Lifeline 1-877-565-8860

Canada 1-833-456-4566

United Kingdom 116 123

Australia 13 11 14

For other countries: Search "suicide crisis lines"

UK: text 85258 | **Ireland:** text 50808

About the Authors

Anne Moss Rogers is an emotionally naked® TEDx storyteller, the 2019 YWCA Pat Asch Fellow for social justice, NAMI Virginia board member, and author of the award-winning book *Diary of a Broken Mind*. Despite her family's best efforts, Anne Moss's 20-year-old son, Charles, died by suicide June 5, 2015, after many years of struggle with anxiety, depression, and ultimately addiction. She chronicled her family's tragedy in a newspaper article that went viral and her blog, Emotionally Naked, has had millions of visitors. After receiving a message from a young lady who wrote that one of her articles saved her life, she sold her digital marketing business and followed her purpose of motivational speaking on the subjects of suicide, substance misuse, coping strategies, and grief. Originally from Fayetteville, North Carolina, and a graduate of UNC-Chapel Hill with a BA in journalism, she currently lives in Richmond, Virginia, with her husband, Randy. Her surviving son, Richard, works in Los Angeles as a screenwriter and filmmaker.

Kimberly O'Brien, PhD, LICSW, is a clinical social worker in the Sports Medicine Division and Female Athlete Program at Boston Children's Hospital, as well as a research scientist and assistant professor of psychiatry at Harvard Medical School. She received her BA from Harvard University, MSW and PhD from Boston College, and completed her postdoctoral fellowship at Brown University. Her research focuses on the development and testing of brief interventions for suicidal adolescents with and without substance use and their families, with an additional specialization on interventions that utilize technology. She has co-authored over 50 articles and book chapters related to adolescent suicide, substance use, and mental health, and was awarded the Young Investigator Research Award from the American Foundation for Suicide Prevention in 2019. She is also the founder and director of Unlimited Resilience, LLC, a private mental health practice for athletes by athletes.

Acknowledgments

Thank you to all who accepted our invitation to be interviewed for this book. These life-saving contributions, examples, and sharing are what makes this book a truly helpful guide. Special thanks to a few we emailed, reinterviewed, and called multiple times to review some of the worksheets and scripts, and to provide extra materials and images, including Jennifer Hamilton, LEP; Jessica Chock-Goldman, LCSW; Jim McCauley, LICSW; James Biela, LCSW; Desmond Herzfelder; and Lea Karnath.

We are grateful to the following people for the contributions and content from interviews conducted for this book (listed in alphabetical order).

Quoted Interviewees:

- Melissa K. Ackley, LCSW (She/Her/Hers), Prevention Services Manager, Chesterfield Mental Health Support Services, Chesterfield Suicide Prevention Coalition

- James Biela, LCSW (He/Him/His), Itinerant School Social Worker, Lower Kuskokwim School District, Bethel, Alaska

- Sam Brinton (They/Them/Theirs), Vice President of Advocacy and Government Affairs at The Trevor Project, Rockville, Maryland, TheTrevorProject.org

- Doris (She/Her/Hers), Science Teacher, Colorado Public School

- Dawn Gallagher (She/Her/Hers), Mother of Kiernan Gallagher who approved Kiernan's written excerpt about her father's suicide

- Kiernan Gallagher, 14, middle school student, suicide loss survivor, Ocean, New Jersey

- Jessica Chock-Goldman, LCSW (She/Her/Hers), Doctoral Candidate, School Social Worker, Stuyvesant High School, Manhattan, New York, JessicaChockGoldman.com

- Jennifer Hamilton (She/Her/Hers), School Psychologist, Director of Psychology and Counseling at Noble and Greenough, Independent School, Dedham, Massachusetts

- Desmond Herzfelder (He/Him/His), Student Mental Wellness Club Founder, Psychology Major at Harvard University, Graduate of Noble and Greenough, Independent High School, Dedham, Massachusetts
- Lea Karnath (She/Her/Hers), SOS Signs of Suicide Senior Program Manager, MindWise Innovations, SOSSignsofSuicide.org
- Michelle Fortunado-Kewin, LCSW, PPSC (She/Her/Siya), School Social Worker and Program Coordinator, San Francisco Unified School District
- Nora (She/Her/Hers), Ninth Grade Dean, East Coast High School
- Scott LoMurray (He/Him/His), Executive Director, Sources of Strength, SourcesofStrength.org
- James Mazza, PhD (He/Him/His), Professor, University of Washington, Author of DBT Skills in Schools, MazzaConsulting.com
- Jim McCauley, LICSW (He/Him/His), Co-Founder and Associate Director of Riverside Trauma Center, Needham Heights, Massachusetts, RiversideTraumaCenter.org
- Sheila McElwee (She/Her/Hers), Chemistry Teacher, Noble and Greenough, Independent School, Dedham, Massachusetts
- Keygan Miller, MEd (They/Them/Theirs), Senior Advocacy Associate at The Trevor Project, Washington, DC, TheTrevorProject.org
- Mr. Nigro, Public High School Teacher, World History II and Economics, Chester, Virginia
- Tammy Ozolins ("Ms. Oz"), Middle School Health/PE Teacher, Pocahontas Middle School, Henrico, Virginia
- Shirley Ramsey (She/Her/Hers), Founder of Virginia Chapter AFSP, Retired School Counselor, *More Than Sad* Presenter, Co-Facilitator of suicide loss support group
- Mike Riekhof (He/Him/His), Survivor of Suicide Loss, Founder of The Peyton Riekhof Foundation, Fishers, Indiana, ThePeytonRiekhofFoundation.com
- Leigh Rysko (They/Them/Theirs), Spanish Teacher and World Languages Department Chair, Kansas Public High School
- Jonathan B. Singer, PhD, LCSW (He/Him/His), President, American Association of Suicidology, author of *Suicide in Schools: A Practitioner's Guide to Multi-level Prevention, Assessment, Intervention, and Postvention*

- Sean Reilly (He/Him/His), retired teacher, Kansas Attorney General Suicide Coalition Task Force, The One Heart Project
- Shelby Rowe (She/Her/Hers), Co-Chair, Indigenous Peoples Committee, American Association of Suicidology (AAS)
- Victor Schwartz, MD (He/Him/His), Former CMO of The JED Foundation, Founder of MindStrategies Advisors, Clinical Associate Professor, Dept. of Psychiatry, NYU School of Medicine, MindStrategies.com
- Laura Stack, MBA (She/Her/Hers), Suicide loss survivor and Founder of Johnny's Ambassadors and Leadership USA, Inc., JohnnysAmbassadors.org
- Dese'Rae L. Stage (She/Her/Hers), Suicide Attempt Survivor, Suicide Loss Survivor, Queer, livethroughthis.org
- Aurora Wulff (She/Her/Hers), Young Adult, Founder of *Active Minds* Student Mental Wellness Club, Graduate of Ithaca High School, student at Binghamton University

Interviewees who asked to remain anonymous

- Beauregard, Young Adult, Graduate of all-boys school in eastern US (agreed name change to protect privacy)
- Anonymous High School PE Teacher, Virginia
- Anonymous High School Counselor, all-boys school in eastern US
- Quotes from those underage whose names have been withheld for privacy
- Many contributions from principals, teachers, school counselors, and students who asked that their names be withheld

Survivors of Suicide Loss Interviewees (adolescent child)

- Kelly Sprecht (She/Her/Hers), Founder of Carl's Cause, Kansas City
- Elaine Alpert (She/Her/Hers), CEO of Mindpeace Miracles, Atlanta
- Ricky Rash (He/Him/His), Mechanicsville, Virginia

Companion Website

Since web links change, we've created a web page with links to resources mentioned in this book, with downloadable guides and resources for your school and classrooms.

wiley.com/go/emotionallynaked

Password is: 988preventsuicide

Preface

ANNE MOSS ROGERS'S STORY

Trigger Warning: Suicide method mentioned briefly

It was June 5, 2015, in Virginia—a warm day, but I was cold and shivering as I sat in the back of a police car in a parking lot. My husband was in the front passenger seat. The officer, dressed in a nicely tailored gray suit and yellow tie, made a quarter turn in the driver's seat so he could see both of us. On some other day, I would have thought him handsome.

"I have some sad news to share. Your son Charles has been found dead this morning. . . ." An electric shock surged though my body and air was siphoned out of my lungs. When my breathing recovered and my lungs remembered what to do, soul-crushing wails of agony and loss erupted. My chest burned, my ears filled with noise, and my mind was watery and unhinged as the unspeakable tragedy that forever changed our lives was delivered in a single sentence.

Moments later, my husband, Randy, paused and asked, "How did he die?" For some reason, this question stunned me. I thought, *How do you think he died? He was addicted to heroin, for God's sake*. I was prepared to hear "overdose." But instead the officer said, "He hanged himself," and my husband banged his fists on his lap and the glove box, wailing in inexplicable emotional pain as I stared at his explosion in shock, unable to move. The statement by the officer dangled in the air outside of my consciousness, trying to get in while confusion and denial obstructed its path. My first instinct was to find the escape route from the agony and slide into another life that was shiny and happy. Rocking back and forth and wailing guttural, inhuman sounds, I had the primal urge to grab the edges of yesterday and bring it back so we could do the day over and achieve a better outcome. *We love him. How could he kill himself?* I didn't understand *why suicide* and it would be a long time before I would.

There was an immediate and desperate longing in my soul for one more hug. My irrational disbelief that this couldn't be true curled around the edges of my trauma and the raw, naked pain of losing my son was forever imprinted on my soul. Bits and pieces of information floated about, screaming their importance with no place to land, only to be retrieved later when my mind had the ability to absorb them and put the pieces together.

I am the mother of a child who killed himself.

Struggling to make Charles's life count, I spent five months after his death writing a newspaper article about my family's tragedy that went viral, creating an audience for my newly minted blog, Emotionally Naked®. This is where I wrote in my public journal to work through my grief. Eighteen months later, my business partner and I sold our successful digital marketing company and I became an author and an emotionally naked speaker on subjects few want to talk about.

Charles was complex, adorable, frustrating, hilarious, effervescent, electric, charming, eccentric, and a creative genius. From the time he came into the world to the time he left, his presence was all-consuming. He pushed boundaries past comfortable, questioned everything, and was relentless and persistent when he wanted something. When Charles waltzed in, the fun had arrived. Faces brightened, bodies turned toward him like he brought the sunshine in his pocket and he was there to hand it out. He was one of those bigger-than-life personalities who exceeded his allotment of space on earth despite his six-foot-two, 130-pound frame. Charles was the younger of my two sons, the funniest, most popular kid in school. Yet this funniest, most popular kid suffered from depression in middle school, and by high school was misusing drugs and alcohol to numb feelings of suicide we never knew about. His substance misuse led to deeper depression and an addiction to heroin, and he took his life while going through withdrawal.

Connection was Charles's gift and he demonstrated it over and over. No child ever entered his school and sat alone at lunch or felt friendless. He was the first to make new kids feel welcome. And given his popularity, that attention was like a social promotion.

It was a teacher who first suggested my child might be suffering from depression. It was a teacher who stars in one of my favorite photos of Charles (Figure P.1). And it was a teacher who wrote me the kindest, most heartfelt note after he died by suicide. My son's education shaped his writing and encouraged daily journal entries—a habit that evolved into his writing hundreds of hip-hop-style rhyme schemes that offered me a window into his tortured, artistic soul after his death. It was those notebooks he left behind that helped me understand the why behind his suicide. Some of these lyrics were included in my first book, *Diary of a Broken Mind: A Mother's Story, a Son's Suicide, and the Haunting Lyrics He Left Behind.*

Figure P.1 Charles on Homecoming Court, escorted by his favorite teacher, Kerry Fretwell.

While there are precious memories from his school days, there were horror stories, too. Zero-tolerance policies and rigid school administrators who defaulted to punitive measures perpetuated my youngest son's feelings of worthlessness, and unnecessary suspensions caused frustrating setbacks to his fragile progress with depression. Misunderstanding shaped their authoritarian responses when what was needed was empathy and compassion.

After students leave school, they rarely remember their test scores. They remember their interaction and experiences with peers, teachers, administrators, teammates, band leaders, school counselors, principals, drama teachers, janitors, bus drivers, cafeteria staff, librarians, school nurses, and coaches. Schools have something few other environments have, and that's opportunity for genuine human connection, which has gotten lost in the digital age. This is the most valuable currency in our universe today and a foundation for emotional wellness.

After Charles died, a young woman who suffered from depression reached out and told me a story that happened in high school. On one particular day, the dark fog of depression moved in and took her motivation hostage, but she made a Herculean effort to get out of bed and go to school. Later that day, she and her friends stood chatting in the hallway between classes. She was struggling to hold onto her mask of a clown, looked up, and was stunned to see Charles staring right at her. She said she knew Charles, since everyone did. But they had never met and she didn't know he knew her. As soon as eye contact was returned, my son walked towards her, stopped about two feet away, and broke out into a rap song he created on the spot, just for her (also known as freestyling). She and her friends were shocked at first but soon burst out laughing.

When he finished his song, he bent over, hugged her, and said, "Pretty girls shouldn't look so sad," and then made his way down the hall. She told me she had never experienced such kindness and it was a moment she tucked away in her mental library of precious memories.

While I will always miss my son's beautiful curly hair and his sense of humor, his tall, skinny hugs and the way he altered his voice when he greeted his dog, what I miss most was his capacity for love. In a world where no one has time to listen, he did. In a disconnected world where no one has time to connect, he made time. As talented and funny as he was, this was his greatest gift—letting other people know they mattered. That is the legacy I carry forward in my son's name. And that is why today, educators invite me into their classrooms and auditoriums to share our family's story, the coping strategies that helped me find emotional healing, and the workshop that helps kids become aware of what defines healthy and unhealthy coping skills.

Many people ask me how I can work with suicide prevention and loss every day after losing a child to this cause of death. My answer is that the universe pushed me towards it. And even after the most devastating loss of my life, I have hope. Because more people survive thoughts of suicide than act on them. And your help and mentorship can prevent tragedy by integrating innovative strategies and small culture shifts in your classes that facilitate connection and healthy coping strategies. You have the relationships. And the goal of this book is to nurture those relationships, empower you with the tools and education to spot students at risk, listen, and introduce them to the next level of care.

There are days when I do want to give up this cause because it's like pushing a spiked ball uphill in a driving snowstorm. But then I get letters from students after a presentation and it reinforces my resolve and rekindles my passion to keep doing what I'm doing.

I want to thank you very dearly for sharing how you changed one of the worst events in your life, to a turning point in your life. The story of your son, Charles' drug addictions and anxiety and depression, has inspired me to speak up if I do need any help. and has encouraged me to reach out to anyone who has been experiencing anything similar.

but every single word that you said in that classroom that day touched my life. You helped me to wanna keep pushing and strive to even be half as strong as you are. So thank you Mrs. Rogers, thank you so much for sharing your story, and helping me in ways I can't even begin to truly explain.

Thank you so much for sharing your story with me. It touched me and it helped me come to some peace with my own grief. I think the way you have turned this situation into such a wonderful lesson to people everywhere is amazing. When I get older I hope to help people like you helped me and my classmates. I have gone through my whole life thinking my father's death was in some way my fault or I did something even though I was so little. You helped me realize that sometimes our loved ones don't mean to hurt us, they make a decision in a place of bad mind. Again, thank you so much.

KIM O'BRIEN'S STORY

My passion for helping suicidal youth runs deep. People wonder how I could do something so dark, so depressing, and often ask me why I got into this field. But I see my work differently. When working with suicidal youth, I see hope and resilience. I see that in that place of darkness that seems never ending, there is a way out other than suicide. I know this because I've been there.

My kindergarten teacher told my parents I needed to see a psychologist. She said I always looked so sad and just stared out the window instead of playing with friends. And so began my journey with depression. Mental health was a foreign concept to my parents, for no fault of their own, so I endured this constant emotional struggle alone. Growing up, I never felt understood by others and never quite understood my sadness. I had two parents and three younger siblings who loved me and I always had a safe, beautiful home to live in. So why was I always so sad?

My childhood turned into an adolescence filled with anxiety and perfectionism, and my depression evolved into a secret source of shame and self-hatred. I would lie in bed at night wishing I could die. I endured some low moments, like when my college roommate died by suicide, when I seriously questioned why I was still living. Life was becoming increasingly too much to bear and I relied on the high moments—accomplishments, excitement, love, and laughter that continued to pull me through.

Shortly after I graduated college, I hit rock bottom. I became angry and sad, closed myself off to others, and drank more alcohol. I cried daily, sometimes all day. I didn't want to wake up in the morning yet I couldn't fall asleep at night. This continued for over a year and I remember going to the doctor one day for a well visit and I couldn't stop crying. She told me I needed antidepressant medication and I agreed. I figured, why not? At that point I didn't care about living any longer but I also thought I had nothing to lose. I was already lost and it was as if my soul had died and I was just going through the motions in a lifeless body.

With the little blue pills, I found myself crying a little bit less and the days became slightly more manageable. I started picking myself up, bit by bit, and began finding more reasons to go on living. There was no magical "aha" moment for me, just continuous introspection with professional support to guide me through. And now, decades later, I can say I live a life full of purpose, love, and even happiness. I still struggle emotionally every day, but I have the skills I need and the love and support around me to get through the difficult times that are a part of every human experience.

That kindergarten teacher spotted something in me that no one else noticed, not even my family. How did she know I was so sad, so tortured inside? And as my emotional state kept getting worse as the years went on, why was no one aware of it? None of my middle or high school teachers ever noticed it. I wonder why but as I look back and ponder, I'm actually not sure I showed too many signs. I was bright, athletic, and relatively social. On the surface I had friends—people to talk to in class and teammates to joke with on the field and ice. So how would they even have known? But the fact remains that no one ever asked me how I was feeling inside. No one inquired about my emotional state or what it felt like to be me. I don't blame my teachers for this—it simply wasn't in the culture back then to address mental health in such a direct way.

But it is now. Today, we are finally beginning to recognize how inextricably linked our physical and emotional health actually are, and how important it is to take care of our mental health. We owe it to our youth to teach them how to identify what they are feeling and what they can do to help themselves when they experience distressing and unwanted emotions. We also need to teach our youth how to recognize when their friends may be struggling, what they can do to help them, and when they need to tell a trusted adult.

Our educators play an integral role in how we can and will affect change amidst this cultural shift where the mental health of our youth is being increasingly prioritized. Many argue that no one knows youth better than their teachers, the adults who are with them every day. Our goal for this book is to help educators see their critical role in suicide prevention, and acquire the knowledge and skills they need to save lives.

Introduction

"The Colorado school where I teach went on lockout and we didn't know why. With our school so close to Columbine, it's hard not to think the worst when this happens. I kept teaching in an effort to distract the students. And myself. Thirty minutes into the lockout I'm looking at my student Emily as a look of horror crosses her face, which triggers a visceral internal response. Then one by one I see other students with their phones out and the same look of shock appears on all their faces. One of them shares that they'd all been sent a picture via the social media platform called Snapchat. It was a body bag photo of a student who had killed himself just minutes before. I never saw the picture. I couldn't. And although we didn't hear it, the rifle shot was heard by many of the classes. Earlier that day, a male who had been in my class as a freshman was in his welding class and referring to his welding helmet, he quietly told another student, 'I won't be needing that anymore.' He then asked the teacher if he could be excused to go to the bathroom. He crossed the football field, went home, got his weapon, then went to a public park near the school. That suicide rocked the community. It was the first one of three student suicides. It was one of the worst teaching days of my life."

Doris, Science Teacher, Colorado Public School

After a death by suicide at a school, tissues are passed around in staff meetings, teachers are encouraged to contain gossip, productivity is arrested by shock and confusion, and in a desperate rush to force premature normalcy in the wake of devastation, the healing step is disregarded or abbreviated. Unresolved grief is a risk factor for suicide but teachers are rarely given tips on supporting grieving students, creating an additional layer of emotional chaos on a school campus that is already hurting. Sometimes lawyers will instruct administrators to say nothing, so they don't engage with the family, which can result in anger, blame, tempestuous lawsuits, and unwanted media attention that can brand the school as a rigid and uncaring. Once the school is moving forward again, administrators resist revisiting the topic.

With this population especially, suicide contagion, also known as copycat suicide, is a real threat and the desperation to contain the chatter and take control of the situation often motivates educators and administrators to act in ways they believe to be safeguarding their school community, when in fact it may be doing the opposite.

Suicide is the number two cause of death for ages 10–34 in both the United States and Canada after accidents, and the leading cause of death for ages 14–15 in the US.[1]

Despite this alarming public health threat, educator training for prevention is inconsistent and school districts tend to implement a plan for suicide prevention only after a student or teacher takes their own life. As one principal said, "It's tragic that a kid with great potential had to die for that to happen." Policies and protocols for identifying students at risk for suicide, information on how to support grieving students, or a commemoration policy on how to handle a death from any cause are not commonplace even though free resources are available.

Overall, researchers have noted that 50–69% of those who die by suicide communicate suicidal thoughts or suicidal intent to others in some way before they die, providing a window of opportunity for intervention and prevention if we know what to look for and what to do.[2] And because youth spend more time in school than any other place in their lives, there is an opportunity to prevent this cause of death and encourage the coping strategies that offer students the tools to manage adversity before it becomes a crisis.

Education has become a frenzy of test taking with little emphasis on students' emotional health. A lot is expected of educators today and the job keeps evolving and becoming more complex. Add to that rapid changes in technology and its influence on students and the teaching profession. The education world can be slow to adapt, leaving gaps in the system and administrators trying to play catch-up, but the good news is that teachers can integrate small culture shifts that are part of a foundation of suicide prevention and student wellness.

"When I graduated in 2000, there was no suicidal ideation happening. For today's students, suicide is embedded in their normal thought processes. It's just part of their language now which is why it should be part of ours, too. I've learned to ask every student that comes by my office if they are thinking of suicide. Because our student population is talking about it all the time. If they are talking about it, so should we."

Jessica Chock-Goldman, LCSW (She/Her/Hers), Doctoral Candidate, School Social Worker, Stuyvesant High School in Manhattan, New York

---

While the conversation on mental health should be open and educators should listen and show empathy, Jessica Chock-Goldman also emphasizes that there is no need for teachers to be heroes but instead they can refer students to school counselors and those who know how to handle the situation since there are many nuances with this age group and even among specific ethnic populations. Sometimes the teacher joins that conversation with the student and counselor if the pupil is showing resistance, since it's only natural that they'd want to connect with the person with whom they have a relationship.

"We had a situation where a student who was quietly struggling with severe depression went on a school trip at the end of the year. One of the teachers who was chaperoning the trip sensed that this kid was really having a difficult time. She continually and gently reached out and kept reaching out, even though the student always responded that she was fine. But then on the last day when they were at the airport, at the last possible moment, the student just opened up and told her teacher how much she was struggling. The teacher called me from the airport and we began the conversation about how to connect this student with support when she returned from the trip. We worked together to help the student open up to her parents and get the help that she needed."

Jennifer Hamilton (She/Her/Hers), School Psychologist, Director of Psychology and Counseling at Noble and Greenough, Independent School, Dedham, Massachusetts

---

Jennifer Hamilton collaborated on what needed to happen next and the student was unwilling to talk with a counselor, having established a trusted relationship with the teacher. This is often the case, which is why it is important to empower teachers with basic talking points on what to say or do to dispel the fear related to those conversations. Because that's all it is. Students want to talk to the person with whom they have a relationship, and that warm handoff sometimes needs to include the person they originally connected with because the pupil is afraid of the process. In this case, the counselor and teacher worked together to talk about what needed to happen next, and it was suitable to contact and inform the parents. After talking with her parents, she agreed to talk to the school counselor with the teacher present. From there, the goal was to include the student in conversations regarding options, which for her included outpatient treatment.

"I believe this teacher saved this kid's life with all my heart. She did. It was so rewarding to see how that all played out because she had a comfort level around knowing what to do when worried about a student. She also knew when she needed some backup. I am so grateful."

Jennifer Hamilton (She/Her/Hers), School Psychologist, Director of Psychology and Counseling at Noble and Greenough, Independent School, Dedham, Massachusetts

---

The purpose of this book is not to make the job of the educator harder, but to make it more meaningful. Our hope is that this book will arm you with the knowledge, tools, resources, and ideas to inspire administrators to integrate new policies and encourage impactful shifts in your school culture and curriculum to prevent suicide and promote health and wellness. It will make you aware of resources for crisis response, as well as give you tips on getting school leadership and the community behind social emotional teaching and suicide prevention, which can mean adding more staff trained in mental health to support those efforts. A lot of what you'll read here is not a teacher's responsibility to implement, but having knowledge of what that collaborative process might look like helps complete your understanding of how it should work and a teacher's role as part of a team effort. So while this book is not intended solely for teachers, that is the point of view from which we will speak. Our intention is to make you more comfortable with an uncomfortable subject because it's one that very few feel qualified to address. But given the pervasive public health problem of suicide in our youth, it's a critical conversation that all educators need to have in order to feel ready and able to effectively engage with their students. Although we refer to students who are at risk of suicide in this book, that's not to exclude educators who might be at risk. They can. And it is our hope that the information delivered will also help you recognize any colleagues, friends, and family members who are struggling and connect them with life-saving and supportive resources in the school and community.

This book is also not meant to train you as an interventionist or a counselor. Enough is asked of you. Instead we hope to help you see, notice, and pick up on which students need intervention. Learning to say, "Tell me more," and actively listen is a powerful first step to help a suicidal student open up. And even if you are not comfortable with that, you can simply look after your students and make the school social worker or counselor aware of your concerns. Mastering the art of listening and empathically connecting to people is underrated in today's busy culture and we are often unaware of how important even the smallest gestures and acts of kindness mean to another human being. One empathetic adult is all it takes to have a positive impact on a student and change the trajectory of their life. Throughout this book we want you to ask yourself, "What kind of educator do I want to be?"

NOTES

1. Kann, L., McManus, T., Harris, W.A., Shanklin, S.L., Flint, K.H., Queen, B., Lowry, R., Chyen, D., Whittle, L., Thornton, J., Lim, C., Bradford, D., Yamakawa, Y., Leon, M., Brener, N., Ethier, K. (2018) Youth Risk Behavior Surveillance — United States, 2017. MMWR *Surveillance Summaries* 67(8):1–114.
2. Coombs et al., 1992; Robins, Gassner, Kayes, Wilkinson, Murphy, 1959, p. 9. https://www.qprinstitute.com/uploads/QPR%20Theory%20Paper.pdf

Chapter 1
Why Are We Seeing More Mental Health Problems with Students?

"In order to achieve, you have to put wellness first."
Jennifer Hamilton (She/Her/Hers), School Psychologist, Director of Psychology and Counseling at Noble and Greenough, Independent School, Dedham, Massachusetts

Mental health includes our emotional, psychological, and social well-being. It affects how we think, feel, and act and drives how we handle stress, relate to others, and make choices.[1] This can be impacted by the home and social environment, economic status including homelessness and food instability, early childhood adversity or trauma, physical health, and a family history of mental health diagnoses and suicide. Mental health concerns, such as depression, anxiety disorders, self-harm, post-traumatic stress disorders, and substance use disorders, significantly impact one's daily functioning, and those are the signs that educators need to look out for.

Many psychiatric disorders have their onset at adolescence. So right at the phase when their brains are still maturing and hormones are driving behavior, teenagers can develop a mental illness, making adolescence that much more challenging. Mental illness often makes teens more susceptible to suicide risk, and family history, medical history, and social stressors like trauma, grief, transitions, and relationship disruption can add to that vulnerability.

THE RISE IN TEEN MENTAL HEALTH PROBLEMS

A study by Twenge and colleagues (2019)[2] found that between 2008 and 2017, mental health problems, including self-harm behaviors, grew substantially for the youth subset of the population. They found that by 2017, 13% of youth had symptoms consistent with major depression in the previous year, which represented a 62% increase in eight years. Scholars and advocates posit a variety of reasons for the rise in mental health issues among today's youth. Technology and too much screen time, constant social comparison exacerbated by social media, emphasis on happiness and nonacceptance of difficult emotions, the academic and extracurricular rat race, helicopter parenting, transitions, and the disruption of relationships (whether that's a family divorce, death of a loved one, or loss of a romantic partner) all contribute.

When the digital age moved in, that which we thought would connect us more instead pushed us apart in many ways. It was during the early 2000s that we began to see an increase in student mental health problems. Poor sleep hygiene, the result of increased screen time and 24/7 Internet access via mobile phones, exacerbated those issues because youth sacrificed precious slumber time for late-night chats and video watching. As the digital revolution has grown, each generation has less face time with friends than the one before, which means youth are getting fewer opportunities to learn, fail, and problem solve. Add to that the fact that extended family often lives out of town and community programs and interactions have a reduced role in our lives, further fracturing the community of connection and support. Humans crave contact with each other, and lack of it can leave teenagers feeling anxious, small, insignificant, and devoid of opportunities to develop important life skills.

If you are an adult who grew up before 1995, think about how much you learned when you played games outside with friends in your neighborhood. You learned to negotiate, compromise, and argue in an effective way. There was no referee other than the peer-appointed kid who lived on the corner, so you had to work it out. Failure is a part of life and a learning opportunity, but so many students have no idea how to manage it because what little unstructured time they do have is now spent on digital screens. Victor Schwartz, MD, Clinical Associate Professor, Department of Psychiatry, NYU School of Medicine, points out that there are fewer community centers, religious-based organizations, and clubs like 4-H or Girl Scouts in today's culture (in some cases for very good reasons). These gathering places and clubs were commonplace in earlier generations and were settings where youth picked up a lot of life skills. This is where kids learned to run a program, organize something, learned how to deal with other people in planning a project. It's not the schools' fault that we've lost the whole notion of community centers, but are there ways to bring more of those skill-building opportunities in a more intentional way into academics? In Chapter 6, "Suicide Prevention Activities for Schools," we present specific strategies and ideas that teachers from different regions are integrating into their curriculums to build that skillset. The effect of doing so reduces unhealthy coping such as self-harm, substance misuse, and suicide, and promotes more positive experiences in school and beyond.

Barriers to Mental Health Treatment for Teens

- Neither teens nor the adults who are close to them recognize the symptoms of their treatable illness.
- Fear of what treatment might involve.
- Belief that nothing can help.
- They don't see help-seeking as a sign of strength.
- They are embarrassed.
- Belief that adults won't understand.
- Limited access to resources (money, insurance, transportation, healthcare).

Source: From the American Foundation for Suicide Prevention, More Than Sad for Parents.

Standardized testing is a measurement strategy that many school systems use. Wherever you stand on the issue, it siphons considerable instructional time and resources during the school day and the casualties of that effort have been innovation, creativity, practical skills, opportunities to build connection, and social emotional skills. In short, there is not enough time. More trigonometry will not help a student learn how to cope with the loss of a sibling. Integrating skills to help students learn and manage life goes a long way in minimizing substance misuse, self-harm, eating disorders, promiscuity, and other unhealthy coping strategies, as well as preventing suicide during the school years and throughout a student's lifespan. What we do know is that several studies have shown that suicide rates increase during the school year and drop off during the summer when most students are out of school and during academic breaks, suggesting that social and academic pressure may play a role in student suicidal behavior.

In a 2018 study, Gregory Plemmons and his colleagues found that the rate of hospitalization of school-aged children for suicidal ideation and attempts increased by almost 300% from 2008 to 2015.[3] Each year the rate of psychiatric hospitalizations is significantly higher in the school months than in the summer. A decrease occurred not just during summer vacation, but also during school vacation weeks, too. So in schools where parents are more involved and academic success and college prep are paramount, for example, the pressure of grades and college acceptance can be a contributor to student suicide risk and attempts.

Social media is another factor that can either boost student well-being or crush it. It's the lollipop land of shiny faces and perfect families, and in our accomplishment-obsessed culture, this highlight reel of influencers, likes, and comments can alter a student's feelings of self-worth. Positive interactions, social support, and connectedness on social networking sites are consistently related to lower levels of depression and anxiety. Conversely, negative interaction and social comparisons on social networking sites are related to higher levels.[4] Extended time spent on these sites results in negative mental health outcomes.[5] With an adolescent population, feelings of inclusion can shift fast, triggering impulsive thoughts and actions. For example, a student who is experiencing a great day can see a status update by another student that includes pictures to a party she wasn't invited to and her mood can transform from happiness to despair in seconds. Teens are more susceptible to social influence, the need for peer approval, and the conformity effect, which drives some adolescents to agree with or engage with what their friends have already commented on or liked.

Teen Worries

What are you and your friends most worried about?

- College is scary and a lot of work.
- Friends feel like they need to do everything every second of the day: volunteering, activities, etc.
- Pressure to get perfect grades.
- Getting acclimated to high school, feeling overwhelmed, figuring out feelings, figuring out who they are, can be very stressful.
- Getting into varsity or JV teams.
- Really worried about junior year, AP classes, preparing for the next year.
- A lot of homework, a lot of pressure.
- Getting along with others.
- Personal appearance, hygiene, being made fun of.
- Gender identity.
- Middle school is a big popularity contest, with nobody winning and everybody losing.
- Gossip, drama, rumors.
- You're in that stage where you're trying to figure it out, but it feels risky to be open about that.
- Feeling threatened threats of violence on social media and in person.
- Not feeling safe at home.

Source: Survey question for teens and sample of comments from Signs of Suicide Youth Focus Group for reviewing new video content.

The trouble lies in how the teenage brain matures. The "let's party now" parts, the hippocampus and amygdala, which are associated with impulsivity, thrill seeking, and emotions, mature way ahead of the "cockpit" or prefrontal cortex part of the brain. That cockpit is responsible for regulating all that emotion as well as planning, focusing attention, following instructions, and juggling multiple tasks. Throughout the adolescent years and up through age 25, this executive portion of the brain lags behind. It's during this period of brain development that kids often act out based on their moods and impulses, misuse substances, and engage in self-harm. Half of all mental health concerns start by 14 years of age but most cases are undetected and untreated.[6] So at an age when their brains are not yet fully equipped, teens with immature coping skills are trying to manage a multitude of complex mental health, social, and life issues.

Teenagers who feel less connected, with underdeveloped coping skills and executive functions, may resort to drugs and alcohol to numb feelings and/or experience highs. People don't heal if they can't feel and this concept is especially unknown to teenagers. The late 1990s and early 2000s brought on a period of normalization for using substances to treat both physical and mental pain. Meanwhile pain clinics that used alternative methods of pain management shut down. And the US, which makes up 4.4% of the world's population, started consuming 80% of the world's prescription painkillers and became the number one consumer of prescription pain medication.[7] The overprescribing meant there were more unused drugs available in medicine cabinets that often ended up in the hands of teenagers more susceptible to dependence and addiction than adults. When adolescents try something and it runs out, they find alternatives in over-the-counter substances that can be bought in drug stores. They get those ideas from online collaboration and sometimes these students will
stalk peers at school for their medications after wisdom teeth removal or athletic surgery.

Just because adults and schools rarely address subjects of mental illness, grief, self-harm, and substance misuse doesn't mean young people aren't seeking answers. Given the gap in that education, young people go online to search for answers on sensitive and taboo topics, the sources of which are not always reliable. This is where they learn to turn cough medicine into a substance to get high and where they look up and find specific ways to kill themselves, often with step-by-step instructions and even videos. Still the most frequently misused substances in this age group are alcohol and marijuana, the effects of which are detrimental to the developing adolescent brain.[8,9] In 2018, marijuana use among middle and high school students remained steady, but the number of teens in eighth and tenth grades who said they used it daily increased.[10] Teens vape it, roll it, smoke it in pipes, cook it into baked goods, and often migrate to waxy-looking globs of high-THC concentrates known as hashish oil extracts, commonly referred to as dabs, wax, shatter, or crumble.

The problem is that parents and students are ill-informed about the detrimental effects and not only consider marijuana and derivatives as harmless but as a viable option to help kids with anxiety and sleep. Compared with conventional marijuana, hashish oil extracts may be associated with a greater risk of psychosis.[11] Laura Stack is the mother of Johnny Stack, who killed himself as a result of high-concentrate THC-induced psychosis. Prior to using high-THC concentrates Johnny had not experienced psychosis, but as his use escalated so did his hallucinations about the FBI and mob pursuing him. After his death, Laura founded Johnny's Ambassadors (JohnnysAmbassadors.org), with a mission to educate parents and teens about the dangers of high-THC marijuana on adolescent brain development, mental illness, and suicide. Laura states, "Using cannabis at a young age, less than 15 to 18 years old, increases the risk of developing a psychotic disorder. Risk is dose dependent and increases with greater frequency of use and with higher potency THC."[12]

Substance misuse, from the stimulants students take for "improving" their SAT scores to the pot they smoke to quiet anxiety, and even the opiates prescribed after athletic injury, combined with impulsivity in this age group, increases risk for suicide. However, school administrators rarely want to talk about substance misuse for fear of being labeled a school with a drug problem—yet another head-in-the-sand approach that has had devastating consequences on our youth. If we don't educate kids, drug dealers and disreputable Internet resources will fill that void.

Of course, other unhealthy coping strategies have also flourished, such as non-suicidal self-harm (e.g. cutting), eating disorders, gambling, retail therapy (buying stuff to feel better), pornography, and promiscuity.

So how can you tell who might be feeling unwell emotionally? Keep an eye out for the kids who are always going to the school nurse with complaints of headaches and stomachaches, who struggle with concentration and motivation or fall asleep in class. A drop in grades or a no-care attitude from a student who used to engage are signs that something isn't right. Other behaviors we don't always associate with depression, anxiety, and other mental illnesses include outbursts of anger, irritability, and aggression such as fighting and bullying. In the past, and sometimes even now, educators label these kids as being lazy, mean, or combative when in fact they are merely acting in response to how they are feeling.

The Impact of Increased Screen Time

Studies have found that spending less than two hours per day of recreational screen time such as browsing the Internet playing games, watching videos, and using social media was associated with higher levels of life satisfaction and optimism, and lower levels of anxiety and depressive symptoms, especially among girls.[13] While there is not enough definitive data specific to remote learning and its impact on student mental health, we do know that high levels of screen time do have an negative impact on a student's mental health.[14]

During the pandemic, calls to suicide hotlines went up 47% nationwide in June 2020 in the US, with some crisis lines experiencing a 300% increase.[15] So it's not farfetched to assume that young people were not insulated from the emotional turmoil triggered by the pandemic, including parental job loss and income instability, and being stuck in a toxic home environment, along with the uncertainty and lack of connectedness of not attending school in person and seeing their peers. During online learning, spotting kids at risk and weeding them out for additional support or assessment became a challenge for educators as schools struggled to adapt quickly to a new digital delivery platform for teaching.

"The kids who were the highest risk were not on the Zoom sessions with their faces in class. Many of them tended to either miss class, sleep through class, or not have a picture in class. So it was very hard for us to find the high-risk kids, which is why our school counseling team sent out a survey. We send it out twice a semester and before the start of the year we were able to weed out the kids who were higher on the scale of showing that they were having more depressive and anxiety symptoms. The kids filled it out and there was a scale of how they were doing during COVID-19, how they were doing during remote learning, and we'd send it out a few times. It's always so important that the school counseling team, either guidance counselors, social workers, whomever is communicating with all the students, to be able to assess who is the most high risk. And honestly, as we know, the kids who are the most high risk are not calling us and saying, 'Hey, I need some help.' At our school, those kids tend to be on the sidelines, who we don't know. So if they're answering these surveys it's actually helpful, especially for the boys. Because again, boys are not calling their friends and saying, you know, 'I'm feeling really sad today. Yeah, I'm feeling depressed, today.'"

Jessica Chock-Goldman, LCSW (She/Her/Hers), Doctoral Candidate, School Social Worker, Stuyvesant High School in Manhattan, New York

NOTE A copy of the survey mentioned can be found in Chapter 12, "Quizzes, Worksheets, Handouts, Guides, and Scripts." Worksheet 3: Student Wellness Surveys features one for distance learning and one for in-classroom learning.

Co-occurring Disorders

Suicide in teens is often linked to the presence of mental health disorders, which can co-occur and further increase risk:

- Major Depressive Disorder
- Conduct Disorder
- Substance Use Disorders
- Eating Disorders
- Generalized Anxiety Disorders
- Schizophrenia
- Bipolar Disorder

Source: More Than Sad Presentation from the American Foundation for Suicide Prevention.

MENTAL HEALTH DISORDERS

Suicide is caused by a constellation of risk factors and underlying vulnerabilities, including mental health issues, environmental and cultural factors (psychosocial), and family and health history, in addition to trying to resolve emotional pain with impaired or underdeveloped problem-solving skills. With most mental illnesses there is treatment and the earlier the intervention, the better the outcome.

The following is a brief overview of some of the more widely known mental health disorders that can affect teenagers and increase suicide risk.[16]

Major Depressive Disorder (Depression)

Major depressive disorder is a mood disorder affecting between 20% and 50% of youth that causes a persistent feeling of sadness, and loss of interest and motivation.[17] It's important to recognize that in children and adolescents, the mood may be irritable rather than sad.[18] Depression affects how an individual feels, thinks, and behaves, and can lead to a variety of emotional and physical problems. Normal day-to-day activities take considerable effort and can lead many to feel that life isn't worth living. Depression is more than just the blues; it isn't a weakness and can often require long-term treatment, including therapy and sometimes medication. These are often the kids who appear unmotivated or tired, fall asleep in class, and are frequently absent.

The total number of teenagers who reported experiencing depression increased 59% between 2007 and 2017.[19] While we cannot pinpoint one single reason that mental illnesses such as depression and anxiety took such a significant jump in this age group, we do know the contributing factors. Adverse childhood experiences (trauma also called ACEs, acesconnection.com), increased digital screen time, grief, marginalization, less in-person face time, sexual orientation, bullying, poor sleep, poor diet, relational difficulties, family history, health history, genetics and more all play a part.

Conduct Disorder

Conduct disorder is diagnosed when children or adolescents show an ongoing pattern of aggression toward others, including property destruction, bullying, fighting, being cruel to animals, and shoplifting. The major characteristic of the disorder is the violation of social norms and the rights of others.[20] Youth with conduct disorder violate these social norms at home, at school, and with peers. These are the kids who often start fights, bully others, skip school, have frequent suspensions on their record, drop out of school, run away, ignore curfews, end up as discipline problems, and at juvenile detention centers. Children with conduct disorders are more apt to become injured and often have trouble with family and peer relationships. Conduct disorders frequently co-occur with depression, but the depression is rarely diagnosed in these cases because the conduct issues are more prominent.

Bipolar Disorder

To be diagnosed with bipolar disorder, the individual must have met criteria for a depressive episode and have had at least one episode of mania, which is defined as a distinct period of abnormally and persistently elevated, expansive, or irritable mood.[21] It can last a week or more and include grandiose feelings of self-esteem, marked by sleeplessness, talking fast, bursts of creativity and ideas, and increased risk taking. Hormonal changes also make it difficult to discern between normal teen emotional behavior versus manic symptoms. In addition, bipolar disorder in teens is often misdiagnosed as ADHD and vice versa, and can be overlooked initially because the teen might have already been diagnosed with depression or anxiety instead of bipolar disorder because mania isn't always the first symptom to express itself. Those experiencing mania can have elevated mood, feel extremely agitated, behave brashly or lavishly, assume superiority or grandiosity, or dress and act flamboyantly. They might post obsessively on social media or start telling dirty jokes at inopportune times and in front of inappropriate audiences. Some with bipolar disorder (and depression) have psychosis and hear voices that can sometimes tell them to suicide.

Substance Use Disorder

Substance use disorders are patterns of symptoms resulting from continued use of a substance, despite harmful consequences. Addiction is the most severe form of substance use disorders, a chronic relapse disease caused by repeated misuse of one or more substances.[22] Substance misuse can lead to substance use disorder but whether it does or not depends on age, family, and health history, as well as environment, which can include mental illness and/or exposure to traumatic events. Developing teen brains are more susceptible to substance use disorders than adult brains and there are many substances to which someone can become addicted. The most common substance is alcohol, followed by marijuana, prescription medications, over-the-counter medications such as cough syrup with dextromethorphan (e.g. Robitussin®), air dusters, and aerosol whipped cream (e.g. Reddi-Wip®). The misuse of easily accessible substances can lead to the eventual dependence on street drugs. The development of physical withdrawal symptoms, which can be relieved by taking more of the substance, is what separates addiction from substance misuse. Teens often start using to fit in, experience highs, "numb" feelings related to an adverse event, or normalize or regulate their moods pertaining to grief or a mental illness. Substance use disorders can co-occur with other mental illnesses and disorders. Drinking alcohol at an early age, binge or heavy drinking, and drinking behaviors that meet criteria for mild, moderate, or severe alcohol use disorder can all lead to increased risk of suicidal ideation and attempts. Persons with heavy alcohol use are five times more likely to die by suicide than social drinkers[23] and toxicology reports on suicide decedents indicate that 75% of suicides involve one or more substances.[24]

Eating Disorder

An eating disorder is a severe disturbance in people's eating behaviors and their related thoughts and emotions. Preoccupation with food, body weight, and shape are other symptoms of eating disorders. Common eating disorders include anorexia nervosa, bulimia nervosa, and binge-eating disorder. A substantial number of individuals affected by an eating disorder may also be suffering with a mood disorder, especially major depressive disorder.[25] Eating disorders are often accompanied by thoughts of suicide or suicide attempts, as this is the most common cause of death among individuals with eating disorders. Eating disorders have the highest mortality rate of all psychiatric disorders.[26] Studies have shown that within the eating disorder population, people with anorexia have the highest rate of suicide death and those with bulimia have the greatest number of attempts. Furthermore, one study also found that half of the people struggling with binge eating disorder have attempted suicide. Suicide attempts by individuals with anorexia tend to be planned, while attempts by individuals with bulimia tend to be more impulsive.[27]

Schizophrenia

Schizophrenia is a serious mental illness that affects how a person thinks, feels, and behaves. People with schizophrenia experience symptoms of psychosis, which can consist of delusions (false beliefs) and hallucinations (seeing or hearing things that others do not see or hear). Experiencing psychotic symptoms is a significant risk factor for suicide, and the early stages of psychotic disorders like schizophrenia represent a particularly critical period of risk. Other symptoms of schizophrenia include incoherent or nonsense speech, and behavior that is inappropriate for the situation. People with schizophrenia may also experience depression, anxiety, sleep problems, social withdrawal, lack of motivation, and difficulty functioning overall. They may seem like they have lost touch with reality, which causes significant distress for the individual, their family members, and friends. Onset of schizophrenia is typically in young adulthood, but the initial and less severe phase of psychotic symptoms may begin in childhood or adolescence. If left untreated, the symptoms of schizophrenia can be persistent and disabling. However, effective treatments are available. When delivered in a timely, coordinated, and sustained manner, treatment can help affected individuals to engage in school or work, achieve independence, and enjoy personal relationships.[28]

Generalized Anxiety Disorder

Anxiety is the most common emotional problem in children. Youth can develop crippling worries about many things, from germs to vomiting to their parents dying. Some anxious kids are painfully shy, and avoid things that other kids enjoy. Some have tantrums and meltdowns, and others can develop elaborate rituals, like compulsive handwashing, aimed at diminishing the fear.[29] Generalized anxiety disorder is a mental health disorder characterized by feelings of worry about multiple things that are strong enough to interfere with one's daily activities. Examples of other anxiety disorders include panic disorder, social anxiety disorder, and specific phobias. The ongoing worry and tension of anxiety may be accompanied by physical symptoms, such as restlessness, feeling on edge or easily fatigued, difficulty concentrating, muscle tension, or problems sleeping. In addition to genetics, brain chemistry, personality, and life events, teens can experience feelings of anxiety that are fueled by high expectations and pressure to succeed, a world that feels less safe than it used to, and digital media sites where teens tend to compare their life and social situations to what others are posting. According to the National Institutes of Health, nearly 1 in 3 adolescents ages 13 to 18 will experience an anxiety disorder. Between 2007 and 2012, anxiety disorders in children and teens went up 20%.[30] Some teens like the pressure and need it to meet deadlines. Others shut down or avoid situations that would otherwise help them learn to manage events that challenge them and build resilience.

Post-Traumatic Stress Disorder (PTSD)

To develop PTSD, an individual must have been exposed to actual or threatened death, serious injury, or sexual violence either directly or indirectly. Someone with PTSD can be jumpy, irritable, violent, or have trouble sleeping and concentrating after experiencing or witnessing a harmful, terrifying, or upsetting event.[31] Any kind of extreme stress can lead to PTSD. For teens this can be the result of physical, emotional, or sexual abuse, undergoing major surgery, loss of a loved one, community violence or unrest, or natural disasters.

The prevalence of trauma exposure among youth is a major public health concern. Youth who have been exposed to trauma, whether a one-time event or repeated, can respond by withdrawing from others or they can be the students who threaten others or start fights. Youth affected by trauma can also have a decreased IQ and reading ability, lower grade-point average (GPA), more days of school absence, and decreased rates of high school graduation.[32,33] Evidence suggests that youth exposed to trauma have decreased social competence and increased rates of peer rejection.[34] Like conduct disorder symptoms, the behavior of these students often challenges the patience of educators. In these cases we encourage teachers to think, "What happened to you?" instead of "What's wrong with you?"[35]

If you notice students exhibiting characteristics that may indicate any of these mental illnesses, do refer them to your counseling staff for assessment because they may need additional intervention to be successful in school.

NOTES

1. www.mentalhealth.gov
2. Twenge, J. M., Cooper, A. B., Joiner, T. E., Duffy, M. E., and Binau, S. G. (2019). Age, period, and cohort trends in mood disorder indicators and suicide-related outcomes in a nationally representative dataset, 2005–2017. *Journal of Abnormal Psychology* 128(3): 185.
3. Plemmons, G., Hall, M., Doupnik, S., et al. Hospitalization for suicide ideation or attempt: 2008–2015. (2018). *Pediatrics* 141(6): e20172426. doi:10.1542/peds.2017-2426. https://pubmed.ncbi.nlm.nih.gov/29769243/
4. Seabrook, E. M., Kern, M. L., Rickard, N. S. (2016, Nov 23). Social networking sites, depression, and anxiety: A systematic review. *JMIR Mental Health* 3(4): e50. doi:10.2196/mental.5842 https://www.ncbi.nlm.nih.gov/pmc/articles/PMC5143470/

5. Primack, B. A., Shensa, A., Escobar-Viera, C. G., Barrett, E. L., Sidani, J. E., Colditz, J. B., and James, A. E. (2017, Apr). Use of multiple social media platforms and symptoms of depression and anxiety: A nationally representative study among US young adults. *Computers in Human Behavior* 69, 1–9. https://doi.org/10.1016/j.chb.2016.11.013

6. Kessler, R. C., Angermeyer, M., Anthony, J. C., et al. (2007). Lifetime prevalence and age-of-onset distributions of mental disorders in the World Health Organization's World Mental Health Survey Initiative. *World Psychiatry* 6(3): 168–76.

7. Rose, M. E. (2018). Are prescription opioids driving the opioid crisis? Assumptions vs facts. *Pain Med* 19 (4, April): 793-807. https://www.ncbi.nlm.nih.gov/pmc/articles/PMC6018937/; or Manchikanti, L., and Singh, A. (2008). Therapeutic opioids: a ten-year perspective on the complexities and complications of the escalating use, abuse, and nonmedical use of opioids. *Pain Physician* 11(2 Suppl): S63–S88 https://pubmed.ncbi.nlm.nih.gov/18443641/

8. Elofson J., Gongvatana, W., Carey, K. B. (2013, Jul). Alcohol use and cerebral white matter compromise in adolescence. *Addictive Behaviors* 38(7): 2295–2305. doi: 10.1016/j.addbeh.2013.03.001. Epub 2013 Mar 15. PMID: 23583835; PMCID: PMC3699185

9. Ammerman, S. (2014). Marijuana. *Adolescent Medicine: State of the Art Reviews* 25(1):70–88. PMID: 25022187

10. NIDA. (2020, April 8). What is the scope of marijuana use in the United States? Retrieved January 14, 2021, from https://www.drugabuse.gov/publications/research-reports/marijuana/what-scope-marijuana-use-in-united-states

11. Pierre, J. M. (2017). Risks of increasingly potent *Cannabis:* The joint effects of potency and frequency. *Current Psychiatry* 16(2): 14–20. https://www.researchgate.net/publication/316647633_Risks_of_increasingly_potent_Cannabis_The_joint_effects_of_potency_and_frequency

12. Ibid.

13. University of British Columbia. (2020, Nov 2). Teens who participate in extracurriculars, get less screen time, have better mental health. *ScienceDaily*. Retrieved November 21, 2020, from www.sciencedaily.com/releases/2020/11/201102124849.htm

14. Trinh, L., Wong, B., & Faulkner, G. E. (2015). The independent and interactive associations of screen time and physical activity on mental health, school connectedness and academic achievement among a population-based

sample of youth. *Journal of the Canadian Academy of Child and Adolescent Psychiatry* 24(1), 17.

15. Pine Rest Christian Mental Health Services, June 2020.
16. American Psychiatric Association. (2013). *Diagnostic and statistical manual of mental disorders (DSM-5®)*. American Psychiatric Publishing.
17. Ibid.
18. Center for Substance Abuse Treatment. (2005). *Substance Abuse Treatment for Persons with Co-Occurring Disorders.* Rockville, MD: Substance Abuse and Mental Health Services Administration (US). (Treatment Improvement Protocol (TIP) Series, No. 42.) Table: What Counselors Should Know About Mood and Anxiety Disorders and Substance Abuse]. https://www.ncbi.nlm.nih.gov/books/NBK64204/table/A75086/
19. 2017 National Survey on Drug Use and Health.
20. INSERM Collective Expertise Centre. (2005). INSERM Collective Expert Reports. Paris: Institut national de la santé et de la recherche médicale; 2000-. Conduct: Disorder in children and adolescents. https://www.ncbi.nlm.nih.gov/books/NBK7133/
21. DSM-5.
22. NIDA. (2020, June 25). The science of drug use and addiction: The basics. Retrieved September 2020 from https://www.drugabuse.gov/publications/media-guide/science-drug-use-addiction-basics
23. Harris, E. C., Barraclough, B. (1997). Suicide as an outcome for mental disorders: A meta-analysis. *British Journal of Psychiatry* 170(3): 205–228. doi: 10.1192/bjp.170.3.205
24. Centers for Disease Control and Prevention. (2018). Surveillance for Violent Deaths: National Violent Death Reporting System, 18 States, 2014. *Morbidity and Mortality Weekly Report* 67(2), 1–36.
25. Mischoulon, D., Eddy, K. T., Keshaviah, A., Dinescu, D., Ross, S. L., Kass, A. E., Franko, D. L., and Herzog, D. B. (2011). Depression and eating disorders: Treatment and course. *Journal of Affective Disorders* 130(3), 470–477. https://doi.org/10.1016/j.jad.2010.10.043
26. Harris, E. C., Barraclough B. (1997). Suicide as an outcome for mental disorders: a meta-analysis. *British Journal of Psychiatry* 170(3): 205–228. doi: 10.1192/bjp.170.3.205
27. Hamilton, G., Culler, L., Elenback, R., and Ekern, J. (2015). Anorexia nervosa – highest mortality rate of any mental disorder: Why? *Eating Disorder Hope.* https://www.eatingdisorderhope.com/information/anorexia/anorexia-death-rate

28. National Institute of Mental Health. Schizophrenia. https://www.nimh.nih.gov/health/topics/schizophrenia/index.shtml
29. Child Mind Institute. Anxiety. https://childmind.org/guide/anxiety-basics/
30. https://www.nimh.nih.gov/health/statistics/any-anxiety-disorder.shtml#part_155096
31. Teens Health. kidshealth.org/en/teens/ptsd.html
32. Delaney-Black, V., Covington, C., Ondersma, S. J., Nordstrom-Klee, B., Templin, T., Ager, J., Janisse, J., and Sokol, R.J. (2002, Mar). Violence exposure, trauma, and IQ and/or reading deficits among urban children. *Archives of Pediatrics and Adolescent Medicine* 156(3): 280–85.
33. Putnam, F. W., and Trickett, P. K. (1997, Jun 21). Psychobiological effects of sexual abuse. A longitudinal study. *Annals of the New York Academy of Sciences* 821(1): 150–59. https://pubmed.ncbi.nlm.nih.gov/9238201/
34. Schwartz, D., and Proctor, L.J. (2000, Aug). Community violence exposure and children's social adjustment in the school peer group: The mediating roles of emotion regulation and social cognition. *Journal of Consulting and Clinical Psychology* 68(4): 670–83.
35. https://www.acesconnection.com/

Chapter 2
Adolescent Suicide: Risk Factors, Protective Factors, and Warning Signs

Trigger warning: suicide methods mentioned briefly

"You need to figure out how worried you are and how uneasy a kid is making you. [Teachers] need to trust their instincts and their feelings rather than dismissing them. If you're up at night worried about a kid in your class, you need to be thinking about why that's the case."

Victor Schwartz, MD (He/Him/His), Former CMO of The JED Foundation,
Founder of MindStrategies Advisors, Clinical Associate Professor,
Department of Psychiatry, NYU School of Medicine

The Centers for Disease Control and Prevention defines suicide as "death caused by self-inflicted injuries with the intention of dying from the result of such actions."[1] Suicide typically occurs when a person has reached a point when they feel their capacity for emotional and physical pain has outweighed the amount of time they can wait for relief, and at the same moment they have access to the means to end their life. That can be anything from pills to firearms. And because suicide has risen to the second-leading cause of death for ages 15–34 and the leading cause of death for ages 10–15, this public health threat can no longer be referred to as a rare phenomenon.

Adolescence is a life event characterized by psychological, emotional, developmental, and physical changes. At the same time all that is happening, young people are challenged with developing their identity and self-esteem, becoming more independent and responsible, while also building peer groups and relationships. They are often challenged with high expectations from relatives and peers, which provokes insecurity, stress, and a sense of losing control.

The presence of suicidal thoughts and behaviors among teens is not uncommon. According to the data from the 2019 Youth Risk Behavior Survey (YRBS), 18.8% of youths had seriously considered attempting suicide, 15.7% had made a suicide plan, and 8.9% had made an attempt.[2] With nearly one-fifth of students considering suicide, educators need to be aware of the risk factors and warning signs so they know when to act on behalf of a student.

"Suicidal thoughts in high school age kids are extremely common. I mean, 15–20% reported for suicidal ideation. Fortunately, even with the increases, the gap between suicidal thoughts and actual death by suicide is about 2000 to one. It's not to say you shouldn't take it seriously, because anybody who's having those thoughts or talking like that is in some kind of distress, and that's the problem. When somebody's telling you they're acutely suicidal, that's easy from a decision-making point of view because you know you need to do something. And the focus for teachers shouldn't be on suicide prevention, it should be on getting to know their students and how they can respond to somebody who's in trouble."

Victor Schwartz, MD (He/Him/His), Former CMO of The JED Foundation, Founder of MindStrategies Advisors, Clinical Associate Professor, Department of Psychiatry, NYU School of Medicine

---

Suicidal thoughts can be active or passive, and may or may not coincide with external events. In those prone to suicidal thinking, those thoughts often vary in intensity, frequency, and duration. Suicidal thoughts that are put into action become suicidal behavior. Intense suicidal thoughts can last 5 minutes to 120 minutes, but the average time for the suicidal process is about 30 minutes with peaks[3] and valleys during that episode.

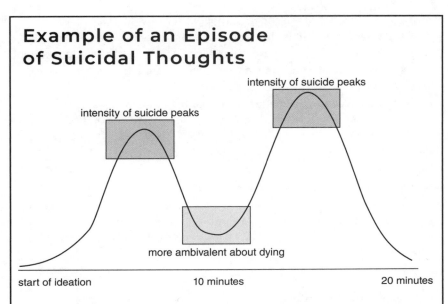

Example of an Episode of Suicidal Thoughts

intensity of suicide peaks

intensity of suicide peaks

more ambivalent about dying

start of ideation   10 minutes   20 minutes

After a stay in a psychiatric hospital following suicidal thoughts with a plan, a 16-year-old high school student described his suicidal intensity as two peaks happening in a 20-minute period. He said that as the emotional pain got worse, the more he wanted to end it. Then it eased off and that was a period where he wasn't so sure he wanted to die and had more fear, suggesting ambivalence. Then he said there was one more peak, more intense than the first, when he really felt worthless, that the world would be better off without him. He managed to endure it without attempting but he very much wanted to tell someone. He texted his counselor and told him and gave that social worker permission to tell his parents.

A survey of 13- to 34-year-old survivors revealed there was less than 5 minutes between suicidal thought and action for 24% of the study subjects.[4] Kim O'Brien's research team conducted a study of 20 teens after they had attempted suicide, and 17 of them reported that the amount of time between thinking about suicide to actually attempting was less than 3 hours, and one teen said they didn't think about attempting suicide at all before acting. In fact, 13 of the 20 made the transition from thoughts to action in 10 minutes or less.[5] With teens, there is often a quick surge of thoughts and emotions that propel the suicidal act, often accompanied by a rapid decline in their ability to cope.

It is often less about the teen's specific thoughts of why they want to kill themselves and what led up to it in that moment, but more about the focus on the immediate emotional pain they are experiencing that drives the suicide attempt.

One teen described what happens for her prior to a suicide attempt:

> "I don't really think about all the factors that go into it before I do it. . . . Just being upset, and you can actually feel it, how upset you are. . . . In the back of your mind, you still think about [suicide], but it's more like what you're feeling at that specific moment."[6]

Another 18-year-old described it this way:

> "Imagine standing in a room and you are on fire. Right next to you is a bucket of water. You are desperate to put out the flames so you grab that bucket of water to put out the fire."

RISK FACTORS

Risk factors are characteristics associated with suicide but not direct causes of suicide. However, being familiar with risk factors helps us understand which teens are more likely to engage in suicidal behavior and to die by suicide. The American Foundation for Suicide Prevention cites three categories of risk factors: historical, environmental, and health.

Suicide Risk Factors

RISK FACTOR: HISTORICAL

- Previous suicide attempts
- Family history of suicide
- Childhood abuse, neglect, or trauma

RISK FACTOR: ENVIRONMENTAL

- Access to lethal means, including firearms and drugs
- Prolonged stress such as harassment, bullying, relationship problems, unemployment, including unemployed family member

---

- Stressful life events, like rejection, divorce, financial crisis, poverty, life transitions, grief and loss, racial/social injustices, and marginalization
- Exposure to another person's suicide, or to graphic or sensationalized accounts of suicide

SUICIDE RISK FACTOR: HEALTH
- Mental health conditions
- Depression
- Substance use problems
- Bipolar disorder
- Schizophrenia
- Personality traits of aggression, mood changes, and poor relationships
- Conduct disorder
- Anxiety disorders
- Serious physical health conditions, including pain
- Traumatic brain injury

Source: AFSP 2020 / American Foundation for Suicide Prevention.

AT-RISK STUDENT POPULATIONS

Although there are student populations with higher risk factors for suicide, the majority of student suicides happen outside these groups. Therefore, it's critical not to dismiss or minimize language that might indicate a student is struggling with suicidal thoughts simply because the individual doesn't fit into one of them. Star athletes and quiet, high-achieving students do die by suicide. However, educators should be aware of student populations that are at elevated risk for suicidal behavior, and the environment, health, and family history that influence it.

The Youth Risk Behavior Surveillance System (YRBS) includes national, state, territorial, tribal government, and local school-based surveys of representative samples of 9th–12th graders in public and private schools and are conducted every two years, usually in the spring semester. While this section will focus on specific populations, your school district could serve a demographic that also has an elevated suicide risk, but due to their small numbers they may not be recognized nationally as such.

_____

"A group of us who are Filipino social workers have focused on this [Filipino] youth population. The Youth Risk Behavior Survey (YRBS) done throughout the different schools in the US has, for our school district, a separate category for Filipino students because of our large Asian populations. In the 2017 survey, 32% of Filipino students reported 'seriously thought about suicide' (SFUSD, 2017). Our Filipino middle schoolers reported the highest rates—even double what we see in the highest risk population, in our case the Asians. So we've done some research of the literature, and also connecting with different professionals in the community, statewide, and in the country, just to see what this is all about. And what we found is that a lot of the Filipino students' ideation is rooted in colonialism. They feel they are not fitting into a model minority because Filipinos can look varied—not specifically Asian or Latino—and this leaves them feeling as if they don't fit in. So we looked into the pressures that they face in terms of their family and we've done specific presentations regarding Filipino mental health with our youth to raise awareness and prevent suicide and suicide attempts."

Michelle Fortunado-Kewin, LCSW, PPSC (She/Her/Siya), School Social Worker and Program Coordinator, San Francisco Unified School District

_____

In those instances where you have high percentage of a particular ethnic culture in your school district, often the YRBS can reflect those numbers for your region.

Gender and Suicide Risk

Females attempt suicide more than two times as often as males,[7] but boys die by suicide over three times the rate of girls.[8] What is behind these gender differences? Males die by suicide more often because they tend to choose more lethal methods,[9] such as firearms or hanging. Females have been more likely to try to kill themselves by self-poisoning, such as overdosing on pills, which has a lower likelihood of death. This gender paradox can be puzzling, especially in understanding why suicidal behavior appears more common among girls. Some scholars argue that seeking help when experiencing emotional distress is more aligned with the female gender, which may result in more male suicide deaths.[10] However, this does not necessarily account for the differences in attempts, except that suicide attempts may be underreported in males due to their being less likely to seek help following an attempt, making the rates possibly more similar than we think.

Sexual and/or Gender Minorities

Lesbian, gay, bisexual, transgender, and questioning (LGBTQ) youth represent another demographic group more vulnerable to suicide. The suicide attempt rate of sexual minority youth is almost five times that of their heterosexual peers[11] and a 2020 survey by the Trevor Project found that 40% of respondents seriously considered attempting suicide in the past year. Over 50% of nonbinary youth (those who don't identify with traditional male or female gender roles), as well as transgender youth, reported having seriously considered suicide.[12] They also found that 46% of respondents wanted mental health counseling but were unable to receive it, emphasizing the importance of schools as safe spaces for these youth and making emotional support by educators even more critical.[13]

> "There's this interesting differential where some say that by treating them [LGBTQ youth] as a high-risk population, you're contributing to the exclusion or ostracism of this group, and not actually supporting them. And in my mind, it's the opposite. You're actually recognizing that this population is going to have a different risk factor than what you're seeing in the general student population. There is something to be said for putting extra resources and watching out for our LGBTQ youth, who face disproportionate rates of homelessness and victimization, along with unique mental health challenges. Part of this is making sure teachers are trained to be LGBTQ competent."
>
> *Sam Brinton (They/Them/Theirs), Vice President of Advocacy and Government Affairs at The Trevor Project, Rockville, Maryland*
>
> **Note: See Trevor Project CARE training in the Resources section (Chapter 11).*

It is not their sexual orientation or gender identity that place LGBTQ youth at greater risk of suicidal behavior, but rather societal and external factors: discrimination, harassment, bullying, violence, victimization, family rejection, and homelessness due to nonacceptance, in addition to mental health history. Two transgender teen suicide attempt survivors express their despair over being invalidated:

> "Telling me I would never be a boy because I had girl body parts, and that I don't look like a boy, and I never would."
>
> "Sometimes it just makes me feel like I'm doing something wrong or I'm in the wrong family or what I am is wrong."

An unyielding religious culture that defines homosexuality in a community as a sin can elevate LGBTQ youth suicide risk, as well as increase the likelihood of being ridiculed at school. And the combination of all these influences con-tributes to their overwhelming feelings of guilt and shame. Lack of tolerance, a confrontational culture on the subject of homosexuality, together with lack of acceptance, is what drives LGBTQ youth to think suicide is the only option. A transgender teen describes this direct relationship to his suicide attempt:

> "I tried to kill myself because my dad and me got in a fight, and he told me that I was not a boy when I was a girl, and I can't hang out with my friends that were also transgender, and that I was a girl no matter what."

A teen who searched a specific way to kill himself and landed on an Emotion-ally Naked YouTube video expressed his despair:

> "My parents do not accept that I'm gay and they want me to rot in hell, they don't physically abuse me. But I want all of the pain inside of me to end. . . . I confessed to the guy that I like and he called me a faggot and now everyone calls me that. . .my sister was the only one who understood my pain and wanted to help me. But not too long ago she got run over by a car while hanging out with her friends. I'm just a worthless piece of crap so I feel there is no point in living."
> *(Note: This young man did reach out to the Trevor Project Crisis Line and joined TrevorSpace, a private forum for LGBTQ youth.)*

How can teachers help? Transgender and nonbinary youth who reported hav-ing pronouns respected by all or most people in their lives attempted suicide at half the rate of those who did not have their pronouns respected.[14] And making sure your teacher roll and attendance sheets reflect that child's preferred gen-der makes your class a more inclusive space.

Race and Ethnicity

Race and ethnicity are other factors to consider in relation to youth suicide. American Indians/Alaskan Native (AI/AN) youth represent the race with the highest suicide rate (17.79 per 100,000), followed by Whites (10.98), Asian/Pacific Islanders (8.01), and Blacks (7.55).[15] With respect to ethnicity, youth who identify as Hispanic have a lower suicide rate (3.98 per 100,000) than non-Hispanics (8.20).[16] Although the AI/AN suicide rate in the US is high, the data do not reflect the variations in suicide by region and tribe.[17]

Behavioral Health Resources for Native Americans

If a Native American student needs behavioral health support:

- Ask the child what tribe they are from and reach out to the behavioral health director for that tribe. Most every tribe now has a director of health or behavioral health. It can make a difference between free care or very expensive care.

- Ask the tribe director of behavioral health what services are available for youth. Because if their tribe has behavioral health, they have access to a robust system of care.

Questions? Go to Indian Health Service at IHS.gov.

Source: Shelby Rowe, Co-Chair, Indigenous Peoples Committee, American Association of Suicidology (AAS).

Historical trauma is one reason AI/ANs are disproportionately affected by suicide. From 1860 to 1978, Native American children as young as five were taken from their families and placed in boarding schools. The official slogan was, "Let's kill the Indian, save the man." The idea was to "Americanize" these kids because it was thought that Native Americans were incapable of raising their own children. These children were beaten if they spoke their native language, and if their name sounded too native it would be changed. Abuse, shaming, and neglect were commonplace in these boarding schools and many of today's Native American parents and grandparents were products of these schools and therefore have extreme mistrust of social workers, schools, government, and other institutions. From the public health level, there are higher rates of substance misuse in some of the more traumatized tribes, and because of that history they may be more susceptible to suicide clusters and contagion within their communities.

"At a public health level [for Native Americans] there are the health disparities: higher rates of poverty, incarceration, addiction but it's not across the board but in different pockets. When we look at the Urban Indian Health National Survey from 2011 to 2014, urban natives actually have a higher sobriety than white people. Whereas on a reservation, that addiction level may be a lot higher. Specifically, when we look at the data of 15- to 30-year-old Indigenous males in reservation-based areas everywhere, their suicide rates are a lot higher. When we look across the lifespan of male and female Native Americans, they have a lower rate than white people. But for our reservation-based and rural native teenage boys, we absolutely need to pay attention."

Shelby Rowe (She/Her/Hers), Co-Chair, Indigenous Peoples Committee,
American Association of Suicidology (AAS)

Despite African Americans having the lowest rate, research demonstrates the suicide rate of black youth is rising faster than any other racial or ethnic group.[18] In particular, suicide attempts have increased by 73% from 1991 to 2017 for Black adolescents. As of 2018, suicide became the second leading cause of death in Black children aged 10–14, and the third leading cause of death in Black adolescents aged 15–19.[19] This group may be at higher risk for suicide due to their lower likelihood of seeking help since mental health is more stigmatized in this community and social networks are not as likely to be supportive. Cultural mistrust of professional healthcare systems and providers also plays a role due to historical inequality and mistreatment. Another reason for an increase in suicide risk among black youth is that trauma is disproportionately experienced in their neighborhoods as compared to other communities. For example, this demographic suffers more exposure to racism, discrimination, neighborhood violence, economic insecurity, abuse, grief, greater access to firearms, and other adverse childhood experiences.

For BIPOC (Black, Indigenous, and People of Color), racial prejudice, colonialism, injustice, lack of acceptance, unrest, and perceived discrimination, including racial, ethnic, and homophobic acts, can contribute to thoughts of suicide.[20] Joblessness can increase risk for youth in communities of extreme violence and poverty who can't see a future for themselves.

Demographic Region

Youth who live in rural areas are less likely to report suicidal thoughts or attempts than those in urban areas, but are almost two times as likely to die by suicide. And this gap is widening.[21] Individuals in rural areas experience unique challenges such as fewer healthcare resources and facilities, mental health workforce shortages, financial constraints, transportation and infrastructure limitations that present challenges to accessing care in-person or remotely.[22]

Perhaps the most relevant explanation for a disproportionate risk compared to urban youth is that households in rural areas are more likely to have a firearm, in addition to higher rates of alcohol and drug use. This, in combination with greater isolation and a lack of social integration, makes rural youth more susceptible to suicide.

Psychological Factors, Including Prior Suicide Attempt

According to the NIMH "Ask Suicide-Screening Questions (ASQ) Toolkit," 90% of suicide attempts among youth are unknown to parents.

Critical psychological risk factors for suicide in students include depression, anxiety, and substance misuse. These underlying psychological issues make adolescents more vulnerable when faced with social, emotional, and environmental stressors. One teenage girl described how her worsening psychological symptoms contributed to her attempt:

_____

"Everything piled up, and it was just like, 'I'm done. Can't do this anymore.' I'd already been to eight programs, and it just seemed like anxiety and depression was never gonna go away, and I couldn't do anything about it."

_____

One of the strongest risk factors for suicide in teens is having made a prior suicide attempt.[23] A common yet highly inaccurate belief is that people who survive an attempt are unlikely to try again. But the facts are that if someone has an attempt, that person's chances of a future suicide are that much higher because a history of previous suicide attempt is the strongest predictor for future suicidal ideation, suicide attempts, and death by suicide.[24,25,26] For attempt survivors, data supports that the year following that first attempt is a critical period for integrative preventive resources to avoid a repeat event. This comment by a teenage girl who lives with depression illustrates the vulnerability:

_____

"Well, I had recently gotten out of another hospital and then it wasn't even a week, a full week being home, and then it was a rough day. I just didn't know what to do and I wanted to give up, so I just took a bunch of medications, to try to kill myself."

_____

Access to Firearms

Having access to firearms, regardless of intent to use them, is the strongest risk factor for suicide among teens. Firearms are used in more than half of all youth suicides. While firearm-owning families are not by nature more at risk emotionally than non-firearm-owning community members, it is the access to means and the lethality of the method that makes youth in these families more at risk of dying by suicide. Safe storage and a willingness to have another gun owner keep firearms for a period of time until a crisis in a family subsides is a wise prevention effort. Neighbors supporting the health and well-being of fellow neighbors is a doctrine in rural America.

Family History of Suicide

A family history of suicide significantly increases suicide risk, whether or not the individual has a personal or family history of mental illness. However, having a mental illness further increases that risk. This does not mean that suicidal behavior is inevitable for students with this family history. It simply means that they may be more vulnerable and steps should be taken to reduce their risk, such as getting an evaluation and treatment at the first sign of mental illness.

Non-Suicidal Self-Injury

Non-suicidal self-injury (NSSI) is the act of intentional destruction of one's own body tissue without suicidal intent and for purposes not socially sanctioned. NSSI is often confused with suicidal behavior (see Chapter 3 on debunking myths), but they are in fact two different behaviors. One teen girl described why she engages in the NSSI of cutting:

"Cutting is usually in people who have suicidal thoughts, but it's kind of in a way to live. It's a coping mechanism that I use or that a lot of people use to be in control of a lot of things. I'm not in control with a lotta things in my life. There were things like disclosing about my sexual abuse that I thought I would be in control of and I'm not. That was taken over by my parents. This was a way that I could be in control."

Teens who self-injure are at higher risk for suicide than teens who do not. This is because engaging in NSSI over time reduces teens' self-protective fears of pain and injury, removing a barrier to attempting suicide.[27] One older teen girl described the slippery slope of self-injury:

"After the relief of [cutting] you get just this welcoming feeling in your body. It just makes it feel like things are just gonna be so much better until you really get into it too much. It becomes an addictive thing to do because you're just getting so used to it. It feels so good that you keep doing it and doing it and doing it to a point where it really can damage your body severely."

_____

Trauma

Physical, sexual, or emotional trauma puts youth at increased risk of suicide attempts and deaths.[28] One teen girl explained the role of bullying-related trauma in her suicide attempt:

_____

"I felt really hated and I guess it brought down my self-esteem. It made me feel what's wrong with me? That in combination with I'm not as popular, I have way less friends, I felt like. . .I felt really like a loser."

_____

There are many reasons why trauma leads to risk for suicide. First, many youth have moments where they feel they are reexperiencing the trauma, or avoiding situations that remind them of the trauma, which can cause them to feel detached from reality and to isolate.[29] This is a key contributor to depression and suicide risk, and suicide attempts often happen as a result of trying to cope with these intrusive thoughts and images of past trauma.[30] Prior trauma can also be indicative of current high-risk and tumultuous family dynamics that contribute to suicide risk.[31] In addition, the characteristics of self-criticism and self-hatred of trauma survivors play a role in the worsening of their suicidal thoughts.[32] Childhood trauma, also known adverse childhood experiences (ACEs), can include any number of issues, including physical or sexual abuse, grief, neglect, or having a parent or parents who are incarcerated, divorced, estranged, or addicted.

ACEs are strongly linked with suicidal thoughts and behaviors. A study of nearly 10,000 US participants by Thompson, Kingree, and Lamis (2019)[33] found physical, sexual, and emotional abuse, parental incarceration, and family history of suicidality each increased the risk for suicidal ideation by 1.4 times and suicide attempts by 2.7 times in adulthood. In addition, they found that the more of these ACEs that youth experienced, the greater the odds of suicidal ideation and attempts. In the same study, compared with those with no ACEs, the odds of seriously considering suicide or attempting suicide in adulthood increased more than three times for individuals who reported three or more ACEs.

Teens with Challenging Family Dynamics

Other domestic dynamics that contribute to suicide risk among teens include family conflict and relationship disruption. Some adolescents experience inner conflict related to family because they feel they are not being a good enough child or sibling, they do not have a parent, the parent is neglectful, or the child is making a conscious choice to distance themselves from a parent. For some, family clashes involve a single argument with a member of that household. And for others, it can be more frequent arguments reflecting a more toxic family environment. Feeling trapped in the middle of a contentious parental divorce can be an event that contributes to an attempt. One teen girl described how her family dynamic contributed to her suicide attempt:

> "Then there was the stress of my brothers. We have a lotta, lotta arguments. When it gets really heated, they start talking about my mom and their mom and how my mom didn't want me, which is why I lived with them—and how she still doesn't want me, which is why I still live with them. It really hurts because just hearing that you're not wanted and that people in your family want to hurt you—is pretty messed up. Apparently, they don't think of that. Whenever it happens I just—it starts running through my mind mostly after we have a giant argument. It's like, your family doesn't want you—at all."

Another teenage boy talks about how his complicated feelings about his mother drove his desire to kill himself:

> "[My mom] loves me to death. It breaks me inside, cuz I love her, but I want nothing to do with her. It's so hard, because I can't help the way that I feel. I can't help that I don't want anything to do with her. . . . I want to have her in my life, but I want to want her in my life, but I don't want to—Yeah, and it's hard, because she loves me so much, and she knows—she doesn't deserve that. It's just her personality—the way she acts, her tendencies. They just drive me up a wall. I don't know, it just—that's another huge reason why I tried doing what I was doing, tried to kill myself, because of that."

For another teen boy, constant fighting with his mom left him feeling invalidated and unheard and was a contributing factor in his attempt:

> "I was getting sick and tired of fighting. . . . I felt like I was trapped, like this was just going to happen until I moved out. Things would not have gotten better. . . .

I have already told my mom I didn't like it, but she wouldn't listen. . . . She needed to know that she was doing something wrong for a while. She needs to listen to me. I felt like I needed to make an impression, by me not being there, now she can feel like she has the burden on her shoulders."

_____

Other high-risk groups include adopted children who are nearly four times more likely to attempt suicide than nonadopted children.[34] Educators, parents, and doctors should be aware of the relatively higher risk among adopted teens who are showing other potential risk factors for suicide, such as substance misuse or problems at school, since co-occurring disorders increase the threat.

A large study in California found that adolescents with parents or siblings serving in the military are at increased risk for suicidal ideation, and for feeling sad or hopeless, and depressed. The deployment of a family member was associated with a further increase in the likelihood of an adolescent's feeling sad or hopeless, or of experiencing depressive symptoms.[35]

Teens who are homeless, in juvenile justice, child welfare, or foster care systems are at higher risk for suicidal thoughts and behaviors than those who live at home.[36] Youth experiencing homelessness are two times as likely to have suicidal thoughts and behaviors than the general adolescent population.[37] And one study found that 25% of foster care youth reported attempting suicide before age 18.[38]

Chronic Illness or Disabilities

Other psychosocial factors that increase suicide risk among youth include chronic physical illness and/or presence of a disability. Chronic pain, loss of mobility, disfigurement, cognitive delays, and constant sickness or surgeries can make day-to-day living more challenging than for their peers. One teen boy with diabetes and chronic pain described the combination of these factors as contributors to his attempt:

_____

"I'd rather not be, so then, there's that. I don't wanna go on with the future. I just don't wanna carry on anymore. Between the diabetes, the pain in my feet—all day, every day, and then just—I don't know, just kind of a blankness. That's why I can describe it as life is like a game, and I'm losing that game, and I just wanna stop playing."

_____

Youth Living with Autism

Research has shown high rates of suicidality in autism spectrum conditions, but there is lack of research into why this is the case.[39] Many common experiences of autistic adults, such as depression or unemployment, overlap with known risk markers for suicide in the general population. Parents of children who live with autism suspect lack of social skills and friends plays into their risk factors.

"My child was 13 years old and he'd never in his life been invited to a friend's birthday party although he had been invited to family ones. His brother, on the other hand, had so many friends and had been to so many I can't count them. I know that really bothered both of my children. The autistic one who never got invited and the brother who hurt for his sibling who never got an invitation."

Precipitating Events

Examples of Precipitating Events

Some adolescent precipitating events include:

- End of a relationship or a parent's divorce
- Death or serious illness of a loved one (e.g. grief and unresolved grief)
- An arrest
- Poor performance (e.g. academics, sports)
- Being the subject of bullying or humiliation

Events that appear to "trigger" a person into an action, or events that mark a critical turning point in the dynamics of a particular pattern of mobilization, may be thought of as precipitating events.[40] In the context of vulnerable adolescents, precipitating events are the stressful life events that can trigger a suicidal crisis.

And it's not just one factor but a cluster of several that happen all at once that increases that threat, and precipitating events can be that one added stressor that collapses the house of cards for a vulnerable adolescent. The humiliation of an embarrassing picture texted to a multitude of peers can be the conclusive precipitating event that inspires an attempt. Relationship disruption, whether that's a romantic breakup, a fight with parents, divorcing parents, the death of a loved one, or loss of friendships, are common precipitators.

Three teens described the events that led to their suicide attempts:

"Me and my best friend got in a really big fight for a really dumb reason. I don't really understand the reason. We've been friends for seven years, so it was really hard for me because when I lose a best friend, I don't really—I care, but not that much, but considering she was pretty much my family, it hit me hard."

"It started at 12 when my parents divorced. I started smoking cigarette butts I found on the side of the street and drinking booze I brewed in my closet. Around 15 I attempted to kill myself by jumping out of my window on Christmas when I was completely alone."

"It is just my time to go i cant live with myself i have made big mistakes and because of that i lost the love of my life i know there is lot of time to live but it is not ment for me."

Life Transitions

Transitioning to middle school, high school, or a new school, from high school to real life or from high school to college, from a gap year to college, or a leave of absence for mental health and the return to school can all be moments of extreme stress for a young person.[41] And these life transitions during the adolescent years can contribute to emotional instability and suicidal thoughts and behaviors. We need students to leave middle school, high school, and college with a stronger level of emotional preparedness for these changes and we know them to be points of vulnerability.

"I transitioned into high school and I went from, you know, performing really well to not really performing at all. I managed to fail marching band one semester, which was the thing I cared deeply about [in school]."

Dese'Rae L. Stage (She/Her/Hers), Suicide Attempt Survivor,
Suicide Loss Survivor, Queer, livethroughthis.org

Gender transitions, moving, and military deployment of a family member are all examples of transitions. We want to make sure students have the skill base, coping mechanisms, and the knowledge to move successfully through these life events.[42]

"We do see surges in suicide at the end of college or the end of high school. More at the end of something. The leaving."

Victor Schwartz, MD (He/Him/His), Former CMO of The JED Foundation, Founder of MindStrategies Advisors, Clinical Associate Professor, Department of Psychiatry, NYU School of Medicine

We can help students by allowing them to discover their individual unique set of intersecting identities and identifying their assets. "What strengths can I draw upon to prepare me emotionally for the transition that's coming?" And in the context of those identities, "Where might I anticipate barriers?" And most importantly, "What can I do when I encounter them?"[43]

Where specifically in that cycle of those transitions do we see the danger zones? Often it's at a point when students actually have the most support and are likely to feel overwhelmed with what the future holds and unequipped to handle that next step, like moving from something known and comfortable to something unfamiliar.

"We know since the early days of psychoanalysis that transitions are difficult. Separations are challenging and they evoke anxiety. [We] do see surges in suicide at the end of college or the end of high school. More at the end of something; the leaving. For many people, this seems to be more difficult than starting the new thing where very often the system is giving [students] quite a bit of support. But ending college or high school are major changes. We need to recognize that changes and separations are both anxiety and depression provoking. They raise people's stress level and are danger points, to some extent. Winter vacations, coming home for Thanksgiving, or for Christmas break, and then going back to school are all again mini transitions.

So, I think it's important for people to understand it's not just the high school to work, or high school to college, but anytime there's a transition. If you move, that's a transition. All of those things present challenges [for students]. So, families and the schools need to be aware of that."

Victor Schwartz, MD (He/Him/His), Former CMO of The JED Foundation, Founder of MindStrategies Advisors, Clinical Associate Professor, Department of Psychiatry, NYU School of Medicine

School and Extracurricular Stress

Of particular relevance to educators is chronic or acute stress related to school or extracurricular activities that can also elevate suicide risk.[44] Some students' stress relates to a relentless pursuit of perfection and constant comparison to others' successes, as it did for this teen suicide attempt survivor:

"Both years I worked really hard so that I got 4.0 in all my classes for the year. I put a lot of pressure on myself to get there. . . . Also the environment I was in was all these people who were college-bound. That's all they talked about, all they thought about was—and every time we got a test back everyone would compare scores, stuff like that."

The presence of conflicting and competing pressures contributes to a concept called strain, which is believed to precede suicide in most cases.[45] Sometimes a combination of acute and chronic school-related stressors (i.e. strain) can put youth at elevated risk, as this teen boy stated when he reflected back on the reason for his suicide attempt:

"I was dreaming about how I'm gonna do well in the world, and then I was over-thinking that. Then I started thinking, 'I'm not happy. I'm at a school that I don't like. I don't get along with people or I don't like the people. I just don't connect there. I fail all my classes, and I don't like the system. I don't like the teachers. I don't like the system. I don't like the students,' but I was like, 'Well, any school you go to, you're not gonna like the teachers or students,' but it was like—I just don't get well with it because it doesn't provide what I need. I want a school with all those academics, but football is my major sport. I love football and that's what makes me passionate. . . . Then I see all of my friends, they're doing well, they're playing football, they're getting scholarships, they're getting looked at, they're doing all sorts of things. I'm like, 'Where am I?'. . . If I didn't get that concussion, if I was good in school. I'm always looking back at the past, and why did I do that when I should have been doing this?"

Suicide Contagion

A community such as a school that has experienced a loss by suicide[46] heightens risk for others in that environment, and in particular for vulnerable adolescents. This phenomenon is known as "suicide contagion" and has also been referred to as "copycat suicide." One teen suicide attempt survivor explains her suicidal thought process as it related to her classmate's death by suicide, helping our understanding of the underlying process of contagion:

"What's the point of being alive. What's the point of doing this, why am I putting myself under so much. . . . It just led to me questioning why am I doing this?. . . and then it was intensified after [a classmate] committed suicide because everyone was so upset and everyone was shocked and everyone was saying, 'how could he have done this to himself?' How could he have felt so alone and how could he have—how come he wasn't able to tell anybody. . . . I realized that made me feel even more alone cuz nobody understood how [my classmate] felt, which meant that nobody understood how I felt. When everyone was saying how could he feel so alone, it was like, yeah, and I am alone. They were like how could he have not told anybody. It was weird realizing that I understood [my classmate] and not the couple of thousand people in the school who were saying this. That was a real scary moment."

SOCIAL MEDIA, TEXTING, TEENS, AND SUICIDE

We have discussed how social media affects teen mental health in both negative and positive ways. As it relates to warning signs, it can serve as an outlet where adolescents post a cry for help. Since 2016, more young people recognize which of their friends' posts are alarming and are more apt to reach out to a trusted adult to alert them to a potential threat to life. In addition, all social media platforms have increased their vigilance when it comes to threats to others or to oneself by using algorithms and artificial intelligence. If someone is commenting dark messages on a YouTube video, for example, an automated message is triggered and sent to the person who might be at risk, giving phone numbers for the suicide prevention lifeline.

All schools should have some protocol when it comes to social media. One middle school asks their teachers to tell students to alert teachers or coaches if there is activity on any social platform that indicates a student might be struggling, or if there are hateful or harmful posts and pages that could escalate. Students are asked to report to a teacher (or use their anonymous tip line on their school website). Teachers then alert the counseling team via mobile text that is reserved for this purpose. Tip line comments go directly to the counseling team.

Figure 2.1 shows a text message sent by someone suffering and expressing a wish to die by suicide. This is a genuine message that was shared by loved ones with Anne Moss Rogers so you can better understand how subtle those cries for help really are.

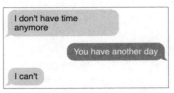

Figure 2.1 Text message from a teen (age 18) to his mother from a work release jail program prior to his death by suicide.
Source: Twitter, Inc.

This next twitter series (Figures 2.2 through 2.6) by Charles Aubrey Rogers, shared by Anne Moss Rogers, are the last social media posts prior to his suicide on June 5, 2015. Only one of these was seen by his mother as she was blocked from his account.

Figure 2.2 Twitter post #1.
Source: Twitter, Inc.

Figure 2.3 Twitter post #2.
Source: Twitter, Inc.

Figure 2.4 Twitter post #3.
Source: Twitter, Inc.

Figure 2.5 Twitter post #4.
Source: Twitter, Inc.

Figure 2.6 Twitter post #5.
Source: Twitter, Inc.

Figure 2.7 shows messages between a teacher and Anne Moss Rogers. The teacher, a subscriber to Emotionally Naked, got the help she needed and worked through her dark period with a therapist and is now managing well and is a mental health champion in her school.

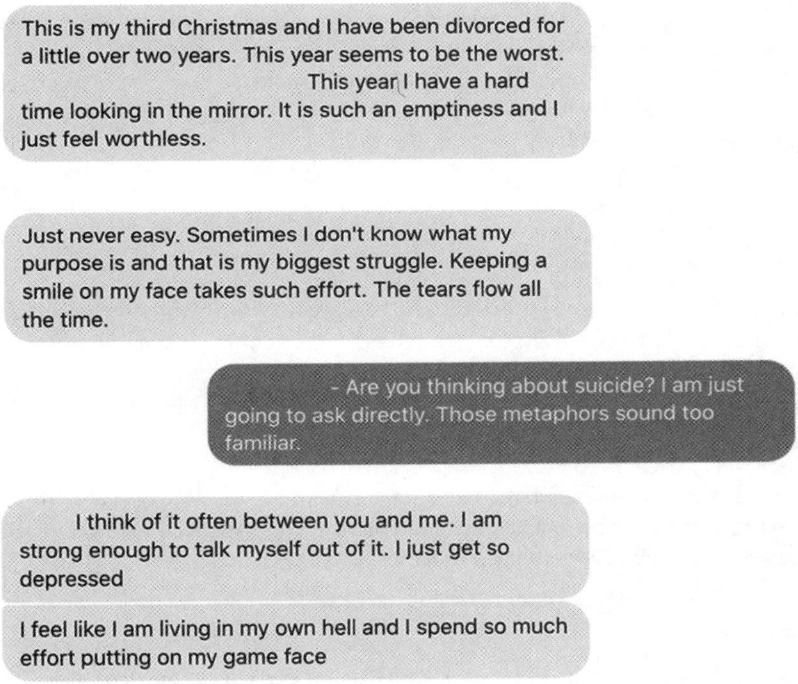

This is my third Christmas and I have been divorced for a little over two years. This year seems to be the worst. This year I have a hard time looking in the mirror. It is such an emptiness and I just feel worthless.

Just never easy. Sometimes I don't know what my purpose is and that is my biggest struggle. Keeping a smile on my face takes such effort. The tears flow all the time.

- Are you thinking about suicide? I am just going to ask directly. Those metaphors sound too familiar.

I think of it often between you and me. I am strong enough to talk myself out of it. I just get so depressed

I feel like I am living in my own hell and I spend so much effort putting on my game face

Figure 2.7 Messages between a teacher and Anne Moss Rogers.

The following is a text message conversation between a male high school junior struggling with thoughts of suicide and his girlfriend, several minutes before he attempted suicide by firearm. It illustrates how hesitant people are to ask for help and how he pulled back because he was afraid of how it would be perceived. This young man survived the attempt, although he was blinded and has undergone multiple facial and head surgeries. It is thought that in a last-second moment of regret, he pulled the weapon away from himself right as the blast went off.

JASON: Can I admit something to you?
    The other day when you said I was depressed I think I am
    don't tell anyone and please don't think of anything of me man cause I'm not
        suicidal I don't wanna die or anything but there has been one time where I
        loaded the shotgun and put it to my mouth but couldn't pull the trigger
    don't think I'm weird please don't man it's just I've gone through a lot and you
        the only person I've ever told this
JILL: I'm really sorry that u went through that
JASON: idk wtf was going through my mind I'm sorry I didn't mean to tell you that
    I did but I didn't
    Do you wanna just go to bed I shouldn't have. . .
JILL: Yeah, I'm going to bed now

These are comments by preteens and teens who were struggling with suicidal intensity at the time they posted the comment or message online, on Anne Moss Rogers' monitored YouTube channel:

"Nothing is helping me. . .it gets worse and worse."

"I have loving parents, amazing friends, financially stable, boys and girls want to date me. I shouldn't be complaining but I still want to die. I dont deserve any of this. Someone else deserves the life I have."

"i do want the pain to stop but there is no other way trust me i have tried there is just not

There is no other options. I've been screamed at for everything I do. Everything I love was taken away. Nobody loves me."

"I'm not sad, I'm fine.

F forever alone

I insecure

N never happy

E everlasting pain."

"I am 10 I have suicidal thoughts on a daily basis I feel like it is just not worth to hang on"

"I've lost all hope my parents are both in jail I've lost Everything my brothers died in a car accident 3 years ago all I have left is my aunt and at this point I'm tired off the bullying since I'm obese I get made fun of started to stress eat overtime and suicide was always on mind at the time"

"I want to talk to someone but I can't seem to get the words out of my mouth"

These preteens and teens want the help but are not sure how to say it or to whom to say it. If there was more discussion on mental health and encouragement for sharing struggles in a safe space at school, kids would be more likely to confide in someone instead of posting anonymously online. We could tell you all it takes is one person. However, it's more effective to show you what that means (Figure 2.8).

> I know nothing will ever take away the pain you must feel but one of the blogs you wrote on your website prob saved my life tonight and you should know your son would be proud. God bless
> Sincerely,
> John
>
> Sent from my T-Mobile 4G LTE Device

Figure 2.8 From Emotionally Naked blog, note sent after 30 minutes on the website (edited for privacy).

Because there have been hundreds of thousands of teens and young adults who have gone to pages on EmotionallyNaked.com and to an article on *The Mighty* by Anne Moss Rogers to look up specific directions on how to tell someone they want to die, we've included those directions on how a student can choose someone and what they should say. See Chapter 12, "Quizzes, Worksheets, Handouts, Guides, and Scripts," Worksheet 1: How to Tell Someone You Are Thinking of Suicide.

Teachers, school counselors, librarians, and coaches can have this as a printed document on a resource table with other materials in a classroom, library, gym, or counseling office so students have step-by-step instructions on who to tell and how. Teens do pick up these resources and use them.

PROTECTIVE FACTORS

"I think, so often, we don't want to ask teachers to be counselors and that's absolutely true. We don't want to ask educators to be the ones carrying the weight of the world on their shoulders. But we all have a part to play, and are a part of that process. And so certainly teachers can be trusted adults. Having a trusted adult in your life is a really significant and powerful protective factor in the life of an adolescent—and so is fostering that kind of connection and trust and relationship."

Scott LoMurray (He/Him/His), Executive Director, Sources of Strength

Suicide prevention efforts rally around reducing the risk factors while bolstering protective factors—those characteristics that help protect people from suicide.

Risk factors and protective factors can vary among demographic and ethnic cultures; however, there are universal protective factors that school populations should strive to bake into to their culture. When protective factors are reinforced, students develop resilience, which has been defined as the maintenance of healthy and successful functioning or adaptation within the context of a significant adversity or threat.[47] Protective factors can relate to the internal skills of the youth in regard to problem solving, emotion regulation, and feelings of self-efficacy. Or it can be external and include positive therapeutic relationships, peer and family support, supportive school environments, and engagement in meaningful activities, including hobbies, and religious or spiritual practices.[48]

Although schools often focus on the identification of risk factors as the way to prevent suicide, it is arguably more effective to focus on the development and implementation of protective factors in their school community. By helping youth to build confidence, self-esteem, and self-worth, you are directly helping them develop internal skills that protect against suicidal thoughts and actions. And by creating a community of connection, empathy, and acceptance, whether at the school or classroom level, you are helping to buffer against the potential risk factors that can emerge in the lives of your students. In Chapter 5, we discuss the culture shifts that bolster these protective factors for students.

Risk and Protective Factors for Suicide[49]

Across all racial and ethnic populations, risk factors include:

- Prior suicide attempt(s)
- Substance misuse
- Mood and anxiety disorders (mental health concerns)
- Access to lethal means (means by which someone can end their life, such as poison or a firearm)
- Family dysfunction and trauma
- Relationship disruption (e.g. romantic breakups, parent divorce, death of a loved one)
- Transitions (e.g. high school to college, trending more towards the "leaving" or the "end" of something, such as high school graduation, leaving for spring break)

Examples of risk factors for special populations:[50]

- Stress resulting from prejudice, discrimination, nonacceptance, bullying, and violence is a known risk factor for LGBTQ youth
- Historical trauma such as that suffered by American Indians and Alaska Natives from resettlement, and destruction of cultures and economies

Across all racial and ethnic populations, protective factors include:

- A sense of belonging and connectedness to individuals, family, community, and social institutions
- A sense of purpose or meaning in life
- Coping ability, life skills, and adapting to change
- A positive sense of self-worth
- Cultural or religious beliefs that discourage suicide
- Availability of physical and mental health care

SUICIDE WARNING SIGNS

In addition to the presence of risk factors and underdeveloped protective factors, there are other warning signs that are important for teachers to look for. Educators need to listen to what students are saying, what behaviors they are exhibiting, and what mood they are expressing.

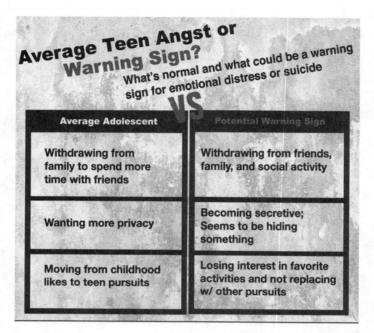

Average Teen Angst or Warning Sign?

What's normal and what could be a warning sign for emotional distress or suicide

VS

Average Adolescent	Potential Warning Sign
Withdrawing from family to spend more time with friends	Withdrawing from friends, family, and social activity
Wanting more privacy	Becoming secretive; Seems to be hiding something
Moving from childhood likes to teen pursuits	Losing interest in favorite activities and not replacing w/ other pursuits

There are some common warning signs and themes of suicidal behavior. But how one student exhibits an alarming change in behavior or expresses his or her suicidality is unique to that individual. It takes those who know that child and teachers with student relationships and knowledge of that child's baseline to see the shifts in behavior that could signal an emotional crisis. Although family will sometimes pick up on changes, they are often not likely to see it as a sign of suicide. Teachers, on the other hand, have the advantage of seeing students interact with their peer groups and have a more objective view, being naturally less emotionally invested in the student than a parent would be and therefore more objective and less likely to embrace denial.

"It should be on teachers' minds that if a student is having a change in their academic performance, chances are they didn't get dumber since last week. So in almost every circumstance, unless they've had a brain injury, if you have a B plus student who's suddenly doing C minus work, chances are something is going on in their psychosocial universe. Now, you know, we're very quick to say, 'Oh, go see the school counselor,' because again, people are afraid to have a personal conversation with a kid because they're afraid they'll be left holding some disaster. But you'd hope that they'd be prepared to have a conversation with a kid, where they say, 'You're not doing as well as you used to. What's going on? Is there some problem or something that I or someone else can be of help with?'"

Victor Schwartz, MD (He/Him/His), Former CMO of The JED Foundation, Founder of MindStrategies Advisors, Clinical Associate Professor, Department of Psychiatry, NYU School of Medicine

Sometimes, but not always, a sudden shift from deep depression to joy can be suspect because the youth has chosen a date and method to end their life and that has brought them a sense of relief. And the keyword here is "sudden." For example, one teen hated camping but her family loved it and she had refused to go on any of their trips after taking one when she was seven. After that, the closest she would get to camping was a bed and breakfast so she often stayed with a relative when the rest of her family would go. Her junior year had been difficult and dark and her family and teachers had been concerned. The family planned a camping trip and even questioned going because they didn't want to leave her. She shocked her parents, brothers, and sisters by telling them she wanted to go and according to the family and her friends, she had a grand time with them, participating in any and all activities with exuberance. Like her family, her teachers noticed her buoyant mood upon her return and thought she was making a miracle comeback when in fact, she had written a suicide note, tucked it away, and that trip was her parting gift to her family, a loving goodbye memory. Fortunately, her mother found the note and they were able to get her into treatment before she attempted.

Another student had played the violin obsessively since he was five years old, practicing two or more hours daily without prodding. He abruptly quit at age 18, which stunned both his music teacher at school and his parents, and his justification was that he wanted to pursue something different, yet he had nothing in mind with which to replace his passion. It's not unusual for a child to be into something as a young child and to change to another interest as a teen. However, if that teen withdraws to the degree that he doesn't pursue some other interest, start asking questions about how the child is feeling. The violin had been this young man's primary focus for over a decade, and two days after his declaration he took his life.

Withdrawal or isolating is also a sign that a person might be thinking about killing himself. This is also known as "ghosting." If you have a student who has been an active part of your sports team or marching band for most of the year and all of a sudden, that student is a no-show, what is your gut telling you? Maybe you left messages and never heard anything back. With some people, the more they don't answer, the more they may be asking for help. You might resist because you don't want to be nosy, but push forward. How are you going to find out what's up if they are not answering you? Change how you are communicating with this student, be thoughtfully persistent, even if that means leaving a note in their locker. You could word it something like this using "I feel" statements:

"Hey Mark, I feel concern because I have not heard from you and that's really not like you. Can we talk during my planning time at 11:30 am? I'm here to listen. I want to hear what's going on. I'll also be in my classroom from 4 to 4:30 pm today if that works better."

We tend to take it personally when people ghost us but often it's because something has happened, so it's a good idea to see if that event has put them in a place of extreme despair. Even if you do reach out and they aren't suicidal, just busy or struggling with some other problem, they'll usually appreciate that you cared enough to reach out and it will allow other students to recognize you as someone they can talk to if they are in distress. Teachers should make sure to alert the school counselor or student wellness team if there is any evidence of emotional stress with a specific student.

WHAT DO STUDENTS SAY WHEN THEY ARE THINKING OF SUICIDE?

We have to consider that teens may offer clues to suicidal behavior by what they say, what they write in class, the art they create, doodles on notebooks, in notes to educators by email or left on a desk, in online chats, by phone, text, and in social media. And it could be that they don't say it but show it in their behavior. While some who struggle with those thoughts will say it directly, most will not. Those subtle offhand remarks and jokes are veiled invitations for you to ask how a student is doing. Because most people, adolescents in particular, do want to tell. And by recognizing and responding appropriately to those clues, we demonstrate a willingness to listen and support.

"I think teachers are more hesitant than they used to be to be involved in a kind of mentoring way with their students. But clearly, if somebody's struggling or suffering, you hope that they see their role as making sure somehow they get the help as just a concerned adult in a young person's life."

Victor Schwartz, MD (He/Him/His), Former CMO of The JED Foundation,
Founder of MindStrategies Advisors, Clinical Associate Professor,
Department of Psychiatry, NYU School of Medicine

We do have examples of what people say; however, this could never be a definitive list. Teachers and coaches in particular are the ones who have relationships with students and it is far more likely that a student will communicate their thoughts of suicide to a person they know and trust, a non–mental health professional, which is why we all need to be empowered to know what people say and how to respond. If we ignore those clues thinking that we're not qualified, we miss the opportunity to help a student save their own life. How do we overcome this imposter syndrome? We learn to be uncomfortable and accept that every time we feel we are out of our jurisdiction, there will be an instinct to pull back and not ask because it is a scary topic that carries with it a feeling of a lot of responsibility. It feels too heavy and your brain puts up roadblocks, makes excuses, and offers exit routes. Your mind will try to coax you into thinking, "Someone else will get this," "This is not my job," "This kid would never kill himself," and so on. Set the expectation that you will feel prickly and fearful that the person might say, "Yes, I am thinking of suicide." Or that they'll have an inventory of problems you cannot resolve. Not intervening at all increases the risk a person will die by suicide. By reaching out you lower that risk. Connecting them to resources reduces that risk even more. So you'll need to override that flight instinct.

Something to look out for when concerned that a person may be suicidal is a change in behavior or the presence of entirely new behaviors. This is of significant concern if the new or changed behavior is related to a painful event, loss, or change, including a relationship disruption (e.g. grief, fight with a parent, or loss of a friend group). Most people who take their lives exhibit one or more warning signs, either through what they say or what they do.

Warning sign: Talk

If a person talks about:

- Killing themselves
- Feeling hopeless
- Having no reason to live
- Being a burden to others
- Feeling trapped
- Unbearable pain

Warning sign: Behavior

Behaviors that may signal risk, especially if related to a painful event, loss, or change:

- Increased use of alcohol or drugs
- Looking for a way to end their lives, such as searching online for methods
- Withdrawing from activities
- Isolating from family and friends
- Sleeping too much or too little
- Visiting or calling people to say goodbye
- Giving away prized possessions
- Aggression
- Fatigue

Warning sign: Mood

People who are considering suicide often display one or more of the following moods:

- Depression
- Anxiety
- Loss of interest
- Irritability
- Humiliation/Shame

- Agitation/Anger
- Relief/Sudden Improvement

Source: American Foundation of Suicide Prevention, AFSP.org.

Phrases that can signal suicidal despair

- "I just want to die."
- "I can't do this anymore."
- "I don't want to live."
- "I feel so worthless."
- "No one would care if I was dead."
- "I'm such a burden."
- "I feel trapped."
- "This pain has to stop."
- "I can't look in the mirror anymore."
- "I hate myself."
- "I just can't go on."
- "I won't be needing _____ anymore."

If you hear any of these phrases, it should trigger an action step of reaching out in private to that student and asking if they want to talk. Listen, and if your gut is telling you something is up, connect them with the school counselor or social worker. Even if it's a chat that leaves you feeling unsure, let the counselor know. Specific directions on what to say and do are outlined in Chapter 7, "Intervention: They've Told You They're Thinking of Suicide. What Now?" with a quick reference guide at the end of the chapter with specific steps.

NOTES

1. Curtin, S. C., Warner, M., and Hedegaard, H. Increase in suicide in the United States, 1999–2014, (2016). National Center for Health Statistics Data Brief. Atlanta, Centers for Disease Control and Prevention. https://www.cdc.gov/nchs/data/databriefs/db241.pdf
2. Ivey-Stephenson AZ, Demissie Z, Crosby AE, et al. Suicidal Ideation and Behaviors Among High School Students — Youth Risk Behavior Survey,

United States, 2019. MMWR Suppl 2020;69(Suppl-1):47–55. DOI: http://dx.doi.org/10.15585/mmwr.su6901a6external icon.

3. Kattimani, S., Sarkar, S., Menon, V., Muthuramalingam, A., and Nancy, P. (2016). Duration of suicide process among suicide attempters and characteristics of those providing window of opportunity for intervention. *Journal of Neurosciences in Rural Practice* 7(4): 566–570. https://doi.org/10.4103/0976-3147.185505; https://www.ncbi.nlm.nih.gov/pmc/articles/PMC5006470/

4. Deisenhammer, E. A., Ing, C. M., Strauss, R., et al. (2009). The duration of the suicidal process: How much time is left for intervention between consideration and accomplishment of a suicide attempt? *Journal of Clinical Psychiatry* 70(1): 19–24.

5. O'Brien, K., Nicolopoulos, A., Almeida, J., Aguinaldo, L.D., and Rosen, R. (2019). Why adolescents attempt suicide: A qualitative study of the transition from ideation to action. *Archives of Suicide Research*, 1–18.

6. Ibid.

7. Centers for Disease Control and Prevention, National Center for Injury Prevention and Control. (2020). *Web-based Injury Statistics Query and Reporting System (WISQARS)* (Non-Fatal Injury Data 2001–2018). Retrieved June 10, 2020, from www.cdc.gov/injury/wisqars

8. Centers for Disease Control and Prevention, National Center for Injury Prevention and Control. (2020). *Web-based Injury Statistics Query and Reporting System (WISQARS)* (Fatal Injury Reports, 1999–2018, for National, Regional, and States). Retrieved June 10, 2020, from www.cdc.gov/injury/wisqars

9. Beautrais, A. L. (2003). Suicide and serious suicide attempts in youth: A multiple-group comparison study. *American Journal of Psychiatry* 160(6): 1093–1099.

10. Moore, F., Taylor, S., Beaumont, J., Gibson, R., and Starkey, C. (2018). The gender suicide paradox under gender role reversal during industrialisation. https://doi.org/10.1371/journal.pone.0202487

11. Centers for Disease Control and Prevention, National Center for Injury Prevention and Control. (2020). *Web-based Injury Statistics Query and Reporting System (WISQARS)* (Non-Fatal Injury Data 2001–2018). Retrieved June 10, 2020, from www.cdc.gov/injury/wisqars

12 See The Trevor Project report at https://www.thetrevorproject.org/survey-2020/

13. The Trevor Project. (2020). 2020 National Survey on LGBTQ Youth Mental Health. https://www.thetrevorproject.org/survey-2020/?section=Introduction
14. Ibid.
15. Centers for Disease Control and Prevention, National Center for Injury Prevention and Control. (2020). *Web-based Injury Statistics Query and Reporting System (WISQARS)* (Fatal Injury Reports, 1999–2018, for National, Regional, and States). Retrieved June 10, 2020 from www.cdc.gov/injury/wisqars
16. Ibid.
17. Substance Abuse and Mental Health Services Administration. Suicide Clusters within American Indian and Alaska Native Communities: A review of the literature and recommendations. HHS Publication No. SMA17-5050. Rockville, MD: Center for Mental Health Services, Substance Abuse and Mental Health Services Administration, 2017.
18. Emergency Taskforce on Black Youth Suicide and Mental Health. Ring the alarm: The crisis of Black youth suicide in America. https://watsoncoleman.house.gov/uploadedfiles/full_taskforce_report.pdf
19. Gordon, J. (2020, Sep 22). Addressing the crisis of black youth suicide. https://www.nimh.nih.gov/about/director/messages/2020/addressing-the-crisis-of-black-youth-suicide.shtml
20. Madubata, I., Spivey, L. A., Alvarez, G. M., Neblett, E. W., and Prinstein, M. J. (2019). Forms of racial/ethnic discrimination and suicidal ideation: a prospective examination of African American and Latinx Youth. *Journal of Clinical Child & Adolescent Psychology*, 1–9.
21. Goldman-Mellor, S., Allen, K., and Kaplan, M. S. (2018). Rural/urban disparities in adolescent nonfatal suicidal ideation and suicide attempt: A population-based study. *Suicide and Life-Threatening Behavior* 48(6), 709–719.
22. Rural Health Information Hub. Suicide in rural areas. https://www.rural-healthinfo.org/toolkits/suicide/1/rural
23. Bridge, J. A., Goldstein, T. R., and Brent, D. A. (2006). Adolescent suicide and suicidal behavior. *Journal of Child Psychology and Psychiatry* 47(3–4), 372-394. doi:10.1111/j.1469-7610.2006.01615.x.
24. Ibid.
25. Goldston, D. B., Reboussin, B. A., Kancler, C., et al. (2003). Rates and predictors of aftercare services among formerly hospitalized adolescents: a prospective naturalistic study. *Journal of the American Academy of Child and Adolescent Psychiatry* 42(1): 49–56. doi:10.1097/00004583-200301000-00010.

26. Zahl, D. L. (2004). Repetition of deliberate self-harm and subsequent suicide risk: Long-term follow-up study of 11 583 patients. *British Journal of Psychiatry* 185(1): 70–75. doi:10.1192/bjp.185.1.70; doi:10.1001/archpsyc.1996.01830040075012.

27. Joiner, T., Ribeiro, J., and Silva, C. (2012). Nonsuicidal self-injury, suicide behavior, and their co-occurrence as viewed through the lens of the interpersonal theory of suicide. *Current Directions in Psychological Science* 21(5): 342–47.

28. Nanayakkara, S., Misch, D., Chang, L., and Henry, D. (2013). Depression and exposure to suicide predict suicide attempt. *Depression and Anxiety* 30(10): 991–996.

29. Weierich, M. R., Nock, M. K. (2008). Posttraumatic stress symptoms mediate the relation between childhood sexual abuse and nonsuicidal self-injury. *Journal of Consulting and Clinical Psychology* 76: 39–44.

30. Calati, R., Bensassi, I., Courtet, P. (2017). The link between dissociation and both suicide attempts and non-suicidal self-injury: Meta-analyses. *Psychiatry Research* 251: 103–14.

31. Johnstone, J. M., Carter, J. D., Luty, S. E., Mulder, R. T., Frampton, C. M., and Joyce, P. R. (2016). Childhood predictors of lifetime suicide attempts and non-suicidal self-injury in depressed adults. *Australian and New Zealand Journal of Psychiatry* 50: 135–44.

32. O'Connor RC, Noyce R. (2008). Personality and cognitive processes: Self-criticism and different types of rumination as predictors of suicidal ideation. *Behaviour Research and Therapy* 46(3): 392–401.

33. Thompson, M. P., Kingree, J. B., and Lamis, D. (2019). Associations of adverse childhood experiences and suicidal behaviors in adulthood in a U.S. nationally representative sample. *Child: Care, Health and Development* 45(1): 121–28.

34. Keyes, M. A., Malone, S. M., Sharma, A., Iacono, W. G., and McGue, M. (2013). Risk of suicide attempt in adopted and nonadopted offspring. *Pediatrics* 132(4): 639–646. https://doi.org/10.1542/peds.2012-3251; https://www.ncbi.nlm.nih.gov/pmc/articles/PMC3784288/

35. Cederbaum, J. A., Gilreath, T. D., Benbenishty, R., Astor, R. A., Pineda, D., DePedro, K. T., and Atuel, H. (2014). Military children and suicide risk. *Journal of Adolescent Health* 54(6): 672–677. http://www.sprc.org/news/military-children-and-suicide-risk#:~:text=A%20large%20study%20in%20California,in%20the%20military%20are%20deployed

36. Scott, M., Underwood, M., and Lamis, D. (2015). Suicide and related-behavior among youth involved in the juvenile justice system. *Child and Adolescent Social Work Journal* 32(6): 517–527. Okpych, N. J., and Courtney, M. E. (2018).

Characteristics of foster care history as risk factors for psychiatric disorders among youth in care. *American Journal of Orthopsychiatry* 88(3): 269–281.

37. Barnes, A. J., Gilbertson, J., and Chatterjee, D. (2018). Emotional health among youth experiencing family homelessness. *Pediatrics* 141(4).

38. Okpych, N. J., and Courtney, M. E. (2018). Characteristics of foster care history as risk factors for psychiatric disorders among youth in care. *American Journal of Orthopsychiatry* 88(3): 269–281.

39. Kirby, A. V., Bakian, A. V., Zhang, Y., et al. (2019). A 20-year study of suicide death in a statewide autism population. *Autism Research* 12(4): 658–666. doi: 10.1002/aur.2076; https://www.ncbi.nlm.nih.gov/pmc/articles/PMC6457664/

40. Whitlinger, C., and Fretwell, J. (2019). Political assassination and social movement outcomes: Martin Luther King and the Memphis sanitation workers' strike, *Sociological Perspectives,* 62(4).

41. Pinder-Amaker, S. Mental health and wellness for students of color: A new kind of college-readiness. McClain College Mental Health Program. https://youtu.be/UkK39QXcVCQ

42. Ibid.

43. Ibid.

44. Czyz, E. K., and King, C. A. (2015). Longitudinal trajectories of suicidal ideation and subsequent suicide attempts among adolescent inpatients. *Journal of Clinical Child and Adolescent Psychology* 44(1): 181–93, doi:10.1080/15374416.2013.836454

45. Zhang, J. (2019). The strain theory of suicide. *Journal of Pacific Rim Psychology* 13. https://doi/10.1017/prp.2019.19

46. Consoli, A., Peyre, H., Speranza, M., Hassler, C., Falissard, B., Touchette, E., et al. (2013). Suicidal behaviors in depressed adolescents: Role of perceived relationships in the family. *Child and Adolescent Psychiatry and Mental Health* 7(1): 8.

47. Garmezy, N. (1993). Risk and resilience. In D. C. Funder, R. D. Parke, C. Tomlinson-Keasey and K. Widaman (Eds.), *Studying Lives through Time: Personality and Development* (pp. 377–398). Washington, DC: American Psychological Association.

48. Szlyk, H. S. (2020). Resilience among students at risk of dropout: Expanding perspectives on youth suicidality in a non-clinical setting. *School Mental Health* 12(1): 1–13.

49. Suicide Prevention Resource Center, SPRC.org

50. Ibid.

Chapter 3
Debunking Myths About Student Suicide

Trigger warning: Suicide method mentioned briefly

"Common myths associated with suicide contribute towards increased stigma and decreased help-seeking and help-providing behaviors. It is important to debunk these myths so that we can encourage people to speak up about mental health challenges and are ready, willing, and able to provide help when it is needed."

Melissa K. Ackley, LCSW (She/Her/Hers), Prevention Services Manager, Chesterfield Mental Health Support Services, Chesterfield Suicide Prevention Coalition

A word like suicide that has spent as much time being whispered, swept under a rug, or tucked away in the family vault of secrecy is bound to have fostered a lot of myths. There is still quite a bit of mystery about suicidal thoughts and the brain, and only in the last decade or so has the field of suicidology included testimony from those with lived experience. Their unique insights into the suicidal mind have been historically undervalued. And it was not long ago that experts thought anyone who had suffered with suicidal intensity was too fragile to discuss the topic or even attend a conference on suicide. We still have a long way to go in terms of understanding suicide, but we know a lot more than we did. Because your response to someone suffering thoughts of suicide or a loss by suicide needs to come from a place of understanding, you should be familiar with popular myths and know what the true facts are.

MYTH: TALKING ABOUT SUICIDE CAN GIVE THEM THE IDEA

Adults, especially parents, fear that talking about suicide will somehow influence a person's thinking and present an option someone had not previously been aware of. But those who have not already had thoughts of killing themselves don't suddenly adopt suicide as an option or strategy just because it's been brought up in conversation.

Research has indicated that talking about suicide doesn't insert ideas into people's heads[1] but instead demonstrates that a responsible and empathetic conversation can actually encourage someone to reach out for help. If talking about a certain behavior did give adolescents the idea, then parent lectures about not drinking, for example, would be an effective way to curb the behavior. And we know how well that works.

There is a caveat, however, in discussions of suicide and especially with this population. Conversation about *method* of suicide, details of the death scene, and grandiose memorials can trigger vulnerable teenagers. So we encourage responsible conversation within guidelines, which you'll find in Chapter 7.

"Our findings suggest acknowledging and talking about suicide may in fact reduce, rather than increase suicidal ideation, and may lead to improvements in mental health in treatment-seeking populations."

Source: Dazzi et al. 2014 / Cambridge University Press.

MYTH: TEENS WHO SAY THEY ARE THINKING OF SUICIDE ARE JUST TRYING TO GET ATTENTION

Let's assume for a moment that a teenager declaring thoughts of suicide is trying to get attention. How else would they get help? Smoke signals? Any teenager who says they are thinking of suicide needs help because something in their life or their mind is gravely wrong. Period. Just because they are declaring it makes them no less at risk than the student keeping it bottled up. And every declaration needs to be taken seriously and referred to the person at your school who handles assessments or makes the call to schedule one.

Suicide is an act of desperation by a person whose brain is telling them they need to die. Educators should avoid phrases like "cry for help" or "just trying to get attention" as it relates to suicidal ideation because they are dismissive. They shame and invalidate the feelings of the person suffering, making them less likely to reach out in a future suicidal crisis.

MYTH: SUICIDE IS SELFISH

Suicide is a public health issue and is recognized as such by the National Institute of Mental Health, the Department of Defense, and the World Health Organization. When a teen is in a suicidal crisis, it can feel like an altered state of consciousness in which thoughts are often distorted. For instance, they may feel completely disconnected or like a burden to others, when that is not in fact how their friends and family feel about them. One teen suicide attempt survivor described this feeling of burden and lack of belongingness:

_____

> "There's no point in me being alive anymore, because no one cares about me, so I need to [kill myself], because I feel bad for being in other peoples' lives when they don't care about me, and I just make it harder for other people."

_____

The emotional distress experienced in a suicidal crisis can lead to a distorted rationalization of suicide, where teens really do believe suicide would offer relief to their family or friends. Two other teens described why they felt that their suicide would have lifted a burden off of their family and friends:

_____

> "They wouldn't have so much to worry about if I didn't have to go through this or even if I wasn't here."

> "A lotta the time I feel like a burden to a lotta people cuz there's things that I need or things that I do that cause people more trouble. It's like why [live]? You're just a burden to them, they're not gonna care."

_____

In short, suicide is an act of despair, not selfishness.[2]

MYTH: YOU SHOULD USE A "NO-SUICIDE CONTRACT" WITH TEENS

In 1973, "no-suicide contracts" were a popular tool for therapists and their suicidal patients. The idea behind this patient-therapist contract was to establish a mindset in which the individual understood that it is never okay to die by suicide. And while therapists had well-meaning intentions as well as the desire to protect themselves legally in the event of a patient suicide, there is no evidence these contracts are effective.[3] In fact, many individuals have found them to be detrimental, because asking an individual to promise not to kill themselves when they have been given no other skills to cope with the crisis at hand is an unreasonable request. This request can make a teen feel ashamed and even more defective than they already feel.

Although "no-suicide contracts" do not work, suicide safety plans do. See the section "Safety Planning," near the end of Chapter 7.

MYTH: ONCE A TEEN GETS PAST A SUICIDE ATTEMPT, THEY'VE LEARNED THEIR LESSON

For any adolescent struggling with suicide, thoughts can be one-time occurrences, cyclical, or chronic, depending on the underlying family and medical history as well as external stressors in their psychosocial sphere. Young people don't always have an established pattern and we don't always know if it's a symptom of past trauma or mental illness, or an acute response to a distressing situation. It's natural to think that if you have a discussion with a student or child on what their death would do to their loved ones that they "see" your point of view, embrace your wisdom, and cease thinking of suicide as an option. But that's not the case. Often, parents of adolescents do think that once their child is past their attempt they are out of the danger zone. It's possible the child might be, but because past attempts are strong predictors for future attempts, their symptoms must continue to be monitored in a supportive way.

MYTH: TEENS WHO SELF-INJURE ARE TRYING TO KILL THEMSELVES

Self-injury is not always an attempt to die. In fact, many teens engage in self-injury like cutting, burning, scratching, hair pulling, and head banging without an intent to kill themselves. This is called non-suicidal self-injury (NSSI) and should be seen and understood as separate from suicidal behavior. Adolescence represents a period of increased risk for NSSI behaviors, particularly during puberty, at the age of 13 to 15 years.[4] NSSI serves many different functions in teens. Some include an effort to cope with their suicidal thoughts so that they don't act on them, helping them feel something when they are numb inside, being able to physically see the pain they feel inside, to punish themselves, push their pain away, feel a sense of control, joy, or excitement, to distract from emotional pain or adverse events, or to communicate their emotional pain to others. Two teen suicide attempt survivors described the relationship between cutting and attempting suicide.

"When I cut, I do it to distract myself and it causes pain on my arm and so it makes me think about that, and distracts me from other things. It was just like I couldn't be distracted and I was like, 'I can't do this. I need more. I don't want to be here. It would just be easier if it all ends.'. . . [The day of my suicide attempt] my first instinct was to try to cut and not just automatically kill myself. . . . I would just be able to use that instead of wanting to just kill myself. [Cutting] distracts me and then I normally don't get like, 'I want to kill myself. I want to kill myself,' and stuff like that unless it's really bad, which was happening that day."

"From personal experience I will tell you that a person has to be in an extreme amount of emotional pain and distress to take a blade or lighter to their skin. We self-harm because we are angry, sad, lost and broken. We hurt ourselves because we want to see the scars we feel on the inside, or as a physical distraction, be it brief, from the hurt we cannot bear."

One teen who struggled with an eating disorder described the thought processes around her self-harm:

"I would self-harm almost every night. My wrists were covered in cuts, but my head just kept convincing me that I deserved it. Convincing me that I was never good enough, pretty enough, skinny enough, or deserving enough of anything."

Instead of telling teens to stop, counselors and therapists must help them transition to healthy coping strategies gradually, like rubbing ice on their body, taking an extremely cold or hot shower, dipping their face in bowl of ice water, or creating a self-harm safety box. Even then, communicating to them that this is "wrong" or "disgusting" may add to their shame and should be avoided because it can escalate the behavior. Both NSSI and suicidal behavior need to be taken seriously and responded to with compassion and empathy. And while self-harm isn't usually with an intent to die by suicide, youth who engage in NSSI do have an increased risk for future suicide compared with those in the general population.[5] Because increasing numbers of teens use NSSI as a coping strategy, it is becoming ever more critical that we help youth learn healthy strategies for managing emotional pain. That's where teachers can help curb this behavior.

"Cutting takes the intangible and it makes it tangible. So it takes what's up in there in the head that hurts and makes you feel crazy, and then you cut yourself and you see the blood and it's like, 'This. . .this is what pain looks like. This is like what I understand pain to mean.'"

Dese'Rae L. Stage (She/Her/Hers), Queer, Suicide Attempt Survivor,
Suicide Loss Survivor, livethroughthis.org

Why Do Teens Self Harm?

Teens self-harm to:

- Help them feel something when they are numb inside
- Be able to physically see the pain they feel inside
- Punish themselves
- Push their pain away
- Feel a sense of control, joy, or excitement
- Communicate their emotional pain to others
- Distract themselves from emotionally painful issues and adverse events

MYTH: THERE IS NO NEED TO SCREEN KIDS FOR SUICIDE BECAUSE THEY WON'T TELL ANYWAY

Most teenagers don't know how or whom to tell about their suicidal thoughts and often fear what will happen if they do. Suicide risk screening provides an opportunity for teens to open up about their suicidal thoughts to a trusted adult. In one study, patients 10–21 years old who presented with both psychiatric and nonpsychiatric complaints to an urban pediatric emergency department were screened using the National Institute of Mental Health Ask Suicide Screening tool (ASQ). In follow-up interviews, these patients were asked if they thought emergency room nurses should ask kids about suicide. Results showed that 96% of them supported suicide screening.[6] They expressed that it's a good practice because it gives them an opportunity to tell someone how they are feeling, and provides a connection to help for their suicidal thoughts. Youth communicated the belief that suicide risk screening saves lives.

However, given what this data shows, why don't more youth who die by suicide tell someone prior to their final act? Think for a moment about the deepest, darkest secret or feeling you've ever had. Is there someone you'd trust with that sensitive information? Would it be easy to tell someone about it?

Thoughts of suicide are the most sensitive feelings a person will ever have. And some of the reasons people don't tell center on their fear of the results, reactions, procedures, and judgments from such a confession. Can they trust you? Will they look weak? What will happen if they do tell? Will telling someone trigger a series of unpleasant events that the student doesn't want or is unprepared for, such as being put in the back of an ambulance in front of the whole school? If the student is African American, might they be subject to a system that hasn't treated them well in the past? Given a student's fear of telling, it's clear that setting expectations about what will happen next dispels a student's anxiety of the process. They need hand-holding, step-by-step instructions, and unconditional support. They need to know that, even if you can't hold their confession in complete confidence because of the nature of it being a danger to themselves, you will at least handle the situation with discretion. They need to know how you will handle the conversation with parents whom they may not wish to know. They need to know that you, their teacher, is as much a partner in the process as possible given limitations on time and privacy. The less information a teacher, school counselor, or school nurse shares about next steps, the more fear a student will have, because what isn't told is fueled by a wild imagination and those gaps in information are filled with projected scenarios far worse than the truth. Students trust their teachers and coaches. They don't know all these ancillary people who will enter the process. It's up to teachers to build the student's confidence, rally for transparency and fairness, and provide a connection to help.

More on suicide risk screening can be found in Chapter 5.

MYTH: IF SOMEONE IS SET ON TAKING THEIR OWN LIFE, NOTHING CAN BE DONE TO STOP THEM

Suicide is preventable and the majority of those who die by suicide communicated their suicidal thoughts or intent to others in some way before their death,[7] demonstrating an opportunity for empathetic intervention. People are ambivalent about dying up until and even at the very moment they take their lives. When Kevin Hines was 19 years old and a college freshman, he acted on the direction of the voices he heard inside his head and jumped off the Golden Gate Bridge. Although it's a 220-foot plunge and only 2% survive, he did.

> "The millisecond my legs cleared it [the rail], the millisecond of true free fall, instant regret for my actions."[8]
>
> *Kevin Hines, Suicide Loss Survivor, Person Living with Bipolar Disorder, Suicide Prevention Advocate, Kevin & Margaret Hines Foundation*

To survive, Kevin knew he had to right himself before hitting the water so the former high school wrestler and football tackle tipped his head back, plunging below the surface feet first.[9] He suffered a number of injuries and went on to become one of the leading advocates for suicide prevention. This regret immediately following an attempt frequently occurs among teens as well.

This comment from a teen suicide attempt survivor describes her thoughts before and after her attempt:

> "[Before my attempt I was thinking] this is just gonna solve all my problems cuz I won't have any more problems cuz I won't be alive. Then as soon as I took [pills to kill myself], it was 30 seconds after I took them, 45 seconds after I took them, I was just like, 'Oh, my God. What did I just do?' I was just terrified and I was like, 'Oh, my God.' ...I was like really mad at myself. I rushed downstairs and I told my mom immediately that I had done it. Cuz my intention was to kill myself, but after I took them I was like, 'I don't want to be—I want to be alive. I do. I want to work this out, so I can be better and stuff.'"

The majority of people contemplating suicide don't really want to die, but in that moment they are seeking to end intense emotional and/or physical pain. Simply listening with empathy and not trying to fix the problem is perhaps the most important part of helping a student feel heard in the midst of their suicidal crisis, and represents a critical step in suicide prevention.

MYTH: THE PARENT IS ALWAYS THE BEST PERSON TO TELL WHEN A STUDENT IS THINKING OF SUICIDE

In an optimal world, we'd like to have a supportive parent to tell when a student discloses to you their thoughts of suicide. But this is not always the case. Sometimes one of the key drivers to a student's suicidal intent is the home environment. It may be that there is domestic abuse and trauma in the home or a lot of academic pressure at a time when a student is vulnerable. Having an experienced school counselor trained in suicide prevention is the key to establishing a protocol of what to do in a school once the student has told someone they are thinking of killing themselves. Sometimes that might mean a delay in telling the parents. For example, suicidal thoughts or behaviors for an LGBTQ student can be related to fear of family rejection of sexual and/or gender identity. Handling that conversation with the parents needs to be carefully planned so as not to make the situation more dire or to unintentionally "out" a student who is not ready to have their gender and/or sexual orientation revealed. In those cases, only the necessary information need be delivered, which is that the child is suicidal.

MYTH: IF THEY DON'T HAVE A PLAN, THEY ARE NOT AT RISK FOR SUICIDE

Many teens who attempt suicide do not have a plan and due to their underdeveloped executive functioning skills, they are more prone to acting on impulse than adults. This is especially the case with respect to acting on suicidal thoughts. One teen suicide attempt survivor described the impulsivity behind her attempt:

"It was like an impulse action, and like I didn't really think about it. I kind of know that like, I didn't want to die, but I still did it. I don't know. It was like, I wasn't thinking. . .Then I just like went upstairs into the bathroom. . .Then I took the pills. . .Then I just kind of realized what I did, and then I told my mom."

All suicide threats should be evaluated by someone who understands the nuances of the population. Even if the student does not reveal a plan, we don't know if the next day or next week they may have a plan to kill themselves. Plans can change over time and still a large number of teen attempts occur that are unplanned.

MYTH: THE HOLIDAYS ARE PEAK TIMES FOR TEEN SUICIDE

The holiday suicide myth is a precarious one because it can give false attributions to the contributors to suicide and masks the real period of risk. In fact, data demonstrate that December is actually a low period of risk, while the suicide rate typically increases in the spring.[10] It is not completely clear why this is the case, although other studies have found the availability of natural light and sunshine to be related to suicide, but not in the way you might think. One study found a higher likelihood of sunshine on the day of suicide and the ten days prior.[11] Another study found that the relationship between day length and suicide to be significantly positively associated.[12] Many are curious about why this might be since people's moods seem to be down during the winter months when the weather is cold and dreary and the days are shorter. However, to actually take one's own life requires energy, which is why many believe that the burst of energy provided by a sunny day can be enough to put suicidal thoughts into action. Spring, when school is in session, is when most students die by suicide, suggesting the importance of educators' awareness of this escalated period of risk.

However, we do want to point out that transitions, including the mini transitions such as leaving school for the holiday break and returning, are times of elevated risk and shouldn't be ignored just because they don't fit within the high-risk months.

MYTH: MOST STUDENTS WHO DIE BY SUICIDE HAVE BEEN BULLIED

Bullying is a practice that has existed for as long as there have been parents and children but never has it been as pervasive and constant as it is now. Social media and texting add fuel to adolescent humiliation that can spread like a viral video. Consider that most kids who are bullied do not take their lives. And both the child being bullied and the one acting as the bully are at risk. A child who is both bullied and dies by suicide is typically also in a vulnerable state with multiple other stressors, contributing to a feeling of overall strain with limited social supports and intrapersonal skills to help themselves. Bullying is often present in the lives of teens who attempt suicide and die by suicide, but that does not mean it is the only reason for their suicidal thoughts or attempts.[13] It is critical in messaging not to create a single cause for a suicide death. When it is singled out as a cause, those words communicate to those being bullied that suicide is the only answer. Media headlines should not state it simply, because it is dangerous, untrue, and only tells part of the story.

NOTES

1. Mathias, C. W., Michael Furr, R., Sheftall, A. H., Hill-Kapturczak, N., Crum, P., and Dougherty, D. M. (2012). What's the harm in asking about suicidal ideation? *Suicide and Life-Threatening Behavior* 42(3): 341–351. https://doi.org/10.1111/j.1943-278X.2012.0095.x
2. Sneidman, Edwin S. (1993) *Suicide as Psychache: A Clinical Approach to Self-Destructive Behavior.* Lanham, MD: Jason Aronson, Inc.
3. Rudd, M. D., Mandrusiak, M., and Joiner, T. E., Jr. (2006). The case against no-suicide contracts: The commitment to treatment statement as a practice alternative. *Journal of Clinical Psychology* 62(2), 243–51.
4. Hawton, K., Saunders, K. E., O'Connor, R. C. (2012, Jun 23). Self-harm and suicide in adolescents. *Lancet* 379(9834): 2373–82. Glenn, C. R., Klonsky, E. D. (2009, Jan). Social context during non-suicidal self-injury indicates suicide risk. *Personality and Individual Differences.* 46(1): 25–29. Nock, M. K., Prinstein, M. J. (2004, Oct). A functional approach to the assessment of self-mutilative behavior. *Journal of Consulting and Clinical Psychology.* 72(5): 885–90. https://www.ncbi.nlm.nih.gov/pmc/articles/PMC4835048/
5. Hawton, K., Bergen, H., Kapur, N., Cooper, J., Steeg, S., Ness, J., Waters, K. (2012). Repetition of self-harm and suicide following self-harm in children and adolescents: Findings from the Multicentre Study of Self-harm in England. *Journal of Child Psychology and Psychiatry* 53(12). doi: 10.1111/j.1469-7610.2012.02559.x; http://www.antoniocasella.eu/salute/Suicide_Australia_2012.pdf#page=37

6. Ballard, E. D., Bosk, A., Snyder, D., Bridge, J. A., Wharff, E. A., Teach, S. J., and Horowitz, L. (2012). Patients' opinions about suicide screening in a pediatric emergency department. *Pediatric Emergency Care* 28(1), 34.

7. Owen, G., Belam, J., Lambert, H., Donovan, J., Rapport, F., and Owens, C. (2012). Suicide communication events: Lay interpretation of the communication of suicidal ideation and intent. *Science & Medicine* 75(2), 419–428.

8. https://www.psycom.net/kevin-hines-survived-golden-gate-bridge-suicide/; https://abc7news.com/golden-gate-bridge-suicides-suicide-survivors-jump-survive/2010562/

9. Glionna, J. M. (2005, June 4). Survivor battles Golden Gate's suicide lure. https://www.seattletimes.com/nation-world/survivor-battles-golden-gates-suicide-lure/

10. https://www.ncbi.nlm.nih.gov/pmc/articles/PMC3315262/

11. https://jamanetwork.com/journals/jamapsychiatry/fullarticle/1901524

12. https://www.ncbi.nlm.nih.gov/pmc/articles/PMC3206457/

13. Alavi, N., Reshetukha, T., Prost, E., Antoniak, K., Patel, C., Sajid, S., and Groll, D. (2017). Relationship between bullying and suicidal behaviour in youth presenting to the emergency department. *Journal of the Canadian Academy of Child and Adolescent Psychiatry* 26(2), 70–77. https://www.ncbi.nlm.nih.gov/pmc/articles/PMC5510935/

Chapter 4
Suicide-Related School Policies

"Many schools, when they learn about our simple process [of creating a school policy for suicide prevention] do want to do something. It's just that they've never been asked. They literally do not think of it as a priority because it hasn't happened in their school. There's also the fear that if we start talking about suicide, it's going to make students think about suicide. And we know from all the research that's not the case."

Sam Brinton (They/Them/Theirs), Vice President of Advocacy and Government Affairs at The Trevor Project, Rockville, Maryland

Across the country, as officials looked for ways to prevent school shootings, which are often saturated in media coverage, states started tip lines, websites, apps, and phone numbers that allow students to anonymously report concerns about classmates. In many places, reports of students self-harming or feeling suicidal have far outpaced the number of shooting threats against schools,[1] according to annual reports compiled by state agencies, forcing communities to confront a crisis cloaked in silence.

The time to create a suicide prevention, postvention, or crisis policy is before the school community has experienced a death or other disaster. It's difficult to respond to students, parents, and community needs and create an effective protocol when emotions are running high in a state of emergency or urgency. Policies and protocols should be put in place proactively so that educators feel prepared to respond to a suicidal student, a student returning to school following a psychiatric hospitalization, or the suicide death of a student or family member, as soon as it occurs.

In this chapter, we emphasize the importance of integrating an overall school crisis plan and focus on a school policy for suicide prevention, commemoration, and confidentiality. These are policies we hope teachers will advocate and be part of, even if it's not their job to choose or implement them.

All policies and protocols need to be created by keeping in mind the sensitivities and traditions of your particular school population, including students who might be at higher risk. How will your student population react to a police uniform or first responder if that's part of an intervention plan? How educated are the parents of this student population in regard to mental health and suicide? Does this school serve a population that stigmatizes mental health? What are the grief traditions of the families of this student population? Are they a religious population, and if so, what theology do they follow? Do the parents in this population know what a licensed clinical social worker is, or do they usually consider this health professional to be part of social services, the one who takes their kids away? Are LGBTQ youth, generally at high risk for suicide, able to find support in the school environment? To create a comprehensive and effective policy, educators need to look through the lens of those they serve and include those individuals in the planning process.

PREPARE SCHOOL CRISIS PLAN

Every school should have a crisis plan that can be executed in the event of a school shooting, suicide, homicide, or other disaster. Who is the designated person to talk to the press? What do students do or where do they go in the event of said crisis? Crisis plans are not new. Back in the days of World War II, teachers were trained to teach kids to crawl under their desks to find shelter from falling debris from the ceiling in the event of an air raid by the enemy. Many schools have some kind of crisis plan in place today, some more robust than others, and many in response to school shootings.

Jonathan B. Singer, PhD, LCSW, president of the American Association of Suicidology and author of *Suicide in Schools: A Practitioner's Guide to Multi-level Prevention, Assessment, Intervention, and Postvention*, recommends PREPaRE School Crisis Prevention and Intervention Training Curriculum.[2] It is a two-day training by the National Association of School Psychologists with both in-person and online curricula, consisting of two complementary workshops. It uses the incident command structure so that if there is anything from a school shooting to a hurricane, there is a structure in place on who does what. And this can be modified to include suicide. So it means that if there is a student who kills himself or herself at school, or a young person who dies two weeks before school starts, or anything in between, there's a crisis protocol in place so people know what their job is. Duplicating effort in a crisis can be embarrassing and detrimental. Imagine for a moment if two people called the parents to discuss the details of their child's death instead of one designated person making the call.

The first of the two PREPaRE workshops is designed to help schools create systems to meet safety and crisis prevention and the preparedness needs of the school community and their families. The next workshop, on day two, focuses on mental health crisis intervention and recovery. The curriculum builds on existing personnel, resources, and programs; links to ongoing school safety efforts; facilitates sustainability; addresses a range of crises (including suicide); and can be adapted to each school's size and needs. While PREPaRE is not itself a suicide prevention program, it does provide the type of training, foundation, and structure that all schools should have prior to the implementation of a suicide prevention program and also provides a structure for schools to use following a student suicide to provide support to staff and students. This can help prevent suicide contagion, which can occur following a student suicide.

SCHOOL POLICY FOR SUICIDE PREVENTION

With youth suicide being the leading cause of death for ages 10–15 in the US,[3] it is critical that school districts have policies and procedures in place to prevent, assess the risk of, intervene, and respond to youth suicidal behavior. A prevention program and a comprehensive school policy can help you deter suicide rather than just acting in response. Given that it is impossible to predict when a suicide might happen, preparedness is critical and it should be a policy that can be paired with others, such as a crisis plan or an anti-bullying initiative.

You do not have to create this policy from scratch. The Trevor Project, the world's largest suicide prevention and crisis intervention organization for LGBTQ young people, in collaboration with the American School Counselor Association (ASCA), National Association of School Psychologists (NASP), and the American Foundation for Suicide Prevention (AFSP) has created a comprehensive overall "Model School District Policy on Suicide Prevention: Model

Language, Commentary and Resources." It is a free download that can be tailored to the needs of your district, school, state laws, and student culture.

> "[When I am working with] school districts in particular, I always look at the demographics and cultural landscape of their region. So when I'm working in Southern California, I'm considering the needs of Latino populations. If I'm working in North Dakota, I'm going to be looking at Native American populations. There's some flexibility to the policy, so that districts can tailor it to their students' needs and make it their own. And that's been a really crucial component of our advocacy when we're talking with school districts across the country."
>
> *Keygan Miller, MEd (They/Them/Theirs),*
> *Senior Advocacy Associate at The Trevor Project, Washington, DC*

This policy was developed by examining strong local policies, making sure it was in line with the latest research in suicide prevention and identifying best practices of a national framework. Comprehensive means that it includes prevention, intervention, postvention (after a suicide), and memorialization. This approach promotes an overall wellness culture that includes multiple strategies, including social, emotional, and mental health, while integrating communities and families in this process. The language is flexible and can be used to draft your own district policy.[4] If you need support in writing and tailoring a policy for your own district, the Trevor Project can act as a consultant. That information can be found in the document itself, and in the resources section of this book (Chapter 11). Chapter 5, "Prevention: The Educator's Role in Creating a Culture for Suicide Prevention," will highlight how aspects of a policy might be executed.

SCHOOL POLICY FOR COMMEMORATION AND MEMORIALIZATION

> "Gail's suicide was not the only death that our school community had to weather in a very short period of time. We suffered a loss the year before her death, the same year she died, and then we had another student who had just graduated die unexpectedly. We didn't know how important it was to have created a commemoration policy so that if we lost a community member, we'd know what was an accepted and safe way to remember them, which is important to healing a community."
>
> *A school counselor from a private school in the northeast*

Since grief and loss raise the risk of suicide, a school's response to the death of a student or faculty member to any cause of death is a critical part of inspiring a healthy healing process and preventing unhealthy coping strategies that can lead to suicide or other causes of early death. By the time children complete high school, most will experience the death of a family member or friend, with 5% of children experiencing the death of a parent by sixteen years of age. Nearly 40% will experience a death of a peer, and 20% will have witnessed a death.[5]

Most educators will experience the death of a coworker or student at some point in their career. So if a commemoration policy establishes that there is a service project or student-led fundraiser and then a donation to a nonprofit chosen by the family of the deceased student or teacher, then the school has something in writing that offers a framework at a time when emotions are fueling action, mood, and conversation. Having that policy reduces the likelihood that there would be multiple yearbook pages dedicated to the football star who died from heatstroke on the field and nothing for the quiet, lesser-known student who died from cancer in that same year. Comparisons and hurt feelings about how one child got greater consideration are less likely to occur. Nora, who has experienced a student suicide at two different schools in which she has been employed, understands that stunned emotional state of both staff and family of the deceased after a death by suicide and the desire to help and appease the family without fueling memorial competitiveness:

"I think policy is helpful, I think structure is helpful. And I think it's really important to go back to someone when you've got such emotional feelings about the way that [a death] was handled and be able to say, 'This is what our policy is.' And I know that can feel almost cold in some ways, right? Because you want to be very supportive of families and friends and others who are experiencing a great loss, and you just want to make them happy. You want to make them feel better. But I think because all situations are different, it's important to go back to a text that just says, 'When a tragic event occurs, this is how we handle commemoration.' And it might not be enough for some families, it might feel great for others. But at least there's more consistency."

Nora (She/Her/Hers), Ninth-Grade Dean, East Coast High School

A commemoration policy should also outline a protocol that treats all deaths the same. Having one protocol for memorializing a student who died in a car accident and a different one for a student who died by suicide reinforces prejudice associated with suicide and may be deeply painful to the student's family and friends. The time to develop a policy on memorialization is now, before a suicide death occurs, so that there is a clear protocol. Because not handling deaths equally sends a message that the student lost to suicide died from a "less noble" cause of death.

"I am having a hard time putting into words what I am thinking and was wondering if you can help. My daughter was an honor and AP student. She was an amazing runner. Won the top underclassmen award her freshman year and had a lot of friends. She died by suicide in January 2018. Another boy who was also an excellent athlete died of a brain aneurism September 2017. They were both sophomores at the same high school. The yearbook company wouldn't publish a tribute to my daughter because of how she died. By suicide. They did, however, publish a page for the other boy. This is wrong on so many levels. A lot of thoughts are streaming through my head. I want to contact the superintendent of our county and the yearbook company. What are your thoughts? Should I reach out to the media?"

Social media comment from a bereaved mother to Anne Moss Rogers after her daughter's suicide

---

Emotions are always stirred up after a student death. But sensitivities after a suicide are especially so and this is a potential tinderbox that can easily explode in terms of negative media and social media coverage, as well as punitive actions toward administrators in an effort to lay blame if it's not handled with thoughtful fairness.

Also consider that in their raw state of shock and naked grief, parents who've lost a child to suicide, or really any cause of death, can make unrealistic demands and requests of the school, like wanting to hold the funeral in the school auditorium, or building a memorial out front, neither of which is recommended since a school is neither a place of worship nor a cemetery. Having a policy helps administrators avoid potentially unsafe and sensitive situations by allowing the school to rely on what has been laid out.

This kind of policy needs to ensure that everyone feels they can be part of it and that no one ever feels one life is worth more or less than another. Otherwise it can also become very competitive, with students and parents trying to outdo one another. Commemoration shouldn't become a popularity contest, and having a policy helps schools avoid that bear trap. Having students involved is one way to create a more balanced procedure, one that works for grieving adults and young people. That can mean having them discuss their thoughts and feelings as a group and allowing them to collectively identify a meaningful way to commemorate even at the policy level prior to any specific event when everyone is more level-headed. That includes language around impromptu memorials, which often appear after a death as a way for students to express their grief.

These impromptu memorials erected after a suicide set off alarms for administrators, who tear them down in fear of copycat events, leaving students feeling angry and dismissed. At no point should administration demolish well-intentioned memorials without meeting with students who erected them, listening to what they have to say, being transparent on why certain suggestions are being made, and attempting to compromise so that ideas fit within guidelines of an established policy. So thinking through these scenarios at the policy level helps schools create one that is more complete and lays groundwork that everyone will be grateful for when it's needed.

Because memorialization or honoring the deceased is one of the more sensitive topics, it needs to be very clear what is an appropriate and inappropriate memorial for adolescents, as this is an area of considerable confusion and has the potential to fuel a lot of anger and frustration, as well as copycat suicide.

Here are some points[6] to keep in mind when creating a memorial policy, and there is more detail on specific memorialization ideas in "Chapter 9: Postvention: After a Student or Teacher Suicide." The overarching themes are: be consistent, don't make the school a church, instead of physical memorials look to events that celebrate life and offer hope, involve students, and run ideas by the family.

- **Treat all deaths the same.** Strive for consistency. If you memorialize student deaths in the yearbook, for example, that should include students who died by suicide as well as those who were lost to other causes of death.[7] There should not be one policy for suicides and another for a student or faculty member who died from an accident or cancer.

- **Avoid planned on-campus erected physical memorials and funeral-type events.** Funeral services, tributes, or flying the flag at half-staff are not recommended at school because it may inadvertently sensationalize a death from any cause and encourage suicide or suicide contagion in a susceptible teen population. Physical structures, like trees or bushes, can begin to look rangy and uncared for, and larger memorials can start to show signs of wear and overall can start to look more like a graveyard over the years.[8]

- **Memorial events like walks to prevent suicide or cancer, donations to nonprofits, and letters written in class about the student (reviewed by staff) to be sent to the parents are all appropriate.** Overall, you want memorial events to allow students to communicate their connection and attachment to the deceased. Active events that encourage connection, celebrate life, and collectively give back to the community in a meaningful way are a healthy coping strategy for grief. At a time when so many feel helpless, it makes people feel useful.

- **Devise a thoughtful and sensitive plan for spontaneous memorials.** Students are more likely to devise spontaneous memorials when expressing their grief (e.g. decorated lockers and hallway displays). Always meet and work with students who erected them, and be transparent. Here are some recommended guidelines for impromptu memorials:

  - Share with students how long such a memorial will be left in place (generally a few days to a week) and discuss what will happen to the items left at the site. For example, students may take photos of the memorial, and gather the items from the site to give to the family of the deceased student. Involving students in these plans to the extent possible is helpful so that they see the decision as fair and respectful of their desires.[9]

  - The school shall then leave a notice for when the memorial will be removed and given to the student's family

  - No permanent writing on property permitted (e.g. graffiti), and objects left must be nonperishable and cannot block exits or hallways or access to student lockers.

  - If necessary, work with the students to relocate a temporary memorial to another site if it's in a main area, and take into consideration that locker memorials can be upsetting to students who also have a locker nearby.

  - The memorial site should be monitored so that inappropriate written comments or objects can be removed right away. Spontaneous memorials constructed in the community can be a problem, especially if they are placed in dangerous locations, such as busy intersections or railroad tracks where a student died. These have the potential to become sites for future risk-taking behaviors, including substance misuse. Offsite memorials are something over which schools have little control but they do affect the school population, so do have someone designated to reach out to community leaders to discuss these if necessary.

- Any school-based memorials or small group gatherings after a suicide should include a focus on how to prevent future suicides; have prevention resources available such as wallet-size cards, and have students think of two trusted adults they'd reach out to if they were struggling.

- **Online memorial pages** should use safe messaging, include resources for information and support, be monitored by an adult, and be time limited. Students use social media to commemorate and memorialize, and schools shouldn't ignore it because it's "off campus." A member of the school staff should review the page, not to police the site but to monitor the mood for the purpose of protecting the health and well-being of the school population. Ask students to bring to an adult's attention any worrisome, destructive, or disparaging comments about the deceased, and any suicidal or homicidal intentions.[10]

- **Include students in planning a commemoration policy.** Invite students to discuss as a group their thoughts and feelings on the subject and allow them to identify collectively a helpful and meaningful way to commemorate. Make it clear in the policy that students should be involved in any postvention activities as well (a walk, fundraiser, volunteer day).[11]

- **Understand that memorializing is often a way for struggling students to express their pain.** Cards, letters, and pictures may be given to the student's family after being reviewed by school administration. If items indicate that additional students may be at increased risk for suicide and/or in need of additional mental health support (e.g. writing about a wish to die or other risk behavior), those students should be triaged to the school counselor to help determine the level of risk and appropriate response.

- **Maintain your structure understanding that it's not business as usual.** Do not cancel school for the funeral or for reasons related to the death, although staff and students may be excused to attend if it's during school hours. Maintaining structure is very important, even if it's not "business as usual."

- **Any school-based class conversations, small gatherings, or support groups should after a suicide should include:**
  - Adult supervision
  - Opportunities to talk about the person's life and what they loved

- Prevention resources
- How to prevent future suicides (don't keep a friend's confession that they want to die a secret)
- Identifying two trusted adults in whom students would confide
- Healthy ways to cope with grief

- **Large memorial assemblies should not be convened.** The emotions generated at such a gathering can be difficult to control. Small groups are encouraged with adults they know in the room for support.

- **Consult with the family about memorials.** The person designated as the liaison with the family needs to be prepared to explain the memorialization policy to the family while respecting their wishes as well as the grieving traditions associated with their culture and religion.[12]

- **Visitation recommendations.** Two people should visit the family of the deceased immediately after getting the news and at least one of them should be a school administrator. This should be the principal or the assistant superintendent (not the superintendent), who goes with someone the family knows, like a favorite teacher or coach. While it is unusual for school administrators to visit the home right after hearing about a student's death, it's a mistake not to. School administrators may get advice from lawyers that the family may sue. But not visiting immediately only increases animosity (if there is any). If, for example, someone dies from heat stroke at soccer practice or a suicide on campus, there is a far greater chance the family will be angry if the school goes silent (more on this point in Chapter 9, "Postvention After a Student or Teacher Suicide"). If there are multiple school deaths at once, such as after a school shooting, this approach may not be possible due to lack of personnel. Consult safeschoolsforalex.org for these visitation guidelines.

If you serve a culture that has some very different ideas about grief, loss, and commemoration, all of that needs to be reviewed and integrated into any commemoration policy and updated when it changes. There are consultants who can act as culture brokers who work with schools on meeting those guidelines and the needs of your student population and their families. If your school has a large population of Native Americans from a particular tribe, for example, you'd want your policy to be culturally competent, and going to the contact form at SPRC.org will put you in touch with those experts.

"[There are] implications of defaulting to whiteness in everything that we do. I think one of the big criticisms of postvention is that it defaults to Western white assumptions about what it looks like to respond to grief and loss. And, you know, after a kid dies is not the time to ask 'what are the culturally different approaches to grief and loss that exist in our school?" You can't survey the school at that point. And so part of postvention is doing that work in advance. Not just making sure that the materials are in the languages that are spoken in the school, but really to understand. I read about postvention in Hawaii where there is this integration of ancestors and spirits and concepts that in your typical white middle-class neighborhood, you would never think of in postvention. So part of postvention that I talk with about at schools is making sure that they understand what conceptions of death look like within these different cultural groups, including rituals."

Jonathan B. Singer, PhD, LCSW (He/Him/His), President, American Association of Suicidology, author of Suicide in Schools: A Practitioner's Guide to Multi-level Prevention, Assessment, Intervention, and Postvention

CONFIDENTIALITY POLICY

Fear of exposure is a barrier to youth sharing a problem that has them emotionally tangled and fighting to find a way out. They may be concerned that their parents will be told, that all their teachers will know, or that it will end up on a record that is sent to colleges (also a concern of parents). To promote help seeking, students need to know that what they say and share with you is in confidence because you want them to disclose problems before they become a crisis. There are times we cannot promise complete confidentiality due to the nature of the confession, a danger to others or themselves, but we can be transparent and outline those boundaries and promise to handle any discovery with discretion and respect for the student's privacy. Preteens and teenagers need to know that before they come forward. Otherwise the fear of what they don't know takes up too much real estate in their minds and decreases the chances they'll seek help. Posting a confidentiality policy in visible areas promotes help-seeking behavior. The editable Confidentiality Policy Template included here can be posted in offices, hallways, lunchrooms, classrooms, and more. It offers the opportunity to establish your teachers and the counseling team as a trusted resource, because students are likely to take a detour to a teacher's classroom prior to seeing the counselor because that is who they know.

Confidentiality Policy Template

(This template also appears as Worksheet 6: Sample Confidentiality Policy for Students, in Chapter 12. Thank you to Jennifer Hamilton of Noble and Greenough School for sharing this policy.)

[Name of School] counselors are available to talk with you about any issue you might be dealing with. All conversations are completely confidential unless we have concerns about safety—for example, if someone is threatening or harming you, if you express suicidal intentions, or if you are talking about harming yourself or another person. In such cases, you can trust that your information will be handled with the utmost discretion, and the goal will always be to ensure that you have the support you need to be safe and well.

Students can confidentially talk about feelings of sadness or anxiety, share personal information, etc., without worrying that teachers, parents, guardians, colleges, etc. will be informed. If a student is having intense thoughts or feelings and is feeling hesitant about coming to talk with a counselor for fear that their information will not be held in confidence, we encourage you to come and share whatever you feel comfortable sharing. We most certainly want to support you and hope that you will grow to trust that talking about those deeper feelings can lead to the greater support that you deserve.

NOTES

1. SafeOregon. https://www.nbcnews.com/news/us-news/school-tip-lines-were-meant-stop-shootings-uncovered-teen-suicide-n1127876
2. The third edition is currently in development and is expected to be live by June 2021. https://www.nasponline.org/professional-development/pre-pare-training-curriculum
3. Centers for Disease Control and Prevention, National Center for Injury Prevention and Control. (2020). *Web-based Injury Statistics Query and Reporting System (WISQARS)* (Leading Causes of Death Reports, 1981–2018). Retrieved June 10, 2020 from www.cdc.gov/injury/wisqars
4. American Foundation for Suicide Prevention, American School Counselor Association, National Association of School Psychologists, and The Trevor

Project (2019). *Model School District Policy on Suicide Prevention: Model Language, Commentary, and Resources* (2nd ed.). New York: American Foundation for Suicide Prevention.

5. https://www.schoolcrisiscenter.org/wp-content/uploads/2017/04/ncscb-guidelines-responding-death-student-or-school-staff.pdf, p. 7.

6. The Grieving Student: A Teacher's Guide Video and pdf, Model School Policy. https://www.schoolcrisiscenter.org/wp-content/uploads/2017/04/ncscb-guidelines-responding-death-student-or-school-staff.pdf

7. American Foundation for Suicide Prevention (AFSP) and the Suicide Prevention Resource Center (SPRC), Education Development Center (EDC) (2018). *After a Suicide: A Toolkit for Schools* (2nd ed.). https://www.sprc.org/resources-programs/after-suicide-toolkit-schools

8. The Grieving Student: A Teacher's Guide Video and pdf, Model School Policy. https://www.schoolcrisiscenter.org/wp-content/uploads/2017/04/ncscb-guidelines-responding-death-student-or-school-staff.pdf

9. Ibid.

10. Ibid.

11. Ibid.

12. American Foundation for Suicide Prevention (AFSP) and the Suicide Prevention Resource Center (SPRC), Education Development Center (EDC) (2018). *After a Suicide: A Toolkit for Schools* (2nd ed.). Memorialization. https://sprc.org/sites/default/files/resource-program/AfteraSuicideToolkit-forSchools.pdf

Chapter 5
Prevention:
The Educator's Role
in Creating a Culture
for Suicide Prevention

"I think educators are a really crucial component in the way we teach and create connection and belonging in our classrooms, and the way we teach learning how to fail. Teachers can be a first line of connection and support for a student who is struggling."

Scott LoMurray (He/Him/His), Executive Director, Sources of Strength

Since teachers oversee millions of adolescents nationwide, your eyes, ears, gut feelings, and observations are a critical part of the workflow of demoting suicide as a cause of death in young people. And your relationships with students are a valuable asset to the process. Without you, there is a canyon-sized hole in the safety net that no amount of superglue can fix. In short, teachers are the vital first link between the students, the school counseling team, their parents, and mental health resources.

While the goal of this book is to promote suicide prevention, that intention does not translate to a constant, exhaustive focus on suicide education for students, but rather striking a healthy balance within an overall Tier 1 framework of positive behavioral interventions and support (PBIS) in secondary education.

The core principles guiding Tier 1 PBIS include the understanding that we can and should effectively teach appropriate behavior to all children, intervene early before unwanted behaviors escalate, use research-based, scientifically validated interventions whenever possible, monitor student progress, and use data to make decisions.[1]

How does suicide prevention fit into that framework? For high schools, efforts to bolster protective factors and coping skills through social emotional learning (SEL) initiatives wrapped with education on mental health and suicide that includes gatekeeper training create an effective foundation for suicide prevention. That might translate to a module for suicide prevention education for all ninth and eleventh graders, an annual module on mental health for all grades, while there are multiple ongoing opportunities for coping skills development (e.g. SEL), peer support, promoting crisis resources, events for emotional wellness, as well as information, education, and support surrounding social issues (e.g. Alateen, What Is Human Trafficking? Body Image Support Group).

Depending on the maturity of the population, however, the emphasis for most middle schools might focus more on mental health education, and developing healthy coping strategies through social emotional learning while also including age-appropriate resources and education.

"You know when you're talking to middle school kids, I don't think there's a lot of added value in speaking to them using language that focuses specifically on suicide. I think you want to focus primarily on wellness and understanding one's own mental life and experience."

Victor Schwartz, MD (He/Him/His), Former CMO of The JED Foundation, MindStrategies Advisors, Clinical Associate Professor, Department of Psychiatry, NYU School of Medicine

---

While many schools like Noble and Greenough School, which has been mentioned many times in this book, have integrated all kinds of suicide prevention training, programs, and social emotional learning over the years, that's not where they started. They began with a basic commitment of prioritizing student wellness. They focused on the simple idea that in order to achieve, you have to put wellness first.

"Last year we had the Stanley King Institute come out and do a day-long training for our faculty on how to be a really good listener. Stanley King works with educators and teaches them some basic counseling skills which will come in handy when working with students. There's a really deep commitment at our school to doing professional development around wellness, mental health, diversity, equity, and inclusion. I think a wonderful thing about Noble is our prioritization of a relational pedagogy; that we are really committed to the relationships kids have with their teachers. In order to do that, you really have to feel comfortable in those spaces. And so, we're just constantly trying to provide ways in which faculty can feel more buoyed to do that work."

Jennifer Hamilton (She/Her/Hers), School Psychologist, Director of Psychology and Counseling at Noble and Greenough, Independent School, Dedham, Massachusetts

Students who are doing well emotionally are absent less, make better grades, cause fewer disruptions, and have fewer conflicts in their relationships. That means that over the years they need fewer disciplinary resources and managing your classrooms is more rewarding. It's in any school's best interest to integrate programs that promote emotional well-being and training because suicide can be prevented, those thoughts can be treated, and the skills you integrate into your teaching can be used by students for a lifetime.

CREATING A CULTURE OF CONNECTEDNESS AND BELONGING

"I just finished my seventh year of teaching at a large public high school. Our school did lose a young girl due to suicide a few years ago. I did not have her in class, but she was involved in sports, so as a PE teacher I saw from a distance how her death affected her friends afterwards. More than once I have had a student either leave a note on my desk, or tell me they wanted to hurt themselves or die. These specific circumstances made a huge impact on my life and how I teach. In addition, I have had personal experience with a daughter who attempted suicide two times while a freshman athlete in college. I always start the year talking about this personal family crisis when doing our units on depression/mental health to try to remove the stigma and then build rapport with young people who struggle with mental health issues. The young lady who ended her life is one I refer to in class because I want my students to know it happens to both males and females. We talk about health history and genetics and I always ask my students to talk to their parents if depression, anxiety, even alcoholism runs in their family. I am open and tell them it does in mine, again trying to build those relationships with each student. Maybe that is why some feel they can turn to me and trust them with something so serious. Anyway, I feel knowing this important health background information can help students navigate through high school and tough times a little better. Knowledge is power and I pump as much life information into them as I can!"

Public High School PE/Health Teacher, Virginia

Research has shown that increased feelings of school and peer connected-ness are related to lower reports of suicidal thoughts and behaviors among students.[2,3] Fostering a culture of connection and belonging can include sharing your own experiences, being culturally sensitive, allowing opportunities for sharing, and amplifying diverse voices.

Cultural sensitivity is being aware of the existence of cultural differences and similarities, how it affects people's values and perceptions of themselves, contributes to their fears, and affects learning and behavior. To adopt cultural competency, teachers have to be open minded, recognize and discard their own preconceived cultural biases, and understand the perspective from which the people sitting in the classrooms view the lessons taught. This is an easier shift in a school already integrating a pedagogy of diversity and inclusion. To understand how this might play out, think about how Native American students might perceive history lessons that focus on Manifest Destiny as a necessary evil to advance progress. How might African American students feel about Civil War history that portrays slave-owning Confederate soldiers as heroes?

More inclusive sex education, for example, means incorporating LGBTQ themes that help youth understand sexual orientation with age-appropriate, medically accurate information emphasizing protection during sex for people of all gender identities. You can't always choose your curriculum as a teacher, but you can shape that interpretation in your classroom to be more well-rounded and inclusive.

"We have seen some states really step up to the plate when it comes to making sure that they have LGBTQ-inclusive history classes. New Jersey teachers are about to transition into having a whole system of making sure that LGBTQ youth will see themselves represented in the history classes. Now that's one form of that support. There are a lot of teachers who do a really great job when it comes to pro-nouns and obviously GSAs [Gender & Sexualities Alliances] are everywhere around the country and those can be really important systems of support. And in DC, we now make sure that LGBTQ youth are counted in the youth risk behavior survey, YRBS. Little things matter. Educators can actually say, 'We see you and we support you where you are. You're spending a third of your day here [in school]. We need to make sure this is a place where you feel safe and supported.'"

Sam Brinton (They/Them/Theirs), Vice President of Advocacy and Government Affairs at The Trevor Project, Rockville, Maryland

Now think of your classroom and teaching methods from the perspective of special needs students who are part of your class, including those with physical disabilities, IEP or 504 plans. For example, a separate desk for a wheelchair-bound student in a class where group tables are the norm isolates that student more. So classroom teachers could ask the special needs representative to present an alternative adaptation so the student can be together with peers. What about that student who is anxious or the one who struggles to stay on task? Calling out students in front of the class can breed resentment and further discipline problems. If you notice a student fidgeting, isolating, arriving late to school, avoiding touching things, or not participating in class discussions, address your concerns privately and let the counseling staff know. When you note symptoms by anxious or restless students, you can develop specific statements to use when supporting your student in a triggering moment without alerting the rest of the class.[4] Ideas for engaging students and allowing them time to share so they are more prepared for learning are in Chapter 6, "Suicide Prevention Activities for Schools."

Part of creating a culture of belonging in a school that serves a particular ethnic or gender group is bringing in teachers and clinicians that mirror the population of the students and their families. At the very least, clinicians and teachers need to be well versed in the traditions of the families they serve. Jessica Chock Goldman, LCSW, serves a large Asian American population. The largest school group is Chinese American, then Bangladeshi American, Korean American, and Indian American. She has established Korean and Chinese parent groups and brings in Chinese clinicians who speak Mandarin or Cantonese, as well as Korean and Bangladeshi clinicians to speak to those groups. Whenever possible, by matching students and their families with clinicians of the same ethnicity, and students with teachers and clinicians who understand or match their gender identity, there is that instant trust bond that goes a long way in helping schools build community and avoid later conflict with students and families, which can be far more damaging and time consuming. While this takes considerable effort, it also helps to normalize mental health within cultures.

Anything teachers can do to facilitate parental and family involvement will make the student feel more included. Because regardless of family income or background, students whose parents are involved are more likely to have higher grades and test scores, attend school regularly, have better social skills, show improved behavior, and adapt well to school.[5] For Native American as well as Latino cultures, offering childcare for after-school events is more inclusive because these families often live in intergenerational homes, which includes mom and grandma, who both want to come and learn and need a place for the younger kids. Single parents also need this type of support.

What needs to follow are specific educational events, and then opportunities such as groups for parents and students to connect, with services that match the needs of those communities.

"What we've been doing is working with our different community organizations and figuring out what culturally appropriate or culturally responsive services [we need] out in the community."

Michelle Fortunado-Kewin, LCSW, PPSC (She/Her/Siya), School Social Worker and Program Coordinator, San Francisco Unified School District

---

For schools with immigrant populations, there is often a language barrier between first-generation immigrants and their kids. Youth who are second-generation immigrants face unique bicultural challenges. This confusion of ethnic identity influences their feelings of belongingness, especially in regard to partial or total affiliation with either their ethnic or host community.

"These are not kids who go to their parents and say, 'Hey, I'm really depressed. I'm having mental health issues.' A lot of times what happens culturally is that mental health and depression are new words for [these] families and you see acculturation play out in this way because the kids are really New Yorkers—fast-paced, high-achieving motivated kids who are part of an immigrant family. So there's a lot of disconnect with many of them in terms of language. They can have basic conversations with their parents about doing homework and eating dinner but when it comes to deeper feelings, kids tend not to speak the parent's language of origin and parents speak limited English. That makes schools a crucial safe place to discuss topics they are uncomfortable talking about at home."

Jessica Chock-Goldman, LCSW (She/Her/Hers), Doctoral Candidate, School Social Worker, Stuyvesant High School in Manhattan, New York

---

LGBTQ students can have similar issues with parent communication and disconnection related more to a lack of acceptance, which can hinder them from talking about mental health or suicide. For these students, a school culture that allows them to navigate the school per their gender identity is critical to their emotional health, especially in cases where they have not yet come out to their family or friends. This is simply meeting students where they are and not forcing them into a specific mold.

_____

"Number one for [LGBTQ youth] is having peers and adults who understand and support you for who you are. We know that just one accepting adult can help reduce the risk of a suicide attempt among LGBTQ youth by forty percent, which is amazing.[6] So having a teacher who is supportive of LGBTQ youth can make a big difference in a young person's life. Access to a school environment [that matches the youth's gender identity] is important—whether that's bathrooms, locker rooms, and sports teams, or making sure that school records can be reflective of the young person's chosen name. So all of those policies that go into school practices and making sure that those are inclusive of a young person's correct name and pronouns. School policies and practices that are affirming of LGBTQ young people's identities work to lower risk for suicide."

Keygan Miller, MEd (They/Them/Theirs),
Senior Advocacy Associate at The Trevor Project, Washington, DC

_____

In addition to any diversity and inclusion training, part of any school's suicide prevention initiative should include teacher training in specific issues that face LGBTQ students since they are at higher risk. Educators should know how to react when a student comes out to them, making sure they know not to "out" their students because that can increase risk for suicide.

Supporting LGBTQ Youth

Data from the Trevor Project's 2020 national survey and a research brief published December 2020 emphasizes the importance of LGBTQ-affirming spaces for suicide prevention.[7] Key findings include:

- For LGBTQ youth, one supportive adult helps lower the risk of suicide by 40%.

- LGBTQ youth who reported having at least one LGBTQ-affirming space had 35% reduced odds of reporting a suicide attempt in the past year—the strongest association being with LGBTQ-affirming schools.

- 62% of all LGBTQ youth stated that their school was LGBTQ-affirming and 55% of transgender and nonbinary youth stated their school was gender-affirming.

Transgender and nonbinary youth who reported having pronouns respected by all or most people in their lives attempted suicide at half the rate of those who did not have their pronouns respected. According to The Trevor Project, one cannot assume someone's pronouns in the same way we cannot assume someone's name. It's always best to confirm with a person what their name and pronouns are and you do that by asking, or by introducing your own pronouns when you meet a person, which gives them the opportunity to share theirs.[8] Given how important names, gender, and pronouns are to adolescent LGBTQ students, you may need to alter your roster from a printed one to reflect names or gender change. Schools can also be proactive for students who identify as transgendered by creating Gender Support Plans available at GenderSpectrum.org so that information can be communicated to staff at the school to support the student. The Gender Support Plan, spearheaded by a school counselor, is a detailed form to help educators create a shared understanding among school staff, parents, and a student about the ways in which the student's gender will be expressed and supported at school.[9]

For educators who want an overview of how to support LGBTQ youth, TheTrevorProject.org provides a free 11-page download, "Guide to Being an Ally to Transgender and Nonbinary Youth."

How else can teachers promote inclusion? Drama, art, English, and music teachers can highlight cultures, expose students to new and different genres, present issues of social justice, and highlight the unique challenges of those with disabilities through their performances or through videos. Coaches can insist that sports teams adopt more culture-friendly mascots so Native American students don't feel irrelevant.

"You can reduce risk [of Native American youth suicide] by getting rid of the native mascot. I think the group that's done the best job of trying to get rid of native mascots is a group called Illuminative. They also do a lot of work to improve the portrayal of Native Americans in film and media. So we look at things like identity. When we look at protective factors for suicide prevention, we look at your connectedness, your sense of belonging, your purpose. You know growing up, 'The only good Indian is a dead Indian' was a national saying. If your culture is telling you your purpose is to die, your purpose is to not exist anymore, of course that affects your mental health."

Shelby Rowe (She/Her/Hers), Co-Chair, Indigenous Peoples Committee,
American Association of Suicidology (AAS)

All of these issues can seem trivial looking from our own cultural perspectives but can carry generations of trauma for those cultures with a history of being mistreated and marginalized.

During virtual learning in 2020, connection and belonging were more challenging to achieve as teachers and students struggled to adapt to the pandemic. Opportunities to connect diminished, and in New York City in the spring and summer of that year, Jessica Chock-Goldman said the isolation and loneliness triggered a lot of ideation with her high-achieving Asian American students, some of whom were not even allowed to step outside due to the fear and high rates of infection in that area. To address this, she hosted a twice-a-week coping and social skills group workshop that attracted mostly boys on Zoom.

"We tend to have most of our attempts in March, April, May. This year [2020 pandemic] it was the end of June, because we were still in kind of a modified lockdown in New York and kids were going crazy with 'What is my summer going to be, what am I going to do, when am I ever going to go back to real life?' I sent so many kids to the hospital at the end of the summer. But these virtual coping skills workshops—they loved talking about how to get through the days during the lockdowns, about not going to school, and remote learning. And they would give each other pointers about what they were doing. That was really was empowering for them to give advice to each other. That said, kids were pretty open about having ideation, like it was pretty across the board that there was mild ideation. So in this coping skills group, we talked about that, about how to normalize that the loneliness sometimes makes you have some ideation. This was the most important work during virtual learning because it was so important that the kids were seeing other faces."

Jessica Chock-Goldman, LCSW (She/Her/Hers), Doctoral Candidate,
School Social Worker, Stuyvesant High School in Manhattan, New York

Connection and feeling included are not only important to adolescents, but are the center of their well-being and an undisputed protective factor for preventing suicide and supporting student wellness. Whatever you do in your classrooms or at your school, seek opportunities for students to work together, learn more about their classmates, and highlight coping strategies that have helped others through times of adversity.

COLLABORATION IS THE KEY TO SUCCESS

To effectively build a school and classroom culture that prioritizes suicide prevention, an understanding of your students' baseline and how this age group evolves to a place of despair helps you effectively prevent them from getting to crisis. The trust you have established is the key ingredient that activates an ethos where a student is more likely to reach out when they are struggling or need to talk, followed by a willingness to connect that student to help. That takes collaboration, communication, passion, and commitment to student wellness.

"I am the only mental health professional in a school of 3,400 students. I speak so highly of collaboration with other departments in schools. So I will meet with the English department every year and just have a quick conversation. 'Hey, guys. If anyone mentions trauma stuff or problems at home, just bring it to me. Send it to me. I'll read it.' And it's pretty remarkable how kids will write a little bit in their English paper, usually using a character in fiction, and then you talk to them and maybe follow with an assessment and discover there is a real issue. There was a kid who wrote about a girl who sometimes worried she was too fat and once I assessed her she ended up going to an inpatient eating disorder treatment. It was a big deal. So it's important counselors have good and open relationships with the teachers."

Jessica Chock-Goldman, LCSW (She/Her/Hers), Doctoral Candidate, School Social Worker, Stuyvesant High School in Manhattan, New York

---

Jessica and other school counselors emphasize setting expectations with parents on the subject of mental health. She brings in the freshmen parents every year, all 950 of them, normalizes the subject, and sets expectations by telling them that they're going to get calls from her and her team about mental health referrals and that's OK. She has to emphasize that these referrals won't be the kind of information that colleges will see. This has to be collaborative with the families, collaborative with the institution, and collaborative with the teachers coming in and being able to spot which kids might need attention. The goal is to normalize mental health topics and promote help-seeking behavior early on, using a wraparound team approach.

Teachers and counselors from schools across the United States send members of their counseling staff to classrooms to deliver presentations and encourage discussion on mental health topics, in addition to coping strategies workshops. This education is not limited to health and PE classes either.

These presentations can happen in person or in virtual classrooms, in math or American history classes. And teachers who become comfortable with the subject can also help by delivering these educational presentations or incorporate that learning in small ways in their curriculums.

CREATE A SAFE DIGITAL LEARNING ENVIRONMENT

"We use Google for Educators and the technology does a sweep at the end of the day every day to go through and find anything that a student has posted that might be alarming—from papers they posted to chats they've had. One student had written her intentions to kill herself in white font in the chat. Human eyes couldn't see it but the technology did. The system sent the name of the student in an alert to our wellness team and one of us was able to reach out to her and later her parents. It was a student we had been keeping an eye on but during the 2020 pandemic that was harder to do. This was a masked cry for help but I'm happy to report this student is safe and got the help she needed. But we must remain vigilant with kids who have struggled even when they get 'better.' Teen moods can shift so quickly."

School psychologist, southeast public school

Kids want to tell and sometimes they tell in cryptic and clandestine ways on digital learning platforms. To find these potential hidden threats, many schools are utilizing technology tools like Gaggle Safety Management (Gaggle.net), which flags harmful online content before it's posted, including drug and alcohol use, intentions of violence, sexual content, self-harm, pornography/child pornography, bullying, and more. It works like a diligent robot to sweep the environment, flag questionable content, find students in distress, and notify someone on staff depending on the predetermined threat level. Immediate risks such as violence to oneself or others would trigger an emergency instant notification to someone on call or even a first responder. For inappropriate language that isn't an imminent threat, the system would prevent the posting and the student would receive a warning for the infraction. This tool has been a valuable low-cost safety tool to help educators prevent tragedy and other potential incendiary incidents. The video about how Gaggle works and videos from educators on how school districts are using it for their digital environments are excellent learning resources.

Gaggle works on these digital learning environments:

- Google for Education
- Office 365
- Canvas

Gaggle scans:

- Chats
- Links to websites
- Documents and online file storage
- Attachments and images
- Outbound and inbound email

Here's how one public school uses this technology in their district.

___

"Our public high school uses Gaggle to sweep the Google Drive of every student. Quite a few school divisions are using this now but many use it only during school hours and on school days. Our school district uses this tool 24/7, 365 days a year. For example, as a support person on call, I may receive a phone call at 1:00 a.m. that a student has written a suicide note on their Google Document, which our students frequently use for chatting particularly when they've lost their phones. Sometimes students will also put a concerning remark or 'plan' on their Google Calendar. Gaggle can pick that up as well. Once we get a call, our mental health team reaches out to the family and/or calls first responders to do a welfare check. We also follow up with the student personally on the next school day. Gaggle is discussed with students and parents and explained in our Student Handbook so they are aware of this supervision."

School psychologist for a large public school division on the East Coast

___

This digital learning environment protocol can be found in Chapter 12, Worksheet 2: Creating a Safe Digital Learning Environment.

CHOOSING THE RIGHT PROGRAM OR TRAINING

___

"[The] biggest barrier to implementing a program like Sources [of Strength] is that it takes time if we are going to shift the culture in a school. The return on investing in mental health, investing in social emotional learning, investing in culture, is profound.

Because you're not spending nearly as much money on all of those negative down-stream outcomes. And so it's actually cost effective to take an upstream approach."

Scott LoMurray (He/Him/His), Executive Director, Sources of Strength

Schools are a widely used setting for youth suicide prevention programs. Suicide prevention efforts in schools are categorized as universal, selective, or indicated.[10] *Universal* prevention programs target an entire population to reduce risk factors or enhance protective factors. *Selective* prevention programs target youth who demonstrate risk factors associated with suicide, but who have not yet reported suicidal thoughts or an attempt. *Indicated* prevention programs are designed to intervene with youth who have already reported suicidal thoughts or an attempt. Examples of suicide prevention efforts in schools include suicide awareness and education, screening, gatekeeper training, peer leadership training, and skills training.[11,12]

You might wonder where to start with your school suicide prevention efforts. Focus initial efforts on training yourself and encouraging the school to sponsor suicide prevention training for the staff if your state has not already mandated it. As far as programs, look at the ones that are evidence-based or evidence-informed, and consider how much buy-in you have with leadership, your resources and goals, the makeup of your student population, state policy, what's already being implemented, and where your school is in terms of social emotional learning (SEL) and mental health education. Budget shouldn't keep you from moving forward because there are many funding options and most of the big programs will help you find it.

There are programs aimed at bolstering protective factors, like SEL, that may already be integrated into your curriculum. SEL does reinforce the protective factors such as coping skills, decision making, and problem solving that can create the foundation for a culture of suicide prevention. And these programs can keep students from getting to crisis, build their emotional muscle known as resilience, and help them find hope and strength in the face of adversity. If your school is implementing SEL, it is vital that teachers have suicide prevention training alongside that effort. Because as students go through SEL role-playing scenarios, many of them will use that opportunity to make a plea for help. These clues can often be subtle and missed, dismissed, or avoided if you've not been trained on what to do if a student is exhibiting signs. Whether or not your school integrates an SEL program, however, should not stop you from integrating those concepts into your own teaching style and modeling these behaviors in your classroom.

In this section, we've highlighted training and school-based programs. Each one focuses on one or more of the following objectives: inspire more open conversation about mental health and suicide, remove the stigma, educate on what to say and do, boost protective factors, promote a culture of connection, instill hope and a vision for the future, and reinforce an ethos of help-seeking behavior.

Some suicide prevention programs are all-inclusive, meaning they include gatekeeper/educator training and are universal school-based suicide prevention programs. A vital first step in educating a school faculty on the signs of suicide is also having a protocol within the school regarding what to do when a student expresses those thoughts. (See the example protocol later in this chapter.) Schools should not wait until there is a student suicide to recognize the importance of having a procedure and integrating these trainings or programs into the school curriculum. You need to know that someone has your back and that you're not in this solo. You already have the skills and the relationships with students to have the conversation or make the referral; training simply increases your confidence and ability to do so.

EDUCATOR/GATEKEEPER TRAINING

"We use SOS [program] one time in the beginning of the semester followed by a second program—either Talk Saves Lives, or More Than Sad; which one is up to the social worker just before school gets out, just as a reminder. We recently started showing the More Than Sad video to parents in some of the communities. Since we've been doing prevention programming twice a year, we have seen a decrease with high school kids dying by suicide. They're still talking about it, 'I wish I was dead,' but we got more people aware of what they're talking about who will intervene."

James Biela, LCSW (He/Him/His), Itinerant School Social Worker,
Lower Kuskokwim School District, Bethel, Alaska
Talk Saves Lives and More Than Sad: 1-hour suicide
primer presentations from AFSP.org

Since student suicides have been on the rise, many states have made teacher training mandatory and states have adopted programs for that implementation. If they have not, consider the following training programs for gatekeepers or seek extra training. Most of these, if not all, include certificates of completion in addition to CE credits, and we've included programs suitable for schoolteachers, school nurses, librarians, coaches, activities directors, students, and any ancillary school staff, because sometimes the person the student tells isn't a teacher but the lunch lady, a friend, a bus driver, or a janitor. Most kids won't seek out and tell a mental health professional.

With few exceptions, most of these programs do have an associated cost but are affordable. Then there are free trainings and programs offered through and funded by state agencies or nonprofits like National Alliance of Mental Illness (NAMI) or American Foundation of Suicide Prevention (AFSP).

QPR: Question, Persuade, Refer from QPR Institute (QPRinstitute.com) is gatekeeper training that is available as a 1- to 2-hour in-person class or online training that is suitable for either individual teachers or school organizations and included on the National Registry of Evidence-Based Programs and Practices.

QPR: Question, Persuade, Refer for School Health Professionals from QPR Institute (QPRinstitute.com) is suicide prevention best practice program training for school health professionals, including school social workers, nurses, psychologists, and school counselors. This course does not teach suicide risk assessment. If you are tasked with conducting suicide risk assessments, you'd take the QPR Suicide Triage course, or if you are clinician who will carry out a treatment plan that integrates suicide risk assessment into that plan, there is the course QPRT Suicide Risk Assessment and Risk Management.

QPR: For Sports from QPR Institute (QPRinstitute.com) is a 3+ hour online training program customized specifically for sports coaches to identify athletes who may be at risk for suicide. This training is appropriate for athletic directors, activity directors, team managers, skills coaches, strength and conditioning personnel, physiotherapists, sports psychologists, nutritionists, and all others who are involved in supporting good mental health among athletes.

Start by LivingWorks (livingworks.net) is a 90-minute customizable, online interactive gatekeeper training program that empowers trainees with the skills and knowledge to keep students, co-workers, and others safe from suicide. It can be taken from any computer or mobile device.

safeTALK by LivingWorks (LivingWorks.net) is for everyone, including teachers, and is an in-person 3.5- to 4-hour course taught independently and through nonprofits and state agencies across the US and Canada. The "safe" letters stand for Suicide Alertness for Everyone and the "TALK" letters stand for the actions one takes to keep people safe from suicide: Tell, Ask, Listen, and KeepSafe. Six 60- to 90-second video scenarios start with a non-alert scene that illustrates a missed opportunity and then an alert video example that represents a more effective intervention strategy for connecting that person with community resources trained in suicide intervention. Videos are used strategically throughout the training to show examples and the program is customized by the trainer to include videos most relevant to the population that will attend the training and includes several school scenarios. The videos cover many "barriers" to why people miss, dismiss, or avoid getting involved, and they empower trainees to step forward and intervene and be the ears and eyes in a community to prevent suicide. Go to LivingWorks.net to see what trainings are in your area.

Kognito At-Risk for High School Educators by Kognito (Kognito.com) is 60–120 minutes of evidence-based online gatekeeper training that features online role-play training simulations that include mental health education and suicide prevention (Figure 5.1). Themes include mental health, self-harm, grief, bullying, alcohol, and drugs, plus other contributing factors of a student suicide threat. "Conversation challenges" are examples of what students might say and how educators can surmise more about that student based on what they are saying, followed by how a teacher should respond, and when to connect the person with the school counseling team. It's designed to drive sustainable, systemic changes in educator behavior to support student wellness, academic performance, attendance, and school safety. It has been used in public, charter, vocational, and parochial schools, and in teacher training programs. The course was developed to be suitable for a variety of settings and appropriate for and acceptable to a broad range of racial and ethnic groups. There is also At-Risk for Middle School Educators, and one for students called *Friend 2 Friend*, which is an excellent learning module that engages youth in a conversation about mental health and drives change in their skills and attitudes toward seeking help for oneself or a friend.

Suicide Prevention: A Gatekeeper Training for School Personnel, developed by Riverside Trauma Center (RiversideTraumaCenter.org), is a two-hour training for licensed school personnel by Riverside Trauma staff in Massachusetts. Taught both in person (they can come to you) and virtually, it is based on current best practices and designed for teachers and school personnel of all grade levels to increase their knowledge about suicide and

Figure 5.1 Kognito uses simulated conversations to give educators talking points to problems teens face.
Source: Twitter, Inc.

crisis issues in youth. It covers basic suicide facts, warning signs, risk, and protective factors. It also offers talking points on conversations with students about suicidal thoughts and behaviors and ways to connect those struggling with resources. The information is presented through lecture, PowerPoint, discussions, role play, behavioral modeling, video, and case studies. This training is relevant for elementary, middle, and high school teachers, administrators, and support staff.

ASIST, Applied Suicide Intervention Skills Training by LivingWorks (Living-Works.net) is a gold standard two-day, in-person training for those who want more role play and practice. Anyone can take ASIST but it's more geared to social workers and school counseling staff. This is usually taught through community-based organizations and is often low cost and even free through state agencies, mental health nonprofits, and the American Foundation of Suicide Prevention, funded by their annual walks and fundraising efforts. ASIST relies more on role play and feedback than other programs and is always taught by two trainers. See LivingWorks.net for trainings listed in your area.

Trevor Project CARE (Connect, Accept, Respond, Empower) by The Trevor Project (TheTrevorProject.org) is an interactive and intensive training that provides adults with an overview of suicide among lesbian, gay, bisexual, transgender, queer and questioning (LGBTQ) youth and the different environmental stressors that contribute to their heightened risk for suicide.[13] The Trevor Project's CARE Training can be combined with the Trevor Ally

Training for audiences who may need additional training in cultural competency in working with LGBTQ young people. The Trevor Project's CARE Training has several modules to provide specific support and tools for adults who work with youth, including K–12 school staff and educators, higher education staff and faculty, and health professionals.

The Trevor Ally Program by the Trevor Project (TheTrevorProject.org) helps adults learn about lesbian, gay, bisexual, transgender, and queer and questioning youth, and the specific risks and challenges they face.[14] This training is designed to create dialogue regarding what it means to be an adult ally for LGBTQ youth by educating about vocabulary used in the LGBTQ community, the process of "coming out," and a discussion of the challenges faced by LGBT youth in their homes, schools, and communities.

Resources for Evidence-Based Curriculums

To find evidence-based universal school-based suicide prevention programs, go to SPRC.org and choose Resources & Programs from the menu, then filter by:

- **Resource and Program Type** > Choose: Programs with evidence of effectiveness
- **Populations** > Choose: Adolescents
- **Settings** > Choose either Middle School or High School

Hit Apply. From there you can add more filters but this will give you an overall view of the available programs that are age-appropriate programs with evidence of effectiveness.

UNIVERSAL SCHOOL-BASED SUICIDE PREVENTION PROGRAMS

One of the best practices and recommendations for all schools who want to address mental health and provide mental health supports is to partner with local community-based organizations, which can be government and county agencies or local nonprofits. For rural areas in particular, those community-based resources can help implement a suicide prevention or mental wellness program within the school. Having partnerships with mental health providers onsite at the school is another way to reduce potential suicide threats. When considering universal school-based suicide prevention programs that include gatekeeper training, look for those that have evidence to support their effectiveness, also known as a "program with evidence of effectiveness." Better yet are programs that are "evidence-based," which means the program has been tested for effectiveness in a randomized controlled trial.[15] Having data on program effectiveness can be used as leverage with leadership, parents, and community partners when considering its adoption.

SOS Signs of Suicide

SOS Signs of Suicide from MindWise Innovations (SOSSignsofSuicide.org) is an evidence-based program for middle and high schools that has been around since 2001, with a track record of having educated hundreds of thousands of students and faculty. The program has gone through three randomized control trials showing a 64% reduction of self-reported suicide attempts, and with the help of the National Suicide Prevention Lifeline, this program was adapted for virtual learning as well as traditional in-person learning. The main message of the program is ACT=Acknowledge, Care, Tell (Figure 5.2): Acknowledge that you're seeing signs of suicide in yourself or a friend, Care by letting your friend know that you worried about them, and Tell, which means to tell a trusted adult in the person's life what's going on. This is a universal approach to educate the whole school community and reframe help-seeking behavior as a being a courageous step and not one of weakness.

Figure 5.2 Signs of Suicide wallet card to remind students of the ACT Steps. © from SOS Signs of Suicide.

"Our resources include student program training in addition to faculty/staff training and parent training. We provide materials so that the whole school community is prepared to watch for warning signs and respond accordingly. Students watch a 20-minute video and then engage in discussion with the class. Next, they take a depression screening, which is called the 'Brief Screen for Adolescent Depression'; this nondiagnostic screening form is used for educational purposes and to encourage help-seeking behavior. We want to empower students with their own health information so that they're prompted to go to their school's mental health professional or talk to a trusted adult. The last piece of the student training is a student response slip that says, 'Based on the video and or screening, I feel like I need to talk to someone,' or 'I do not need to talk to someone,' and then schools will determine whether follow-up is needed. We have schools that have been using the program since 2001, schools that have just started using it, and we have schools in very rural communities who have limited mental health resources. And we have school districts that have a lot of mental health resources. Schools have noticed over the time that they've used SOS that it really shifts the culture within the school [and] students are more comfortable talking about mental health."

Lea Karnath (She/Her/Hers), SOS Signs of Suicide Senior Program Manager, MindWise Innovations

Across the country, there is a lack of counselors and school mental health staff. So if a school district has one counselor they share with the entire district across thousands of students, then implementing a program with hundreds of students in one week is unrealistic. However, Lea encourages them to roll it out as a pilot program, first with a classroom of 20–25 students. This pilot helps establish the follow-up rate of how many students will speak up and tell a trusted adult, which students to keep an eye on, and which ones require mental health services. Once a pilot is completed, the school can use this information as a framework for how many students are likely to seek services right away and then continue to educate that student body over the course of the semester that year.

The idea of all these programs is to empower teachers to look out for warning signs and be able to provide information to the school mental health professional. For students, their trusted adults tend to be teachers, not necessarily counselors, because teachers are the people with whom students interact daily.

In 2019, SOS also launched a scholarship program that schools have already utilized, and they encourage schools who are concerned about funding to apply to that and then SOS Signs of Suicide will connect schools with funding opportunities. This program can be taught by teachers, counselors, school nurses, and community resources.

SOS Signs of Suicide Second ACT

SOS Signs of Suicide Second ACT (mindwise.org), an all-digital program designed as a booster to SOS Signs of Suicide for high schools, includes a short video for older students, a depression screening tool, and student response slips. The program is for upperclassmen, preparing and empowering students to take care of their own mental health as they transition from high school to the workforce or college. SOS Second ACT is consistent with the messaging of other SOS Signs of Suicide programs.

Sources of Strength

Sources of Strength (SourcesOfStrength.org) is a popular evidence-based program for middle and high schools designed to build protective factors and reduce the likelihood that vulnerable youth will become suicidal. Although each can work as a stand-alone program, some schools have integrated both Signs of Suicide and Sources of Strength into their school because they complement each other. The Sources of Strength program is different in that it trains students as peer leaders and connects them with adult advisors at school and in the community. We know that students often tell their friends most often and those friends are at a loss about what to do. Advisors support peer leaders by conducting well-defined messaging activities with the goal of altering peer group norms by bolstering coping practices and minimizing problem behaviors such as self-harm, substance misuse, and promiscuity.

"When we were creating of Sources of Strength, we were trying to meet several of the gaps we saw in the prevention space at the time. We wanted to move upstream. A lot of what was out there was very reactionary, crisis driven, and risk based—focusing primarily on talking about risk factors [and] warning signs. But when we went in and talked to teenagers about risk factors and warning signs for suicide, pretty much everywhere we went, they could just fire those off.

But when we asked them [students], 'How does somebody who is feeling suicidal get better? How does somebody who is addicted to drugs or alcohol recover? How does somebody who has been abused or harassed or raped? How do they get through that?' It was crickets. We started to realize that there's a lot of dialogue happening about risk, but there's not a lot of dialogue on talking about what strength looks like. What does resiliency look like? What does recovery look like? And how do we get through the ups and downs and twists and turns and storms that life throws our way in ways that are healing and healthy?

Another gap was that a lot of public health messaging and prevention messaging and certainly in the suicide prevention space had been kind of stuck in this paradigm of sad, shock, trauma—a lot of sad images, a lot of shocking statistics, a lot of traumatic stories. We saw that this could be contributing to a false normalization effect, making suicide seem even more common than it really was. The truth is that the vast majority of people who struggle with feeling suicidal do not go on to die by suicide. Recovery and resiliency and connection are the true norm, but that's not what we communicate when we just throw out these shocking statistics, or images, or stories. We really wanted to tell those stories of strength, connection, recovery, and resiliency and help normalize those pathways towards knowing we can get through it, and we can get better. Because what we've seen is that some of our students that were struggling, most would see those sad, shock, trauma messages and say, 'Yeah that's me,' and it would reinforce a sense of inevitability and hopelessness. We want to highlight how people get through this, so they can say, 'Yeah, that could be me,' and find hope and a pathway to help.

The last gap I would say sort of differentiates us is that if we're going to move the needle in a school, we have got to have students involved—that their voice is going to be critical to moving and shifting that culture."

Scott LoMurray (He/Him/His), Executive Director, Sources of Strength Program

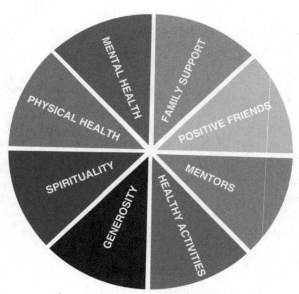

Figure 5.3 Sources of Strength®.

Depending on the size of the high school, 10–50 students are recruited through staff and student nominations. They form a team of peer leaders, mentored by 2–5 adult advisors. Certified Sources of Strength trainers then provide peer leaders with interactive training, which the adult advisors also attend. Adult advisors facilitate peer leader meetings over 3–4 months to plan, design, and practice tailored messaging activities that include individual and media messaging, and classroom presentations, which also reflects local cultural adaptations. The peer leaders develop messages to be delivered via video, the Internet on social media or website platforms, or through text messaging.[16]

The program is often a 3- to 6-month project, but it is designed as a multi-year effort with ongoing peer messaging and contacts growing over time. The idea is to bake this into the school culture and normalize the conversation. But what about religious schools where tenets of a suicide prevention program are oppositional to the religious doctrine?

"So I started getting involved in student suicide prevention, which then led me to partner with this organization, Sources of Strength. They started coming to Kansas City and have done a great job in certain school districts and communities, a really good job. So we've seen now that in those places, the suicide hasn't gone away but it's definitely been yielded to a certain extent. We have a large private school here, a wonderful school. The graduating class this year [2019] had five kids die by suicide. So I knew many of the administrators and I knew many of the teachers, I knew many of the coaches. And they said, 'OK, help us. Is there anything we can do?' So I said, 'Let me introduce you to the Sources of Strength people.' And they liked it. But said, 'You know, there's concepts in here that may be very applicable in a public school. But we have a hard time within a Catholic school.' So we created a Catholic model with Source's permission. And so now we're introducing that. We've done three large Catholic high schools and they're asking us down to consider going into the grade schools, the middle schools, along with the public school model, which to me, having clergy actually call us and say, 'We want to talk to you,' was a huge step."

Sean Reilly (He/Him/His) retired teacher, Kansas
Attorney General Suicide Coalition Task Force, The One Heart Project

---

If your school does have religious teachings or cultural issues that compete with some of the curriculum or needs adaptation, do not hesitate to call one of the programs mentioned in this book and see what kind of accommodations can be made. Sean Reilly is also part of an advisory board for the state attorney general's office in Kansas and in discussing reaching more kids, especially those in rural areas, it was suggested at one point that one way to do this would be to bring together all six thousand kids in an arena at once. It's not recommended to bring this many kids together to talk about suicide where it would be impossible to oversee and triage students who need help. Sean knew that the program needed to be broken down by community, so he encouraged the rural schools to utilize the help of the staff at community mental health centers to deliver the program through the schools and be supervised the way it was intended.

The Sources of Strength peer model works well with middle and high school students. However, in thinking about programs even farther upstream for younger students, Sources focused on translating the protective factors into a SEL-type curriculum for elementary age kids with some of the prevention and mental health components that are often traditionally lacking in in other SEL models. This strengthens the foundation of prevention early in a child's development.

Lifelines: Prevention

Lifelines: Prevention, an evidence-based student curriculum by Hazelden Publishing (hazelden.org), is one of three components of a comprehensive, school-wide suicide prevention program for middle and high schools called *Lifelines: A Comprehensive Suicide Awareness and Responsiveness Program for Teens*. This universal school program's three components are Lifelines: Prevention, Lifelines: Intervention, and Lifelines: Postvention. This series of programs is the only model of its kind available for adolescents. The overall goal of the Lifelines Prevention program is to promote a caring, competent school community in which help-seeking is encouraged and modeled, and suicidal behavior is recognized as an issue that cannot be kept secret. Lifelines Prevention educates middle and high school faculty, parents, and students on the facts about suicide and their roles in suicide prevention. It empowers students to know how to listen, what to say, and ultimately to help connect at-risk peers to the right personnel through role-playing while demonstrating the importance of self-help in the event they are struggling with thoughts of suicide. It includes training of school faculty and staff to prepare them for their role in identifying and responding to suicidal students, training and teaching students regarding their role in suicide prevention, and providing a workshop and informational materials to educate parents. Like many programs, Lifelines will conduct an audit to ensure that the district has procedures, training, and supports in place prior to delivering the curriculum to students.

Hope Squad

Another program for consideration is **Hope Squad** (hopesquad.com), an evidence-informed peer-to-peer suicide prevention program that started in Utah and is now in several states. It was founded by a principal, Dr. Gregory A. Hudnall, who was motivated to create it following the loss of a student at his school. The peer-to-peer curriculum was developed in partnership with a local mental health agency, University of Utah, and Brigham Young University. Hope Squad members are trained to identify suicide warning signs in their peers and refer them to a trusted adult. After the first successful year, Dr. Hudnall implemented Hope Squads in every school in the Provo City School District: three high schools, three middle schools, and thirteen elementary schools—forever changing the district's approach to suicide prevention. For nine years after this program was implemented, suicides in the Provo City School District dropped to zero.

JED High School

Based on the success of their widely praised signature program called JED Campus for universities, The JED Foundation has created the Comprehensive Approach to Mental Health Promotion and Suicide Prevention for High Schools (JEDFoundation.org/jed-high-school). This program, introduced in 2021 and in response to results from a 2019 research survey with partner Fluent Research, aligns well with the widely accepted Multi-Tiered Systems of Support (MTSS) framework for implementation of supports and interventions in schools. Like the MTSS framework, this approach recognizes that no single intervention will be effective for all students, that systems change in the boundaried high school community can and should be aimed at supporting all students effectively, and that the promise of a multitiered prevention/intervention system is intended to "catch" students with different levels of need and connect them to needed treatment.

With this technical assistance model, JED High School team members work with schools to create an environment where students feel like they belong in the school community; feel connected with their peers, teachers, coaches, and staff across the school; learn key life skills to manage their daily tasks and activities, academic requirements, relationships, life transitions, and physical and mental health; learn skills that will help them communicate, manage emotions, and deal with stress; and feel comfortable asking for help.

Each school creates a team of school staff, parents, students, and community members to work on the initiative with support from school leadership. The team completes JED's assessment measuring school policies, programs, and systems that promote student mental health. Students complete an online student survey developed in partnership with Healthy Minds Study (HMS2). The survey reveals information about student attitudes, awareness, and behaviors related to mental health. JED puts together the information from the assessment and survey, shares with the school, and works with the team at the school to create and carry out a plan over 18–24 months. (Research Report 2021: Understanding and Addressing the Mental Health of High School Students).

CAST, Coping and Support Training

CAST, Coping and Support Training, (ReconnectingYouth.com), by Reconnecting Youth is an evidence-based program that aligns with the National Health Education Standards of CDC's School Health Education Resources. It is a school-based small group counseling program for at-risk youth, although CAST can be offered to an entire population as universal prevention; to a high-risk group, which is called selective prevention; or to specific at-risk students, known as indicated prevention. It has twelve 55-minute sessions facilitated by an adult who works well with at-risk youth and trained to implement the program. The twelve CAST sessions are offered twice a week for middle or high school students as a pull-out or referred program that can be inside or outside the school setting. When facilitated outside the school, it's usually run by community-based youth-oriented agencies, by mental health professionals, and in community centers. Goals include decreasing substance misuse, decreasing emotional distress, and increasing school performance. It can be delivered by trained CAST teachers, counselors, social workers, or others with similar experience.

American Indian Life Skills (AILS)

AILS (SPRC.org) is a universal, school-based, evidence-based, culturally grounded, life-skills training program focused on reducing the high rates of urban, rural, or tribal American Indians/Alaska Natives (AI/AN) adolescent suicidal behaviors.[17] The curriculum is designed to reduce suicide risk of AI/AN youth by improving protective factors, and the course teaches life skills in communication, problem solving, depression, stress management, anger regulation, and goal setting. Aimed at American Indian adolescents 13–19 years old, the curriculum includes anywhere from 28 to 56 lesson plans covering topics such as building self-esteem, identifying emotions and stress, increasing communication and problem-solving skills, recognizing and eliminating self-destructive behavior, learning about suicide, and role-playing, as well as setting personal and community goals. The curriculum is typically delivered over 30 weeks during the school year, with students participating in lessons three times per week.

PREPaRE Crisis Training

PREPaRE (NASPonline.org) School Crisis Prevention and Intervention Training Curriculum[18] is a two-day training by the National Association of School Psychologists with both in-person and online curriculums, consisting of two complementary workshops. The first is designed to help schools create systems to meet safety and crisis prevention and preparedness needs of the school community and their families. The next workshop on day two focuses on mental health crisis intervention and recovery. The curriculum builds on existing personnel, resources, and programs; links to ongoing school safety efforts; facilitates sustainability; addresses a range of crises (including suicide); and can be adapted to each school's size and needs.[19] While PREPaRE is not itself a suicide prevention program, it does provide the type of training, foundation, and structure that all schools should have prior to the implementation of a suicide prevention program and also provides a structure for schools to use following a student suicide to provide support to staff and students. This can help prevent suicide contagion, which can occur following a student suicide.

The PREPaRE model emphasizes that members of a school crisis response teams must be involved in the following hierarchical and sequential set of activities:

P—Prevent and prepare for crises

R—Reaffirm physical health and welfare, and perceptions of safety and security

E—Evaluate psychological trauma risk

P—Provide interventions

a—and

R—Respond to mental health needs

E—Examine the effectiveness of crisis preparedness

MENTAL HEALTH TRAINING PROGRAMS

These mental health training programs will help educators spot students who might be at risk, although not all who live with a mental illness are suicidal, and not all who live with suicidal thoughts have a mental illness. We simply know that mental illness is prevalent in most suicides and can make people more vulnerable. Trauma trainings and social emotional trainings are all additional tools that will help you recognize students who may be at risk, how to communicate, and what to do.

Youth Mental Health First Aid (YMHFA)

Youth Mental Health First Aid (MentalHealthFirstAid.org) from the National Council for Behavioral Health is an 8-hour training on the National Registry of Evidence-Based Programs designed for adults who interact with young people including parents, teachers, school staff, and peers, on how to help an adolescent (age 12–18) who is experiencing a challenge or a mental health, substance misuse, or addiction crisis. The course introduces common youth mental health issues and teaches a 5-step action plan on how to help young people in both crisis and noncrisis situations. Themes include anxiety, depression, substance misuse, disorders that have a component of psychosis, eating disorders (e.g. anorexia and bulimia), and disruptive behavior disorders.

Teen Mental Health First Aid (TMHFA)

Teen Mental Health First Aid (MentalHealthFirstAid.org) from the National Council for Behavioral Health and Born This Way Foundation is an in-person training for high school students on how to identify, understand, and respond to signs of mental illnesses, substance misuse, and substance use disorders with their friends and peers. This is training that offers students the tools to have supportive conversations and refer friends to a trusted adult. It empowers young people with the knowledge and skills they need to foster their own wellness and to support one another.

More Than Sad

More Than Sad (AFSP.org) teaches parents, teachers, and youth leaders how to recognize signs of depression and other mental health problems, initiate a conversation about mental health, and get help from the American Founda-tion of Suicide Prevention and can be found by searching "more than sad afsp." Included in the free download are facilitator tools, the Model School Policy, and the *After a Suicide Toolkit*. The educator's version and parent's presenta-tion (English and Spanish) both have a PowerPoint presentation for those audiences. It's about 45 minutes to an hour long in person or virtual. A teacher, parent advocate, or school counselor can present the program to educators or parents and the recommended versions are:

- More Than Sad: Suicide Prevention Education for Educators
- More Than Sad: Suicide Prevention Education for Parents: Available in English and Spanish

There are few evidence-informed presentations that are free. And if you are in a school that isn't getting much leadership support, has to wait for grant money, or needs to get some education in front of teachers or parents right away, More Than Sad is a great mental health education primer that can be pre-sented online or in person. The quiz for adults and teens plus the depression guide in the facilitator downloads serve as good tools to facilitate a classroom discussion for depression and signs of suicide in a health class.

"Community members who want 'More Than Sad' can get in touch with their local AFSP chapter to present it, or someone in the school can as well. The parent ver-sion is good. I get good feedback from parents when I present that module."
Shirley Ramsey, Retired Elementary School Counselor, Substitute Teacher, Founder of AFSP Virginia Chapter, AFSP Virginia Chapter Chair: Loss and Healing

---

PROGRAMS THAT BOLSTER PROTECTIVE FACTORS FOR STUDENTS

This section focuses on programs that integrate universal coping strategies into a school curriculum before any problems arise with the understanding that kids have fewer opportunities in the digital age to learn those skills. These are examples of two specific programs that focus on two different aspects: one that emphasizes social and emotional learning (SEL), and another that is an experiential program that exposes students to new ideology by helping them understand their passion and see a future for themselves.

CASEL

The Collaborative for Academic, Social, and Emotional Learning (CASEL.org) is a trusted source for knowledge about high-quality, evidence-based social and emotional learning (SEL). It provides a systematic framework for identifying and evaluating the quality of SEL programs, especially those with potential for broad dissemination to schools across the United States. The CASEL guide also shares best-practice guidelines for school teams on how to select and implement SEL programs and recommends future priorities. CASEL's guide can be found for free on their website (CASEL.org/guide/).

DBT STEPS-A

DBT in Schools: Skills Training for Emotional Problem Solving for Adolescents STEPS-A (MazzaConsulting.com) is a universal SEL curriculum designed for middle and high school students in educational settings. This program was first introduced as a teaching curriculum in 1993 and developed by Dr. James Mazza, Dr. Elizabeth Dexter-Mazza, and colleagues.

DBT STEPS-A is designed to complement academic learning and sets a foundation for suicide prevention by offering kids ways in which they can work through adversity and manage a stressful situation before it reaches crisis levels. When Professor James Mazza saw his incoming college students arrive with few emotional regulation skills, and knowing that suicide is also the number two cause of death on college campuses, he decided to teach the skills course to college students, too. And each year at the University of Washington over a thousand kids go through his course in an academic year.

Several different DBT exercises are taught before each of the skills training classes, which include Orientation and Goal Setting, Dialectical Thinking, Core Mindfulness Skills, Distress Tolerance Skills, Emotion Regulation Skills, and Interpersonal Effectiveness Skills. Middle schools, high schools, and even colleges focus a lot on the academic child and infrequently on the emotional child, and DBT STEPS-A is an approach to teach the whole child.

Teachers have learned the curriculum from the book *DBT Skills in Schools: Skills Training for Emotional Problem Solving for Adolescents (DBT STEPS-A)*, by watching *DBT in Schools* online videos, and from in-person or virtual trainings.[20] The DBT STEPS-A curriculum includes 30 lesson plans that are designed to fit within a general education curriculum. Each lesson is 50 minutes long and adapted from the skills training program in Dialectical Behavior Therapy (DBT) developed by Dr. Marsha Linehan, a professor at the University of Washington.[21] The idea is to teach kids important life skills way upstream, before they are in crisis, because once they get in that fast-moving current it's hard to pull them out. Teachers who are using the program report that kids are using these skills in the hallways or during discussions and as a result the number of fights and disciplinary measures have decreased and with that comes a feeling of personal pride and success, which builds self-esteem.

"Schools have to work with these kids regardless. These kids [with disciplinary problems] are going to demand a lot of attention, take up a lot of resources. And all this is reactionary and these kids struggle, struggle, struggle. They get disciplined, they get expelled. Instead of doing that, why not start to give them skills before this happens? A middle school or high school principal knows there's going to be kids that are going to struggle, so why not give them skills ahead of time? So their struggle is less. And so I think it's just a more proactive approach to empowering kids, rather than reacting to the kids. The kids' mental health when they're being scolded, punished, assigned detention, and suspended, is that they feel like failures. So let's give them skills that they know they can use in their own lives at age 11, 12, 13 and say, 'Okay I can use this skill and this skill and this skill before I get into trouble, before I start self-medicating, before I yell at my parent.'"

James Mazza, PhD (He/Him/His), Professor, University of Washington, Author of DBT Skills in Schools

---

Don't have time to teach all the skills? Teach half of them, or a quarter of them. Because, as Dr. James Mazza says, two skills are better than zero skills as long as they get the foundation step first, which is mindfulness. The idea is not to get rid of all the baggage but to figure out how to manage it. When we think of mindfulness, we default to breathing and meditation, sitting cross-legged and chanting om. But there are mindfulness games that are more active (mindful Jenga) and quiet mindfulness skills (sitting and paying attention to your breath and body) and a blend of the two, which are integrated into the curriculum. Many of these are demonstrated on their DBT in Schools YouTube channel.

Mindfulness is being aware of where you are in this moment and being present and in control of your mind instead of it being in control of you. The opposite of that, mindlessness, is something you do when you are not thinking, like pouring the wrong gas in a lawn mower because you are not concentrating on the activity.

How Mindfulness Contributes to Emotional Wellness

Research confirms that for youth, mindfulness can:

- Mitigate the effects of bullying
- Enhance focus in children with ADHD
- Reduce attention problems
- Improve mental health and well-being
- Improve social skills when taught and practiced with children and adolescents

Source: Ackerman 2020 / PositivePsychology.com.

For DBT STEPS-A, there are two kinds of mindfulness in play: focused mind and open mind. Focused mind is about being here, right now, and putting your attention where you want it to be, recognizing when your mind starts to wander, being aware, and bringing focus back to the moment. Open mind is being aware of the present moment without judgment and without trying to change it—aware of what's around you with mindful awareness of what your body is doing in a particular moment. Part of this is taking a pause between the urge to do the behavior and actually doing the behavior. For example, helping students recognize when they are thinking about pulling a phone out of their pocket to check text messages, recognizing the urge, pausing, and making the mindful choice of leaving it where it is. It's in that pause where one makes a mindful decision and it's an effort to give kids control over their impulses.

The Emerson Model

A lesser known but positive program curriculum called the Emerson Model (OneHeartProject.org) was developed by Sean Reilly, a retired Kansas schoolteacher and a suicide prevention advocate. Typically delivered over an eight-week period to help youth gain valuable personal insight with potential career options, the primary goal is to get adolescents thinking about their passion, future, and potential—one filled with hope and possibilities. This is especially suited for areas where there are few job prospects or for kids who feel they have no future. The Emerson Model is a curriculum he teaches with Jim Clark of the One Heart Project that has four major components (two weeks per topic):

positive peer relationships, trusted and normalized adult relationships, real-world experience, and artistic expression in the form of creating their own branded "Heroes Journey." This has been integrated in schools with special populations—one is Sumner High School in Kansas City, a magnet school of about 98% high-achieving, inner-city African American youth. Sumner is one of the highest-performing schools in the state of Kansas, located in the middle one of the rough-est neighborhoods. The students who piloted the program were hesitant at first because they'd never done anything like it but became very engaged in the project.

The other school where the program was run is a last-resort youth ranch for foster kids who have run away or cannot live with their foster family. There are 20 teenage boys at this youth ranch from all over the state of Kansas at any given time.

"Emerson is not a competitor at all to programs like Sources or Strength. It's a different approach. And a child might be suicidal. A child may be filled with anxiety, or a child may not have any of those things. I would say with these kids, it was so amazing to watch them go through Emerson. We know those kids are going to hook into that journey because they are seeing people care. We have a saying: 'Kids don't care what you know until they know that you care.' It was like a catharsis for them. You know, we've talked to more schools and want to bring it into targeted schools and grow with it. So I don't know of anyone else in the country who's doing a program like that. There may be, but this was something we designed. Actually my colleague Jim Clark was the inspiration and driving force of the design. But then especially at the youth ranch, the young guys would work on it during the week with the counselors there. And I think the schools are now beginning to change their paradigm and saying, 'You know, we are pretty good at teaching physics and we have a great language department but this idea of mental health and how to develop strength, resiliency is not our forte.'"

Sean Reilly (He/Him/His), Retired Teacher, Kansas Attorney General Suicide Coalition Task Force, The One Heart Project

---

CUSTOMIZING/ADAPTING SUICIDE PREVENTION PROGRAMS

Many times, schools want to "customize" suicide prevention programs and screenings and if you are considering such steps, make a list and consult the team that supports it. The big three universal school programs that have been implemented for many years—Signs of Suicide, Sources of Strength, and

Lifelines—have support staff that is motivated to have a conversation about how to adapt because all advocates want to do what it takes to remove barriers to integrating this education into schools. Given that most prevention programs are carefully constructed to meet specific guidelines that prevent suicide and the amount of scientific data supporting how they are disseminated, freelancing your own adaptations and changes can be tricky, problematic, and have unintended results.

Jonathan Singer, author of the book *Suicide in Schools: A Practitioner's Guide to Multi-level Prevention, Assessment, Intervention, and Postvention,* cites a very specific example of customizing that was likely a barrier to suicide prevention. He was working with a school district that was doing a good job of it and they had a real commitment from leadership and even a community advisory board made up of parents, students, a resource officer, and representatives from local mental health agencies and nonprofits.

The school asked if they could offer one of the tools from his book, a suicide risk monitoring tool, and post it online through Google forms instead of distributing it on paper. Having a more accessible form for mobile devices or even virtual learning environments is important for engaging students, so he gave permission. One of the questions on this tool asks, "How hopeless are you?" and offers a 1–5 rating scale by which the student can grade their state of mind. The higher the number, the more hopeless the student feels. And as that number increases, the risk of suicide does, too.

When he returned the following year to train the educators, he pulled up their version of the suicide risk monitoring tool, which they had renamed the Progress Monitoring Form. With good intentions and to make it more consistent with their strengths-based wellness focus, they had changed the question "How hopeless are you?" to "How hopeful are you?" They had kept the 1–5 rating. So if a student had listed a 4 on "How hopeful are you?" it indicated that that student was in a high-risk category, although given how the question had been reworded, the opposite was true. The result was that it was no longer a usable tool for monitoring suicide risk and inadvertently earmarked students who were not at risk. You might think this would be a simple change to make it right. But given that the whole form had gone through the school district's legal department and gotten their stamp of approval, they couldn't just open and edit the form. To do so would mean going back and resubmitting the form and repeating the whole approval process.

For reasons like these, it's vital to consult with the company or consultant who has developed the program. And bring in the legal department early in the process so they are in it every step of the way.

SCREENING FOR SUICIDE RISK

Some of the universal suicide prevention programs have self-assessment screenings to empower students to take charge of their own mental health. But when it comes to assessing or screening students for suicide risk, not all schools have the personnel qualified to do them and some experts advocate that these should happen at a therapist's or doctor's office where there are specific established healthcare pathways. However, many schools do have the resources, staff, and protocols in place for suicide risk and assessment screenings. No matter where your school district stands on the issue, teachers, counselors, school nurses, coaches, and activity directors should encourage primary care doctors who do their school and sports physicals to incorporate a suicide risk screening such as the twenty-second Ask Suicide-Screening Questions (ASQ), a 5-question brief suicide risk screening tool developed by the National Institute for Mental Health (NIMH) for ages 10+, in addition to any anxiety and depression screenings. Anxiety, depression, and general mental health screenings will not catch all students at risk for suicide.[22] The direct, suicide-specific questions in the Ask Suicide-Screening Questions are critical in accurately determining risk and take 20 seconds to implement.[23] The more doctors hear this from school personnel, the more likely they are to include mental health and suicide-specific screenings for the overall health and wellness of the whole child in their protocol, because physical fitness is influenced by mental fitness. Our culture may separate physical and mental health. But to our brains, the two are mixed together like cake batter and if something is off with either, both the mind and the body are affected.

Since so many are curious about the questions that are included in the Ask Screening Tool (ASQ), we've included those here:

Ask Suicide Screening Questions: Suicide Risk Screening Tool[24]

- In the past few weeks, have you wished you were dead? Yes / No
- In the past few weeks, have you felt that you or your family would be better off if you were dead? Yes / No
- In the past week, have you been having thoughts about killing yourself? Yes / No
- Have you ever tried to kill yourself? Yes / No
- If yes, how?
  When?

If the patient answers Yes to any of the above, ask the following acuity question:

- Are you having thoughts of killing yourself right now? Yes / No

If yes, please describe:

Quick, Validated/Evidence-Based Suicide Screeners

- Ask Suicide-Screening Questions (ASQ) NIMH, 4 questions
- Columbia-Suicide Severity Rating Scale (C-SSRS), Screening version for schools, 6 questions

Source: Suicide Prevention Resources to Support Joint Commission Accredited Organizations (pdf).

Jessica Chock-Goldman, LCSW, is adept and comfortable doing interventions and suicide risk assessments on her students. She has the expertise and is in sync with the nuances of her population, although she validates her decisions by calling off-campus colleagues, checking in with teachers and co-workers to double-check, and has established pathways for student mental health triage that include internal and external collaboration. However, many schools don't have this expertise on site. All of this points to having a discussion with your student care team on the protocol that suits your school best, but in every case the care team should have relationships with outside community resources, including inpatient hospitals and providers, and advocate for mental health and suicide-specific screenings and assessments.

Example Protocol

Example of the basic steps that describe the protocol that one counseling department uses for a student who is struggling with a behavioral health issue:

1. If the referral comes to us through an advisor or teacher, a school counselor will encourage the advisor or teacher to talk with the student and make a connection with someone in the counseling team so the student feels some agency and does not get surprised that someone on our team is reaching out. We will then follow up with the person who made the referral to let them know we are working to take care of the student.

---

2. When someone on our counseling team finds out about a pressing mental health issue, we tell the student that we need to involve parents/guardians and give them the option to talk to the parents first if it's urgent. Otherwise, we give them the option of being present when one of us makes the call.

3. Then, the assigned counselor will generally make a referral either to the ER or to an emergency services team in their town that can do an in-home (or virtual) evaluation to assess for risk and/or make treatment recommendations. Our counseling team always informs the student as to who needs to be "in the know" so that they understand who might learn the broad strokes of the situation. Generally, this would be the division head and class dean since often a medical leave is on the horizon.

4. Then, in terms of communicating about the medical leave, we ask permission from the student and parents/guardians to share with their teachers that they are on medical leave to address a mental health challenge. Or, if they prefer, we will just say medical leave.

5. Our policy is generally to have students return to school as pass/fail for the term so that they don't need to worry so much about making up lost work, but rather focus on being able to learn the essential content so that they are not lost when they return.

6. We will often hook up the student with academic support services to help them get back on their feet in terms of schoolwork, and the school counselor will have regular meetings/check-ins and will also be in communication with outside treatment providers.

Source: Jennifer Hamilton (She/Her/Hers), School Psychologist, Director of Psychology and Counseling at Noble and Greenough, Independent School, Dedham, Massachusetts.

GETTING LEADERSHIP BUY-IN FOR SUICIDE PREVENTION EDUCATION

Leadership frequently makes many excuses for not implementing a suicide prevention program: it will take too many resources, we don't have the time, it's not a priority, we don't have the funding, it's not the right time of year, it's the wrong time of day, the subject is too dark, the parents will object, the moon and stars aren't lined up with Pluto. But having leadership committed to a suicide prevention culture is the key to making the transformation happen.

According to Lea Karnath, SOS Signs of Suicide Senior Program Manager at MindWise Innovations, and Scott LoMurray, Executive Director from Sources of Strength, there are five common barriers to leadership adopting a curriculum of suicide prevention education. These are fear of liability, putting the idea of suicide in student's heads, pushback from teachers uncomfortable with delivering the curriculum, avoidance because it will take too much time and effort to implement, and finally, anxiety that there will be a deluge of struggling students requiring urgent support the first day of the program and a lack of resources to help them.

Knowing how to address each of these specific concerns can help advocates win support. Because the best and most effective school prevention efforts happen when staff and leadership are singing from the same song sheet.

"One of the big facilitators [to suicide prevention] is having leadership on board. When you have the superintendent or the assistant superintendent, the principal, or whomever it is saying, 'This is important and we're gonna do this,' then people get on board. And there are a couple of ways that I've talked to school districts about doing this. One of the ways that seems to be pretty effective is having loss survivors who are parents in the district come and talk and give presentations and making sure that it's the administrators who are in the room. I also think it's always important, like if you've got a larger district, to ensure that the communications person and the legal department are in the room when that conversation happens. Because if you're talking to the superintendent or the principal and they're all on board, they're gonna go into a meeting with legal and legal is going to be like, 'No way, sorry, we're shutting it down.' They haven't been there, they didn't have the same experience, and they don't understand how proactively addressing suicide mitigates risk."

Jonathan B. Singer, PhD, LCSW (He/Him/His), President, American Association of Suicidology, Author of Suicide in Schools: A Practitioner's Guide to Multi-level Prevention, Assessment, Intervention, and Postvention

---

Barriers to School Suicide Prevention Efforts

Five common barriers to leadership adopting suicide prevention education:

- Fear of liability
- Worry that suicide education puts the idea of suicide in student's heads
- Fear of pushback from teachers who are uncomfortable with delivering the curriculum

- Avoidance because it will take too much time and effort to implement
- Anxiety that there will be a deluge of struggling students requiring urgent support the first day of the program and a lack of resources to help them

The first barrier with leadership is that if they incorporate suicide prevention education, it will increase their liability that a family is going to sue the school. The counter argument is that schools are doing their legal duty to take care of students when they do evidence-based suicide prevention training as well as saving young lives and helping others recognize signs in their family and friends in the community. In the case of SOS specifically, a universal school-based prevention program that has been around since 2001, three randomized control trials have illustrated a 64% reduction in student self-reported suicide attempts.[25] Crisis response always uses up more resources and time, and any effort to avoid that is helpful for any school administration.

In Chapter 3, we addressed the myth that talking about suicide puts the idea in people's heads. In fact, talking to students about suicide is one of the most helpful prevention strategies because it lets the student know you care and creates a culture where more students feel less shame and are more apt to come forward. We've kept it tucked in a dark corner for years, cloaked it in silence, and even whispered the word. And still the suicide rates have refused to fall, which tells us that silence has been a sorry solution to reducing this cause of death. The science is telling us that talking about it does. That suicide-specific education piece is a small part of a more holistic approach buoyed by a smorgasbord of other education and life skills efforts, including healthy student/teacher relationships and mentorship.

Those in leadership positions also express concern that teachers are going to push back because they are uncomfortable with the subject, or don't think it's their job.

"Every year when the advisory lesson is sent out [prior to Suicide Prevention month learning curriculum] there's a note included. 'If you're not comfortable leading these discussions or reviewing the information, please contact a social worker and we will have someone cover this advisory for you.' It just so happened that I'm the world languages department chair. We had three teachers new to our building in my department—brand new to the profession. . . . [One teacher] had said, 'I'm concerned about students taking this seriously. I want them to take it seriously. I want to do it right.' So I did reach out to the social worker and they teamed up with him for the lessons. It was nice just to have a second adult in there. He still led it and did it independently, but I think it just made him feel supported [having the social worker in there]. If he got emotional or whatever, he could turn to the other adult."

Leigh Rysko (They/Them/Theirs), Spanish Teacher
and World Languages Department Chair, Kansas Public School

So if you know there are educators who aren't ready or will push back, don't ask them to teach it but leave the option open for when they may feel more comfortable. Instead pair them with other teachers or school counselors to build their confidence, find other teachers willing to teach the module, or have a community mental health resource deliver the information. Even in states where suicide prevention training and school programs are mandated, no one should feel forced. Teachers have to get CEs and there are many suicide prevention and mental health trainings that can fulfill that requirement and go a long way to help alleviate the fears associated with teaching on the subject of suicide. It's also important to set the expectation for your school and for yourself that delivering the content is uncomfortable and there is a level of fear that comes with the subject but that does ease over time and with practice.

"I'll be honest, after Paula* died, when we decided to run the SOS Signs of Suicide program with the whole school, I felt somewhat anxious about ensuring that our faculty felt equipped and comfortable to lead these discussions with over six hundred students. But we brought in clinicians to help train our faculty, and we rolled out the program without a hitch. We made sure to have two adults per group and we set aside a special time for the whole school to participate. The next year, it was so much easier, and even easier the year after that. Now, we integrate SOS annually into the regular academic program for every student in seventh and ninth grade, and some years we also offer the booster for students in other grades. We've experimented with running SOS during health classes, and even during English and history classes. It's always run by teachers with whom the students have a good rapport. Every year it feels more comfortable because we have normalized having discussions about mental health and suicide prevention. And the more normal it feels, the more effective it is. One thing I've learned is the importance of having kids do some behavioral rehearsal around thinking of adults that they'd talk to both in and out of school in case they are ever worried about themselves or a friend. We've also found that it's important to offer to have a counselor reach out to talk if they want to connect after the program."

Jennifer Hamilton (She/Her/Hers), School Psychologist, Director of Psychology and
Counseling at Noble and Greenough, Independent School, Dedham, Massachusetts
*name changed for privacy

Usually, after a school runs a program that includes suicide prevention education, there is an uptick in help-seeking behavior. Kids come forward because they are worried about a friend or wonder if something they've noticed is a sign of depression or suicide risk. It opens up a discussion and not all of these kids need immediate care but simply have questions. The more comfortable we can be talking about mental health challenges, the more likely it is that kids are going to reach out for support in high school, college, and later in life. We need to emphasize that students can come forward if they are wrestling with other emotional issues such as anxiety or cutting and not just crises like suicide.

The fear factor over delivering any suicide prevention program is that it's really time intensive and schools are under the impression that on the first day they start, there will be a deluge of students needing urgent care and not enough resources to support them.

"Data from a partner organization shows fewer than one percent of students who went through the program were identified to be in immediate crisis. Our goal is to reach those students but also to reach the many students who are not yet in crisis but could use support today. Elyssa's Mission, an organization that has delivered SOS to hundreds of thousands of students over the years, found that thirteen percent of students were identified for follow-up through the screening and/or asked to speak to school staff using the program's student response slip. Following a conversation with school-based mental health staff, less than one percent required crisis intervention but half of those students required additional support services in the school or community. We're identifying students who are struggling, so now schools know about them and can do something."

Lea Karnath (She/Her/Hers), SOS Signs of Suicide Senior Program Manager,
MindWise Innovations

What if you are in a school that lacks the staff to deliver the program? Most will tell you that if you make the commitment to do it, there is a way to deliver it. Many schools start with a small pilot program and the SOS Signs of Suicide staff state they never want delivery resource shortages to be a barrier to implementation. Most of these program managers are accustomed to working with schools of all sizes on how to implement with the resources they have and where to find additional help in community agencies. Some programs, such as Lifelines, will do an audit to ensure that the district has procedures, training, and supports in place prior to delivering the curriculum to students.

When it comes to funding, the programs are well versed in helping schools know where to look for financial backing. Schools can look to community partners, education foundations, or community organizations to help braid funding together to support any program implementation.

"We have a grant writing resource and help in that regard. If schools don't have the funding, we can help them explore what funding might be available or if they're writing a grant proposal, we can support them with that proposal. So we help with the administrative side and have some support resources available but I would say it's certainly a minority of our schools that are actually paying for the program out of their own budget. Most are using some level of grant funding or outside support and resources to fund the program."

Scott LoMurray (He/Him/His), Executive Director, Sources of Strength

---

It's never a good idea to wait until you've had a suicide to decide this is important. All teachers should have mental health and suicide prevention training. And by adopting a program that incorporates SEL and mental health/suicide prevention education you are setting the precedent that student wellness is a priority.

Healthy School Culture

Overall, a healthy school suicide prevention culture should include:

- Support of leadership that student mental wellness is a priority
- Collaboration and commitment among staff
- Healthy relationships and mentorship between adults and students
- A sense of connectedness and belonging within the school that creates a safe space
- Integration of healthy coping exercises that include decision-making and goal-setting skills for students into the curriculum or extracurricular activities (with or without a formal program)
- Evidence-based or evidence-informed mental health and suicide prevention education
- Opportunities for students to share personal stories to educate, inspire, and connect as well as promote acceptance and reflection
- Reinforcement of help-seeking behavior
- Communication that life-threatening behaviors can't be kept secret but can be shared discreetly with a trusted adult or coworker

NOTES

1. https://www.pbis.org/pbis/tier-1
2. Marraccini, M. E., and Brier, Z.M.F. (2017). School connectedness and suicidal thoughts and behaviors: A systematic meta-analysis. *School Psychology Quarterly* 32(1): 5–21
3. Matlin, S. L., Molock, S. D., and Tebes, J. K. (2011). Suicidality and depression among African American adolescents: The role of family and peer support and community connectedness. *American Journal of Orthopsychiatry* 81(1):108–117. Horowitz, L., Tipton, M. V., and Pao, M. Primary and secondary prevention of youth suicide. *Pediatrics* 145(S2): S195–S203. https://doi.org/10.1542/peds.2019-2056H
4. https://anxietyintheclassroom.org/
5. Henderson, A. T., and Mapp, K. L. (2002). *A New Wave of Evidence: The Impact of School, Family, and Community Connections on Student Achievement.* National Center for Family and Community Connections with Schools, Southwest Educational Development Laboratory.
6. TheTrevorProject.org, and The Trevor Project's 2020 National Survey on LGBTQ Youth Mental Health.
7. Ibid.
8. Ibid.
9. GenderSpectrum.org, Gender Support Plan. https://genderspectrum.org/
10. Singer, J. B., Erbacher, T. A., and Rosen, P. (2019). School-based suicide prevention: A framework for evidence-based practice. *School Mental Health* 11(1): 54–71.
11. Erbacher, T. A., and Singer, J. B. (2018). Suicide risk monitoring: The missing piece in suicide risk assessment. *Contemporary School Psychology* 22(2): 186–194.
12. Singer, J. B., Erbacher, T. A., and Rosen, P. (2019). School-based suicide prevention: A framework for evidence-based practice. *School Mental Health* 11(1): 54–71.
13. The Trevor Project, https://www.thetrevorproject.org/
14. Ibid.
15. Suicide Prevention Resource Center. https://www.sprc.org/keys-success/evidence-based-prevention#:~:text=Programs%20labeled%20as%20evidence%2Dbased,outcomes%20reviewed%2C%20and%20evidence%20ratings
16. SourcesofStrength.org

17. Suicide Prevention Resource Center. https://www.sprc.org/
18. The third edition is currently in development and is expected to be live by June 2021. https://www.nasponline.org/professional-development/pre-pare-training-curriculum
19. https://www.nasponline.org/
20. www.mazzaconsulting.com
21. Linehan, M. (2014). *DBT: Skills Training Manual*. New York: Guilford Press.
22. Conwell, Y., Duberstein, P. R., Cox, C., et al. (1996). Relationships of age and axis I diagnosis in victims of completed suicide: A psychological autopsy study. *American Journal of Psychiatry* 153:1001-1008.
23. NIMH, Ask Suicide-Screening Questions (ASQ) Toolkit, https://www.nimh.nih.gov/research/research-conducted-at-nimh/asq-toolkit-materials/asq-tool/screening_tool_asq_nimh_toolkit_155867.pdf
24. Ibid.
25. Schilling, E. A., Aseltine, R. H., Jr., and James, A. (2016). The SOS suicide pre-vention program: Further evidence of efficacy and effectiveness. *Prevention Science* 17(2): 157–166. Summaries of all three randomized control trials: https://www.mindwise.org/evidence-behind-sos-program/* *name changed for privacy*

Chapter 6
Suicide Prevention Activities for Schools

"I think most good educators do this already. But the more vulnerable we are in sharing our own humanity—failures and fears—the more kids will open up."
Leigh Rysko (They/Them/Theirs), Spanish Teacher and
World Languages Chair, Kansas Public High School

Activities, clubs, projects, displays, and events focused on skill building, educating, forging connection, conflict resolution, feeling safe, anti-bullying support, emotional regulation, setting expectations, and acceptance all work to help students create a toolbox from which they can manage adverse experiences.

Before engaging in activities for students about mental health, ask students to identify two trusted adults they would talk to or confide in when things get tough—one trusted adult in the school and one trusted adult outside the school. Who would they turn to in a crisis? Who would they talk to or call? How would they cope? They don't have to share this with the class. The next step in this short exercise could be to have them think of how the conversation might go and to picture themselves speaking to this adult about a sensitive matter. When someone thinks about how they'd manage a crisis when in rational thought, it's likely that person will rely on that strategy when there really is one. By having students picture it in their heads, it bakes in a behavior modification that can kick in when they need it the most. Teachers and counselors can take this one step further by creating or having students create scripts and act out scenarios in small groups with problems that students suggest should be on a list. This has the added benefit of promoting connection.

Life happens. There are beautiful moments, tragedies, roadblocks, successes, failures, recoveries, discoveries, and meaningful life events. Happiness is not a holy grail one reaches and maintains forever, because emotions—all of them—are temporary. Everyone is assaulted by life at some point and some meet tragedy that takes them to their knees and challenges all inner resources. The question is how does one feel the feelings, manage the pain, find hope, and eventually move forward again? How do people work through adversity in a healthy way?

"We did a 'What Helps You?' campaign. 'What are your strengths that got you through school closing during COVID-19?' They have the strength. We just have to help them realize. Point out situations where they got through a difficult time or a crisis and say, 'Look you succeeded here. What did you do?' Talk about that when there is no crisis so they identify those coping strategies they have used that were successful. Take pictures and post it on their bulletin boards. We want to celebrate their strengths."

James Biela, LCSW (He/Him/His), Itinerant School Social Worker,
Lower Kuskokwim School District, Bethel, Alaska

While goal setting is a great exercise, it's more important for adolescents to understand how they might handle it when life explodes in their faces—when problems come at them all at once like swarm of angry hornets. Adolescents need to develop the skills to work through those challenges more than they need algebra, although hopefully teachers can do both by incorporating these strategies into their everyday teaching. That's when the real growth happens. So how can you integrate small cultural shifts to help students build their toolbox?

In this section, we focus on the ideas that teachers and school counselors have shared for the purpose of healthy social and emotional development. Ideas that build confidence and skills in handling adversity help to create a foundation for suicide prevention, and have the potential to reduce incidents of self-harm and minimize dropouts and substance misuse. It helps if teachers also practice some of the tenets they teach, by modeling behavior such as taking a deep breath when presented with a stressful situation. And don't think because you have a math class instead of an English class you can't incorporate creative ideas to bolster life skills. You can. Even small strategies can make a difference and you can integrate these ideas into your pedagogy.

SIMPLE IDEAS/CONCEPTS ANYONE CAN INTEGRATE

"Integrating stories, ideas, and concepts into the curriculum makes it easier to have conversations around things that might be distressing to youth. That could be specifically related to suicide risk or could be some of the things that we think of as sort of the distal risk factors. And I know that some schools have integrated that in what they call their social emotional learning curriculum."

Jonathan B. Singer, PhD, LCSW (He/Him/His), President, American Association of Suicidology, author of Suicide in Schools: A Practitioner's Guide to Multi-level Prevention, Assessment, Intervention, and Postvention

A distal risk factor is one that represents an underlying vulnerability for a particular condition or event. It doesn't predict that a student will develop a condition or that an event will definitely happen, but rather identifies that a person may be at risk for the condition at some time in the future. Some examples of distal risk factors include poverty, having endured abuse or trauma as a child, and certain personality and/or genetic traits.

By telling your own personal stories of how you worked through adversity and encouraging students to also share theirs, you are introducing the concept that it's possible to work through emotional storms. Teachers who present a personal story need to consider the emotional maturity of their audience and tailor the message appropriately, including messages of hope, healing, endurance, perseverance, and present examples of help-seeking as a courageous step and weave in the idea of "I wish I would have asked for help sooner," whenever appropriate.

James Mazza, PhD, from the University of Washington and one of the developers of the DBT STEPS-A Program and author of the book *DBT Skills in Schools*, expresses how important it is for students see that educators are mortal beings and have struggles. He says that his students perceive he has it all: past president of the American Association of Suicidology (AAS, Suicidology.org), a successful author, a PhD at a prestigious university. He tells them what they don't know and don't see is the battle it took to get where he is, and he is authentic about some of the relationships he had that didn't work, times he got too upset with his kids, and his failures as a partner to his wife.

"I want them to see that I need these skills too. Just because I have letters after my name and titles, I still have challenges. And so I try and make sure that I point out and talk about my failures. Because of that, they see me as somebody that's real that they can relate to. And I get that as good feedback, usually from the students at the end of the quarter. They feel like that's what makes my class meaningful."

James Mazza, PhD (He/Him/His), Professor, University of Washington,
Author of DBT Skills in Schools

Tammy Ozolins has been a middle school teacher for the past 17 years. She was named "Teacher of the Year" for her school in 2016 and "Secondary Health and Physical Education Teacher" in the county in 2017. As a NAMI (NAMI.org) In Your Own Voice presenter, she has been outspoken on the issue of mental health because she is a suicide attempt survivor and lives with a mental health condition.

"I manage and live with Bipolar II Disorder. Back in high school, I would cry myself to sleep at night, just praying the pain would stop. I kept all of it inside and struggled my senior year in high school and through college. By my mid-twenties, I had attempted suicide to escape the feeling of being alone. So, when our counseling department at school asked if any staff member wanted to make a video about something our students would probably not know about us, I decided to tell them about my struggle with the depression part of my illness. I was not sure middle schoolers would understand the mania part. I told them how I used to spend a lot of time in my room crying and feeling helpless and would wear a mask all day, but then fall apart once I got home. I told them how I finally did open up and tell my parents to get the help I needed.

"In the video I made, I mentioned how it takes just a few words to help me: strength, love, and hope. Then I asked if they had me as a teacher or knew of me, and if I was in a room with a bunch of people, would they have been able to pick me out as the one with depression? Many staff members told me their students just shook their heads 'no' when they watched the film. They had no idea because I am outgoing at school—loud, and very energetic. I then decided that if I can be open about my mental health on video, why can I not do it with my classes and help them open about their own? Opening to my class allowed them to see me as a 'real' person with challenges, not just a teacher. I wanted them to also see that it is an illness that will never go away—that this was something I had to cope with and manage for the rest of my life. But with the right treatment plan, it will be okay and never defines who I am. One of my favorite quotes is 'Sometimes the strongest among us are the ones who smile through silent pain, cry behind closed doors, and fight battles nobody knows about.'"

Tammy Ozolins ("Ms. Oz"), Middle School Health/PE Teacher,
Pocahontas Middle School, Henrico, Virginia

When you present stories that illustrate how you worked through adversity, or live with a chronic illness, it wipes away the associated stigma. Students see hope in the person they witness in front of the classroom every day. Tammy kept her story simple and put it in a context that middle schoolers could understand and relate to: crying, hopelessness, and depression. She then went on to say how she reached out for help and that's when her life started to turn around, but she also emphasized that, as with any health condition, there is daily maintenance, just like someone with diabetes might have to take medication or manage their blood sugar level.

At the beginning of every class, Tammy often does a "meet and greet" exercise to help students get to know each other better. She'll tell them they have to find someone they have not spoken with before and gives them 15–20 seconds or so to share what their favorite movie is or some other fact she highlights that day. Another year she asked the students to create a unique handshake, hand gesture, or other greeting like a thumbs-up that they would use only with that student when they passed each other in the hallway. She's brought in tin foil and told everyone to shape it into something that represented a hobby they liked. One kid made a tin foil guitar and talked about how playing helped him relax when he was feeling anxious. Students know if they are late, they miss this part of class and are motivated to make it on time because they don't want to miss the "meet and greet."

Leigh Lysko, a Spanish teacher at a public school in Kansas, has experienced the loss of a student to suicide. As a result this teacher is more open with students and begins the school year by setting expectations for failure by minimizing the fear associated with making errors or a low test grade. That starts with a lot of icebreakers so students get to know each other better. Leigh emphasizes that in order to get better at Spanish, students have to make mistakes, and that all of them as a group are going to accept that. The rules are that everyone should be gracious towards themselves and others regarding errors because mistakes are not catastrophic failures but learning opportunities that promote progress and build a path to success. Many perfectionists in particular need to hear that because often it's the quiet straight-A student who is struggling on the inside.

No matter what you teach, every class should include resources available to students. Whether you post the counseling department's confidentiality statement (see Chapter 12, Worksheet 6: Sample Confidentiality Policy for Students), have cards with crisis lines, and flyers on community resources like Alateen for those who have a loved one with addiction, what you have lying around your class or posted on your walls could provide a much-needed resource at a time when a student really needs it. In an online environment, you could integrate a virtual background that you create in image editing software with the Suicide Prevention Lifeline, Crisis Textline, Trevor chat, text, and phone line, Trans Lifeline, and any school-related or local call-in resources. You can also drop these in the chat in every online class or arrange a sign on the wall in the background that you print out with those resources. By having these numbers visible at all times, you are communicating an "I care" message, signaling your openness to sensitive topics, normalizing the idea of seeking help, and providing a lifeline for students you don't even know are in need of it. Help-seeking behavior should always be positioned as a sign of strength and not a weakness.

One example would be to print out an 8.5-by-11-inch poster with the crisis text line. Or enlist the help of students to name some problems that students face and provide resources such as the phone numbers or text lines and have them create the artwork to display in a prominent place. (See Figures 6.1 and 6.2.)

In crisis?

Text HELLO to 741-741 and speak anonymously with a crisis Counselor.

CRISIS TEXT LINE | Free, 24/7 support for people in crisis.

Figure 6.1

Suicide Hotline 1-800-273-8255

USA Crisis Text 741-741

USA Crisis line for LGBTQ Youth 1-866-488-7386

US Crisis Text for LGBTQ Youth 678-678

TrevorSpace chat room for LGBTQ youth who want peer support.

Any school or community resources?

Figure 6.2

"Parents divorcing? Feeling overwhelmed by schoolwork? Pregnant? In crisis? There is help. Text HELLO to 741-741 and speak anonymously to a crisis counselor."

To find printable posters, google "crisis text line shareables." To access 8.5-by-11-inch pdf posters, business cards, and images for hallways, classrooms, and websites to let students know about confidential resources, go to **emotionallynaked.com > resources > suicide > scroll to Crisis Text Line Posters and Shareables**.

A simple classroom icebreaker, especially for middle schools, is to have students share one skill they are good at with the whole class. Offer examples and say that this skill could be anything from being good at making sandwiches to having great handwriting, having strong fine motor skills with video games, or coordinating events for a church. "Hi, my name is Latisha and I am good at handstands." This activity encourages kids to start thinking of their good qualities. By listening to others, they also have moments where they think, "I'm good at that, too." They can start to form a picture of the future and understand that they do have skills. Pinning these to a bulletin board or taping to a whiteboard and leaving it in the class allows students to learn more about their classmates and discover common interests.

A favorite student game is one in which you ask students to present two unknown facts about themselves—one that is false and the other true—and have the class try and figure out which one is the real fact. If you have a large class, you can go down the roll and pick 5–10 students on Monday and then continue each day until all of them have had a turn. This allows each child to have a moment to share something interesting, which builds connection and shows that there is always more below the surface that they see. At the same time, it helps students become more accustomed to speaking in public. What's more, they love this activity and they make sure to get to class on time so they don't miss it.

Wendy Turner, MEd, a second-grade teacher in Delaware, shared an idea on the *Cult of Pedagogy Podcast* "(Episode 143: Social-Emotional Learning: Not Just for Kids)" about how students can display current feelings without words by choosing a red, green, or yellow rubber bracelet from the basket near the door of the classroom. Red means someone's not having a great day; yellow is for a so-so day; and green means feeling good. This could also work for middle and high school students, and could be done on a specific day of the week, such as Mondays or Fridays. The value is offering a visible way of expressing how one feels inside—something others wouldn't necessarily know otherwise. But you need to remember to have them deposit the bracelets in the baskets as they walk out the door.

Mindfulness is a foundation for coping skill development because it focuses on breathing and physiological response to stress and creates space for thoughtful action. There are many mindfulness activities, both active and quiet, and they can help you and your students manage stress and anxiety, and you don't have to be a guru to take two to three minutes to do one exercise. There might be resistance at first but eventually your students will look forward to them. Here are a few thoughts:

- **Box Breathing:** Ask your students to start by breathing in for four seconds, then hold their breath for four seconds, and then breathe out for another four seconds. Repeat four times. There is also three-part breath or alternate nostril breath, as well as simple deep breathing, to change things up. These can be found online.

- **Objects in a Bag:** Add various types of objects to a bag, making sure the objects are different in texture and shape. Pass the bag around and take turns asking students to use their sense of touch to guess what each object is, observe, and describe the sensations.

- **Making Sounds:** Go around the room making funny sounds, one person at a time. "Pass" the sound from one person to another. The person "receiving" the sound repeats it and then makes up a new one and passes that sound to the next person. This one promotes paying attention and appeals to your more active students.

- **Mindful Jenga®:** The goal of this game is to present proactive skills practice and relieve stress. It does require some initial work, minor expense, and more time and it's best used in small groups. Each of the 60 Jenga pieces includes mindful and emotionally regulating strategies to encourage healthy methods of managing stress. You print out the skills and tape them onto the Jenga pieces. When the students pull out a block from the stack, the goal is for them to use the skill printed on the block. This can be used in small groups, for students who need a brain break, or it can be used during high-stress times such as midterms or exam week. You can download labels for a small fee from Teachers Pay Teachers.

- **Robot and Rag Doll:** This short exercise allows students to notice when they are tense or relaxed and is especially helpful before a test or quiz or other times when the class might be keyed up and anxious. Ask students to tighten up all muscles like a robot, starting with the legs and moving on to the bottom (this always gets chuckles), trunk, arms, hands, shoulders, and face. Hold for a few seconds and then cue them to relax completely like a rag doll, bending forward and dangling. Point out that shoulders are not relaxed if they are hunched up around the ears and encourage kids to wriggle a little bit to make sure they are loose. You can do this a couple of times and then end with a deep belly breath or two. Chances are any pent-up anxiety will be alleviated.

CREATIVE ACTIVITIES FOR BOLSTERING PROTECTIVE FACTORS

By introducing mindfulness strategies in the classroom, having guests that speak on the topic, and integrating social emotional learning into the curriculum, teachers can help students build their toolbox on managing anxiety episodes throughout their life span. People can learn to trigger their parasympathetic nervous system to immediately reduce their sense of anxiety and stress with a simple strategy of pausing and using breathing exercises.

"High school students have more anxiety symptoms and are 2X as likely to see a mental health professional as teens in the 1980s."
Source: Twenge, J.M. (2015). Time Period and Birth Cohort Differences in Depressive Symptoms in the U.S., 1982–2013. Social Indicators Research 121(2): 437.

This section highlights creative ways to allow students to express themselves and learn more about others by promoting problem solving, connection, and empathy. Not all of these will work with every student population, and ideas can be adapted to suit the culture of your school and the students you teach.

The following creative activities are from Leigh Rysko (They/Them/Theirs), Spanish Teacher and World Languages Department Chair, Kansas Public High School.

Advice Column Activity

"I do a 'Dear Abby' kind of assignment in my class. It's an intermediate Spanish class, so they have enough vocabulary to be able to express a problem. When I first did this, I told the students they could make up a problem. But now I say, 'How many of us are stressed about something in life right now?' and everybody raises their hand. I then tell them to pick a problem they are wrestling with or have wrestled with. I assure them it's going to be anonymous and basically they write out the problem in Spanish, and they list things that they've already tried that haven't worked and in as much detail as possible. I then put codes on them so later I know who to give the advice back to. Then I circulate the papers around the room and other students handwrite their own advice. I'm blessed in world language to be able to do creative activities like that which I think are so important. It combines using their Spanish and working through solutions to a problem that they or someone else is struggling with."

Leigh Rysko (They/Them/Theirs), Spanish Teacher and
World Languages Department Chair, Kansas Public High School

Leigh says the assignments the kids present get better each year because they have more examples on which to build and one or two of the ideas come from the school social worker. Another exercise they do for Spanish class is a social justice movie.

Social Justice Movie

This film project is based on the World Language Film Festival. The student projects can be different genres: horror, comedy, animation, documentary style, and so on. Given that students dedicate so much time to the project, learning the technical side, script writing, acting, collaboration, and editing, it makes sense to create a movie with a message that needs to be heard. So it has to focus on some kind of social justice cause. Leigh says the students have really covered a lot of important and relevant topics and educated on issues about which other students had little awareness, such as age discrimination, poverty, mental health, gender identity issues, racism, the environment, school-to-prison pipeline, and animal abuse.

One of the movies Leigh remembers was about a student who is transgender. In the film, there is a bully who harasses the student and also struggles with mental health issues and ends up confessing his own problems. After the class saw the film, Leigh expressed how amazing it was and the student said it was a story with which he was familiar because he lived it. This film project is a creative conduit through which students can tell their story and learn at the same time. As a result, they are more motivated and enthusiastic to learn the Spanish in order to communicate their message.

So the exercise has multiple facets of learning embedded in the process, including the reward of raising awareness for a cause that most students had never heard about or considered.

Dia de los Muertos

While some Spanish teachers celebrate Cinco de Mayo, Leigh feels this is highlighting a drinking day, which isn't what they want to promote. So instead, they do *Dia de los Muertos,* also known as the Day of the Dead celebration, rooted in Mexican culture. The only day in the US that is roughly similar is Memorial Day, but this one is for the nonmilitary. Day of the Dead is a much more meaningful celebration of life and death and a time to reflect and commemorate people. Skulls are often created with a smile to symbolize laughing at death itself and those take on many forms, such as clay decorations, sugar candy, and face painting. Students are encouraged to commemorate those they've lost and Leigh always includes a picture of her student who died by suicide and shares the memory with the class in a thoughtful way. It destigmatizes talking about death, grief, and those we've lost. While a schoolwide memorial showing pictures of a recently deceased student or having a display in a grandiose way is not always supported by postvention experts, this is an exercise done with a small group, doesn't follow a specific suicide death event, and is a relevant part of a curriculum of learning Spanish.

Hope and Care Video

Teachers at Leigh's school filmed a video for students focused on letting them know the faculty was there to listen. Different students, administrators, the school nurse, and teachers were filmed stepping out from the dark and saying, "I will listen. I care. You matter." Then it was shared with the student body to foster a culture of connection.

The following creative activities are from Sheila McElwee (She/Her/Hers), Chemistry Teacher, Noble and Greenough, Independent School, Dedham, Massachusetts.

> "As much as I love the one-on-one relationship with kids [that being a teacher provides], I love the community feel of the classroom. I like that dynamic and I think you can really help kids a lot when you have the opportunity to observe them in their natural setting with their peers—see what their rhythms are as opposed to having them in isolation come in and report to me as they would a therapist. I think I've enjoyed much more just becoming a skilled observer of young people and trying to home in when I think it's important."
>
> *Sheila McElwee (She/Her/Hers), Chemistry Teacher, Noble and Greenough, Independent School, Dedham, Massachusetts*

Sheila considered being a therapist at one point but chose instead to become a teacher because she loves the community of a classroom. Sheila has been through many devastating student and faculty losses. The suicide of one of her AP chemistry students in 2016 was especially hard because of the small class size and how close the class had become. Even though she is a chemistry teacher, she employs a number of social emotional strategies to allow students to share and open up, including icebreakers and mental health check-ins so students can unload what's on their mind before the lesson begins.

Mental Health Monday

Every Monday at the beginning of class, Sheila has a check-in called Mental Health Monday, which, during the COVID pandemic, became a really important component when it came to getting kids engaged in virtual learning when so many were struggling with the isolation and loneliness of quarantine. This is an activity where kids rate how they feel, with 5 being the best and 0 meaning the worst.

"Kids will say things like, 'Well, I'm a 2 because, you know, we found out this week-end that my grandmother's only got a week and a half to live.' Or I've had a kid say, 'I'm a 2 because nothing's bright right now, nothing's going right.' This activity offers an emotional window into the lives of my students. If somebody says that they're a 1 or a 2, they immediately get a lot of very genuine empathy. And there's quite a bit of problem solving that happens, too. Pretty quickly the kids really want to know why their classmate feels so down. Sometimes they're down because of a really bad grade they got on an assignment and didn't sleep well. What this activity does is create a culture where it's okay to not be okay and to talk about it openly. It has also opened up a line of communication between me and a lot of our students who are a little bit more vulnerable. I'm also very open about the fact I had a brother who lived with a mental illness, and my daughter, who has a diagnos-able disorder. My daughter is extraordinarily successful with a master's degree in autism studies. And she accomplished all this despite having a panic disorder. From anxiety and depression and so on, we talk very openly. As a society, we're not at the point where we feel like there is no shame, but we all have a responsibility to work to that point with this generation of kids."

Sheila McElwee (She/Her/Hers), Chemistry Teacher, Noble and Greenough, Independent School, Dedham, Massachusetts

With Sheila's smaller classes, around 10–15 kids, this activity takes about 10 minutes. Most kids will say they are a 3 or a 4, rarely a 5. What has evolved in her class is that is if someone is a 3, they will explain why they're not a 4. They're very apt to say, they are at a 3 because they are stuck with an English paper, or unhappy about a parent's new curfew, or a failed learner's permit. This is a time when she finds out things about her students that she didn't know, like one of them has two moms. It's a chance for them to learn more about their classmates and ask questions without judgment. She's worked hard to create a safe space and have guidelines around these activities, which is a vital component to having that cohesive relationship.

For her AP students, the struggles revolve around achievement, tests, papers, and grades, while her other classes focus more on successful or failed sports or music performances, and whether or not they got a role in the school play. She shared a story about one young female student who expressed dis-appointment that she didn't have a prom date yet. One of the boys intervened and expressed he had no idea she didn't have a date because he had assumed she had already been asked and admitted he wanted to, and she replied she'd love to go with him to the prom. While this may seem counterintuitive to getting a chemistry lesson plan completed and maybe even too "kumbaya" for some educators, Sheila has found that if she offers students an opportunity to vent and share at the beginning of class, they are more focused on chemistry after. It's not too far-fetched to understand why students would struggle to get engaged if something else is on their minds. And since she does many of these exercises often, students know that it's not a 30-minute therapy session but instead they have the expectation that it will last a few minutes and there will be many opportunities to share on other days. No one is obligated and students who are quieter warm up to the activity at their own pace. To do this in a larger class, there could be a check-in on Monday and then again the next time class meets.

Connect/Disconnect

Connect/Disconnect is an activity Sheila does when there are five minutes left in class. It offers students an opportunity to focus on the nature of their connections and identify moments when they feel included and connected, and other times when they feel excluded and disconnected. Students self-select when they want to share and not everyone shares every time. This activity helps students understand the perceptions they make about themselves and each other. Often, adolescents compare themselves to others and have a skewed sense of the real lives of their peers, especially since social media portrays a wonderland of highlight reels. Students tend to overestimate how much fun someone else is having, see the lives of others as being more idyllic, and are unaware others feel as they do, and this exercise blows apart those misconceptions.

In those instances where a student feels disconnected and excluded, when they express their feelings, classmates dive in to support their peer. To them, it's eye-opening what assumptions others make about themselves and others. Sheila points out an interesting pattern she has noticed over the years and that's when females express a desire to do the Connect/Disconnect activity, they almost always start off with an example of how they felt or feel disconnected. Conversely, when males initiate the game, they almost always have a connection they want to share first. She does this activity regularly enough that students will request it because they have an example they want to share.

Hope Versus Fear

At the very beginning of the year, students write a letter to Sheila about their learning style. She offers the students guidance and asks them to share a challenge when a teacher really helped them over the wall. She wants to hear about a time when they faced that challenge, what they did, their hopes both academically and personally, as well as their fears about the upcoming academic year. They upload this personal letter to her on Google Docs; these are confidential, as is her response to each letter, which includes how she plans to work with them on their fears and goals. When she and the student meet later for their one-on-one, she goes back and looks at this letter and they review the contents to measure whether the student feels progress has been made.

During class time, she'll also utilize Hope Versus Fear as an activity using what's happening in the larger community to spark a current events conversation, whether it's about political unrest, or something more benign like whether the Patriots will win their next football game. They share hopes ranging from doing well on an upcoming test or in a sporting event, to hopes that a dad gets really good news on a cancer biopsy. A lot comes out and it's a window into what the kids are experiencing in the context of what is happening around them and how they are processing that experience. At that point she can ask questions that help that child and the class think about how they'd manage the situation, face the fear, cope with the anxiety, or solve the problem.

The following creative activities are from Tammy Ozolins ("Ms. Oz"), Middle School Health/PE Teacher, Pocahontas Middle School, Henrico, Virginia.

"One year, I did pass out a paper with the outline of a T-shirt and I told them they had to write something positive on their T-shirt to describe themselves because I think, especially in middle school, their self-image is so important to them. It's like, the biggest thing they care about is being liked."

Tammy Ozolins ("Ms. Oz"), Middle School Health/PE Teacher,
Pocahontas Middle School, Henrico, Virginia

Tammy Ozolins, also known to the students as Ms. Oz, is lucky to have the full support of her principal and the school counselors in her efforts to have open conversation on mental health topics. For her students' school projects about mental health, she includes how her struggle strengthened her emotional muscle, built her resilience, and made her the person she is today. Her message to her students is never presented as a therapy session or a hopeless situation. For Tammy's health classes, she began with an anonymous survey to see where her students were in terms of their own mental health. (See Chapter 12, Worksheet 3: Student Wellness Surveys.) Her survey had these basic questions:

Answer Yes or No

1. Have you gotten nervous about taking a test or quiz?
2. Do you get nervous or anxious about meeting new people or being in a new situation?
3. Do you know the difference between being sad versus depressed?
4. Do you know what the word stigma means?
5. Do you know anyone with a mental illness?

After each class responded, she got the data and then read them the anonymous peer results of the survey. It indicated that a large number of students experienced anxiety and most either lived with or knew of someone with mental illness. After seeing the results, she mobilized and got the necessary blessings to be educated and trained on the topic and started out the unit with a discussion about mental health. The dialogue in some of the classes was remarkable. Some students were vocal about their anxiety and others discussed dealing with their depression.

Mental Health Presentations by Students

For the mental health presentations they would create, Tammy provided a list of mental illnesses and disorders from which they would choose, earmarking a few for eighth grade due to maturity, and divided them into small groups to create a presentation on a behavioral health topic. Below is the list of mental health conditions or developmental disabilities from which the students could choose to do their presentation:

- ADHD
- Anxiety
- Autism Spectrum Disorder
- Depression
- Post-Traumatic Stress Disorder
- Obsessive Compulsive Disorder

- Types of Phobias (like claustrophobia)
- Bipolar Disorder (8th grade only)
- Anorexia Nervosa (8th grade only)
- Bulimia (8th grade only)
- Binge Eating (8th grade only)

Student Mental Health Presentation Guidelines

Presentation Steps

1. You may work with 1 or 2 other partners. No groups larger than 3.
2. Choose a mental health topic listed.
3. Research your topic using the 11 guidelines below.
4. Put together a Google slide presentation that includes the information from the guidelines listed below.
5. Make your presentation "Anyone with a link can view" and then submit the link.

Presentation Project Guidelines

(Research will need to be done using credible resources. Do not plagiarize—put it ALL in your own words.)

1. Name of the condition.
2. Description of the condition.
3. Physical symptoms of the illness/effects on the body.
4. Percentage of teens diagnosed with that condition each year.
5. How is it diagnosed?
6. Who can diagnose mental conditions?
7. What treatments are available?
8. From whom and where can the teen get help?
9. Name 3 myths about this condition.
10. Name 3 truths about this condition.
11. What ways can a friend/family member support the person with this condition?

While she was walking around, Tammy could hear students sharing stories about their own challenges, with comments like "I deal with this illness," "This is what I do or how I work with a doctor," and "This is how I feel at times." This project is not only educational but allowed students to share how they had managed and coped with aspects of their own emotional health struggles.

It's one thing to say, "You are not alone." But it's a different thing altogether when students do an experiential activity and arrive at a place where they *feel* they are not alone, where they feel heard and understood. And that should be the goal in our schools and classrooms—to provide the opportunity for students to make that discovery in a safe space and experience connection, belonging, and feeling like they've been heard.

License Plate Project

Many states offer specialized license plates for vehicles that enable people with a common interest to identify or promote themselves or their cause. Specialized plates can be ordered through the department of motor vehicles. The special plates usually cost a little more and proceeds from those plates financially support college scholarships, foundations, charities, or preservation. The project Tammy created for mental health awareness month was for students to design a specialty plate to support the cause of mental health. They could do this for any state, as long as they looked up and followed the motor vehicle department guidelines. Once students finished, the license plate art would be printed by a 3D printer and posted on the walls outside the classroom during May, mental health awareness month (see Figures 6.3 and 6.4).

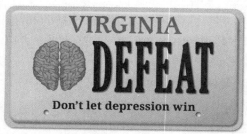

Figure 6.3 Example of one of the license plate designs for the project. Special thanks to Carolyn Tye McGeorge, Art Director, for rendering this student design in high resolution.
Source: Carolyn Tye McGeorge

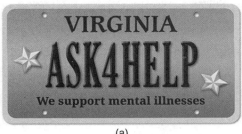

(a)

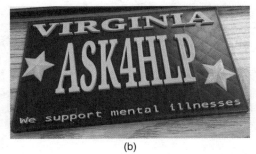

(b)

Figure 6.4 Ms. Oz used the school 3D printer to render real-looking plates for display from the student designs. Special thanks to Carolyn Tye McGeorge, Art Director, for rendering student design in high resolution.

Student Directions for Creating a Specialty License Plate

Many states offer specialized license plates for vehicles. To learn more about specialty plates, visit your state's DMV website. To see some of these plates quickly, go to Google and search for "[State's name] specialty license plates" and click the images for examples of plates and the causes. To bring awareness to mental health and the need to support people who struggle with mental health issues, you are going to design a specialty license plate using Tinkercad.

License Plate Requirements

- Design using Tinkercad.
- Plate must measure no more than 9 inches long by 6 inches wide by .5 inches tall.
- You can only include 2 of these colors: red, orange, yellow, blue, purple, pink, white, black, gray, gold.

- The plate must meet the state license plate requirements.
- The design must represent the mental illness your group chose.
- The design must be submitted as TWO .obj or .stl files—one file per color. To do this, hold shift and click on each piece that is the same color. Then go to Export → .stl or .obj and repeat with the next color.
- Upload both files to the same form submission.

Podcasts

To further embed the concepts they learned by creating their mental health topic presentations, students were also assigned to create a 2- to 3-minute companion podcast. Ms. Oz discussed the format and offered an example so the kids would know what the end product should sound like. The first year she did this, she and another educator made the sample podcast. At the end of the project and once reviewed for content, a few of these podcasts were selected to play on morning announcements and/or be shared on the school website.

Tammy's Mental Health Topic Podcast Guidelines/Requirements for Students

As part of our effort for mental health awareness month, you will create a podcast that teaches your audience about the mental illness your group chose for their presentation.

- You must record on Audacity.
- Podcast should be a question-and-answer session.
- Podcast should have some form of introduction.
- Length should be between 2 and 3 minutes.
- Create a script.
- Podcast must teach the listener about the illness—include symptoms, treatments, how relatives can help (using your Google Slides presentation to guide your script).
- Both partners must speak.
- Export as an .mp3 file.

AFFINITY GROUPS

An affinity group is one that is formed around a shared interest or common goal and bring together people with similar backgrounds, interests, or struggles and can have a powerful influence in the school environment. They were mentioned several times by teachers, counselors, and students as being the primary support resource that helped many students find their way out of darkness. Think of it as a support group sponsored by the school. These differ from mental wellness groups in that they are more specific and usually have a confidentiality agreement. Affinity groups can be formed around any subject but the ones brought to our attention were confidential groups specifically for LGBTQ students, student of color, victims of sexual assault or abuse, groups for students who live with mental illness or a disability, or for those struggling with body image. Many teachers and school counselors have also sponsored parent groups at schools specific to ethnicity, like Jessica Chock-Goldman's Korean Parent Group or a group for parents of children who live with mental illness established at Nobles by Jennifer Hamilton. These should have an adult facilitator, and if you are short-staffed this support can be a community member. Never underestimate the number of parents and community members whose lives have been touched by suicide loss, mental illness, or substance misuse and their passion to be involved in a meaningful way.

STUDENT-LED MENTAL WELLNESS CLUBS

"A student took her life my sophomore year and it was definitely the catalyst for me and Michaela to start a mental wellness group at the school. By the time we graduated, I felt there was a big shift, and mental health is definitely discussed more by students."

Desmond Herzfelder (He/Him/His), Student Mental Wellness Club Founder, Psychology Major at Harvard University, Graduate of Noble and Greenough, Independent School, Dedham, Massachusetts

Over the last few years, students have become more engaged in the topic of mental health because they have, as one student put it, "been to enough funerals." Many students are tired of the silence and of waiting for adults to start talking about the subject because they are suffering and are hearing the struggles of their peers. So they are putting that frustration into action. When students become involved and make it a priority and a passion, it can have a bold trickle-up effect, meaning that the young people start influencing adults, including their parents.

We saw this phenomenon with recycling. While it started in the 1970s, it wasn't until the 1990s that this environmental movement was embraced by school-age students. In areas where recycling education was part of the curriculum, those kids would go home and stop parents from throwing away items that were recyclable, show the family what they learned, and after a while, parents adopted it as a habit because their kids "guilted" them into separating their trash. By 2000, it was the norm in most households, due in large part to so many youth having learned in school how important it was in saving our environment.

Groups of students can be far more persuasive in both a school and a policy setting. It's due to student efforts that many schools have had American Foundation of Suicide Prevention "Out of the Darkness" walks on campus. Having adults in the community support students in this effort can go a long way in helping community leaders warm up to the topic and recognize its importance.

Mental wellness clubs operate under the guidance of student leaders and a sponsor, usually a member of the school counseling team, a teacher advocate, and supported by national or area nonprofit leaders and parents.

Not long after a student in their school died by suicide, Desmond Herzfelder and a fellow student, Michaela, made the commitment to start a mental wellness club, Nobles Heads Together (NHT), for students at Noble and Greenough School in Dedham, Massachusetts. Desmond had remembered his own struggles in middle school and started by sharing them in a school assembly. Inspired by the grief of her cousin's suicide, her own struggles, and a presentation by the local NAMI group (www.NAMI.org) at her school, Aurora Wulff started a mental wellness group at Ithaca High School in upstate New York called Active Minds. And after a number of mental health events and the opiate overdose death of a vivacious former student who had graduated named Billy Derr, Godwin High Principal Leigh Dunavant, new to the role, got together with her counseling team and asked some junior and senior students if they would like to spearhead a mental wellness club, which they called No Eagle Left Behind. These groups were started out of a need or a wish to open the conversation on mental health and most were started with small budgets or no budget at all. The education sector is slow to change and this is one way that students can jump-start an effort to support their peers and create a mental health awareness and suicide prevention culture. Student-led efforts are very effective because young people listen to other young people.

Nobles Heads Together was similar in title to Heads Together, a mental health initiative in the UK spearheaded by the Royal Foundation of the Duke and Duchess of Cambridge. Nobles staff did reach out and were granted permission to use the NHT name. Similarly, Aurora Wulff was at Ithaca High School in New York when she started their mental wellness club. Together they decided on the name Active Minds (AM) before they knew it was a national non-profit for student mental health. When their counselor shared that newsflash, they officially registered their club with that organization.

We know that mental health problems affect a student's energy level, concentration, dependability, mental ability, outlook, and performance, and research suggests that untreated depression is associated with lower grade point averages, and that co-occurring depression and anxiety can increase this association. Although there are not data on whether a mental wellness club can improve school or individual performance, anecdotal evidence suggests that it can, especially because peer relations are of primary importance to adolescents.

The goal of student wellness clubs is to educate, empower, and engage students committed to raising awareness and reducing stigma around mental health. These groups promote inclusion and connection, and normalize the conversation. Activities promoted by these groups often include mental health panels and speakers or just fun events to bring people together.

Mental Wellness Club themes include:[1]

- Resource Awareness
- Stigma Reduction
- Social Systems of Support
- Respect
- Healthy Habits
- Coping Skills
- Healthy Mindset
- Mindfulness in Adversity
- Compassion in Action (kindness)

Many groups have started with a sponsor, usually teacher advocates or school counselors, who got together and made plans, all from scratch, with ideas generated by students with their sponsors. (There are nonprofits who have set agendas for these clubs, which will be mentioned later in this section.) The goal is to create an environment where suicide, substance misuse, self-harm, and other high-risk unhealthy coping behaviors are minimized by offering social support and access to coping skills and professional support.

The clubs mentioned here—Nobles Heads Together, No Eagle Left Behind, and Active Minds—collaborated with school counseling teams, administrators, community partners, and nonprofits focused on mental health. The students who started these clubs developed leadership skills that also made attractive additions to their high school résumés when applying for colleges. With suicide being the number two cause of death on university campuses across the US, when student applicants show leadership on this subject, it is an asset that catches the attention of admissions professionals looking for students who can shape a culture of mental wellness on their university campuses. For students not considering college, the lessons learned from leading a club or participating give them important coping tools they take into the next stage of life, whether it's trade school or apprenticeships, nursing programs, or other job training.

Initiatives and Ideas for Student Wellness Clubs

Ideas can include simple icebreakers, poetry slams, speaking panels on mental health topics, personal stories, campaigns through the library, poster campaigns advertising resources, and more. Usually there is a monthly topic with extra emphasis on activities during September, Suicide Prevention Month and Recovery Month, and May, Mental Health Awareness Month. The year's activities should be outlined by month and any proposed materials, costs, and volunteers needed for the effort.

Walks, either live or virtual, can be planned with the help of your local chapter of the American Foundation of Suicide Prevention (AFSP). While cities across the United States have annual "Out of the Darkness Walks," schools and colleges can have their own "Out of the Darkness Campus Walks" in support of suicide prevention. Usually community organizations that provide mental health resources set up tables, feature short student speeches about their story that have been reviewed prior to presentation, and then participate in the walk. AFSP Campus Walks, launched in 2010, sparked a grassroots movement at high schools and colleges across the country as students started finding their voice for this important topic.[2] The message is that together, students and educators can bring mental health conditions like depression and anxiety out of the darkness, erase the stigma surrounding the conversation, and prevent this loss of life. The organization has toolkits, promotional materials, and a variety of templates to help organize the event.

Nobles Heads Together

Desmond and friend Michaela started Nobles Heads Together (NHT) from a need to offer a safe space for a small group of grieving students to meet in the aftermath of a student suicide their sophomore year, and the group evolved into a mental wellness club from there. In May 2018, as part of a school assembly, Desmond, a junior at Noble and Greenough School, kicked off the effort to destigmatize the topic of mental health by speaking to the student body about his own experience with teenage depression in a "NED Talk." (The N stands for Nobles; YouTube Keywords: Desmond Herzfelder NED Talk.)

When Desmond and Michaela were planning events for their club, they created these categories for activities, which were either events or projects:

- **Education**, e.g. A film about depression by local filmmaker Desiree Adams. Panel discussion to follow.

- **Events intended for those who are struggling or to help students support their peers**, e.g. November: Men's mental health! Toxic masculinity: Why is it hard for men to talk about mental health? The first 10 guys who show up get a prize.

- **Fun events meant to bring people together**, promoting belonging, connection and raising awareness of the existence of a mental health club. In the first year, 50% of the NHT events fell in this category. e.g. Come join us for a marshmallow and hot chocolate toss. Test your aim and winners will walk home with their very own bag of marshmallows!

- **Activities that promote stress-reduction and connection**, including decorating gratitude journals, painting rocks with inspirational sayings and putting them around the school, and bringing therapy dogs onto campus.

NHT Video Project

The NHT club also did a video project, each one featuring a student telling their story about struggling with a mental health issue. Students, a lot of them members, volunteered and filled out a consent form (parents also filled out consent forms for their child's participation), which included the goal of the video project:

> "The project's primary purpose is to show students who are struggling that they are not alone. Mental struggles can sometimes feel unbeatable, but the project will show real examples of students who have been able to move past dark times and offer potential strategies to those still fighting."

While a project like this takes a lot of resources, time, effort, and oversight, NHT repurposed those videos by making an online library after airing them to the student body and these videos are accessible today by students with a school login.

They also created a page for Mental Health and Wellness at Nobles that included crisis lines, strategies for managing anxiety, study strategies, places to go to get help at the school, a link to The Trevor Project for LGBTQ students on how to "Protect Your Space and Well-Being on Social Media," suggested podcasts, videos, and book recommendations.

Jennifer Hamilton is the school psychologist who sponsors NHT and works with the students to develop ideas. They collaborate with teachers, coaches, students and student groups, deans, counseling staff, and administrators. She says there are a lot of inspiring ideas on Pinterest and good keywords can include "teen activators," "teambuilding activities for high school students," and "teambuilding activities and icebreakers for virtual environment."

During mental health awareness week, the students found inspiring quotes from celebrities who have struggled with mental health challenges. Then the NHT group members created the artwork by framing a photo of the celebrity with their quote on colorful construction paper and posted them throughout the school as a way of raising awareness. An activity that has been one of Jennifer's favorites is "Am I the only one who. . ." They handed out sticky notes to every middle school student and each of them wrote down how they would complete that sentence and stuck it on a large bulletin board on wheels. Jennifer says, "Any time I'm working with a kid who has that imposter syndrome or is struggling in some way, I pull out the bulletin board with those quotes to remind them that they are not alone."

Fishbowl

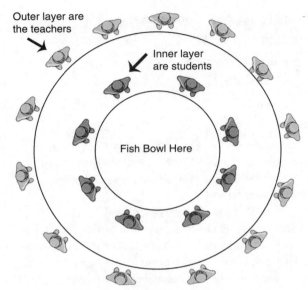

Outer layer are
the teachers

Inner layer
are students

Fish Bowl Here

Figure 6.5 Fishbowl Game.

A really powerful activity that Jennifer has done as a school activity is Fishbowl, which involves handpicking about 10 students ahead of time. She bought pizza for the group and explained the game.

The students stand in the inner circle with faculty members around them. During the whole game, the faculty are not allowed to say a word and both groups are facing inward, so the faculty are actually looking at the backs of the students in front. The students helped come up with statements. These are written on slips of paper, folded, and added to a bowl. A student leader draws a statement out of the bowl and hands it to one of the students. Then that student comments on it.

Here are some examples of statements they created together, which could also be phrased as questions:

- Something I wish my parents understood about me. . .
- Something I wish my teachers understood about my life. . .

- What I do during my downtime. . .
- The things that keep me up and make me worry. . .
- If I could change something at school it would be. . .
- An adult who has impacted me in my life is. . .
- When I am afraid, this is what calms me down. . .
- The bravest thing I've ever done is. . .
- If money didn't matter, I would do. . .
- A special talent I have is. . .

(Go to EmotionallyNaked.com and in the search field use the keywords "fishbowl game" to download a template for the editable questions that go in the fishbowl. It's also included in the packet of downloads at wiley.com/go/emotionallynaked; password is 988preventsuicide.)

The students start talking, and after a while they talk openly as if the adults aren't even there. The educators can't ask questions—nothing—but they have the privilege of listening in and learning more about the students. There could also be an audience of students and faculty on the outer layer in a gymnasium and in this case a microphone would be needed. To adapt this virtually on the Zoom platform, students who will be making the statements are designated in the admin section as "panelists" and they get a different login so their faces will show. The rest of the audience are the attendees, which might include a mix of students and faculty.

To adapt this activity for a classroom of 30, have 10 students on the inside circle, 20 on the outside. The 10 students in the center draw from the fishbowl and take turns talking, while the outer circle students listen. If you have 30 students in your class, it will take three sessions to give all students a chance to be in on the "inner circle."

Rock Painting

Gather a bunch of stones large enough to paint. Let the students paint them with sayings like "You're not alone," "Believe in yourself," and other short, inspiring messages. Or just paint beautiful images that don't have writing. Then you can place them on school grounds for other students to discover. It's so much fun to hear about students who found them, some of whom carry them in their backpacks the whole year to touch and hold as a ray of hope on a dismal day.

Middle School Visit

For this event, a group of seniors from NHT spoke to the middle school about times when they thought they were the only ones who felt they weren't smart enough, strong enough, athletic, beautiful, or talented enough. They talked about times they failed or thought they were a failure. Their stories were often embarrassing and funny, with a focus on ending with a recommendation about not keeping struggles secret. Optionally, they broke into small discussion groups, one senior per group of middle schoolers. No teachers. It gave the Nobles club members such a feeling of agency to be able to share their fears with their younger peers. And the younger kids really appreciated it and because they looked up to these older kids, they listened and participated.

No Eagle Left Behind

The No Eagle Left Behind (NELB) club at Godwin High School in Henrico, Virginia, focuses on spreading kindness so all events and education revolve around this core central theme. Their goal is to make it difficult for a culture of bullying to thrive and to empower students to facilitate change. For opening day in September 2019, NELB students at Godwin High School created stickers for notebooks, backpacks, and laptops that said, "You can sit with me," so students who were nervous about the first day and where to sit in class or at lunch could see a dotted sea of stickers designating available spots where they were welcome to join the crew and feel included. (See Figure 6.6.)

Figure 6.6

They also created a bulletin board with a headline that said, "Take What you Need," which was covered edge to edge with positive Post-it Note messages that students could choose to take with them. Some of the messages were "You matter," "You are loved, valid, important." "You've got this," and "Take a smile." They further extended this concept to drawing messages in chalk on the sidewalks on random school days when students were arriving.

When school shut down due to the COVID-19 pandemic, they took their campaign online to Instagram and focused on self-care topics. They made a bigger virtual footprint to step up to support students by creating a website called Henrico Real Talk and made a space where students and faculty could send a message that would be delivered virtually to another person to keep students connected to one another at a time when it was a challenge to do so. This was an effort to combat feelings of isolation. On this site were also resources, quotes from other students, and their mission for creating the site.

To support African American students during and right after the Black Lives Matter protests in the summer of 2020, the NELB group created a "Wall of Solidarity" on their Real Talk website with messages students sent to support their peers who were additionally stressed in light of those protests.

"Black lives are human lives and I will fight for equality in this country until the day I die."

"Always standing by your side. Know that you are loved!"

"This fight is far from over. We're going to stand as allies with you until the very end."

"It is unfathomable to me that we have to fight for basic human rights in 2020, but I will fight for equality and stand alongside every black person in this country."

Godwin Real Talk Was Created with One Goal in Mind

We plan to promote positivity and enrich the social atmosphere that students are surrounded by. With this in mind, we wanted to create a place where people had the ability to compliment each other and make others feel better, or recognize them for a small act of kindness that they might not even have realized they have done. We acknowledge that speaking in person may be difficult for some, especially if the topic is serious, so we have made the ability to send personal advice easy through this Real Talk website page. Along with a clean and easy-to-use interface, we also wanted to preserve the user's privacy. Through this protected website, you are free to send any compliment or word of advice to a person who may need it. Feel free send a compliment on the home page!

Active Minds

Aurora Wulff, founder of Active Minds Mental Wellness Club at Ithaca High School in upstate New York, says their most memorable event was a panel event that featured club members telling their personal stories. They decided to have the event during the school's social justice week, which allowed several assembly-style events to happen during that period from multiple clubs and the community. Students could ask permission from teachers to leave class and attend featured assemblies, and the Active Minds panel event drew a crowd of over 200 people. From anxiety issues to eating disorders, panel members had a slot of time in which to share their stories, which none of the students had ever heard. The stories were about hardship, healing, hope, and seeking help. They followed up this successful event by partnering with a women's rights club at school and a community non-profit partner to hold a discussion on body image that started with a brief presentation followed by a panel discussion, and they packed the room.

The club also had a peer-to-peer sharing space once a week on Wednesdays at zero period, which was a time slot before the first period of the day. The club had permission to use their sponsor teacher's classroom and students would come and talk while club members listened and provided emotional support. The 50-minute sessions usually started with an activity or icebreaker and segued into peer-to-peer sharing. Still other times, the activity was ditched in favor of the peer-to-peer sharing if attendees needed that to happen. The club members feared no one would show up but found that there was always healthy attendance and it provided a much-needed outlet.

When schools do have club events about mental health, it is advised to have a member of the counseling team, the club sponsor, or an adult volunteer trained in mental health or suicide prevention to facilitate or just be present. Active Minds also partnered with the library and a community bookstore. They coordinated with the librarian to use the library's digital screen to advertise their upcoming events and choose books to put on display. They had poetry readings at a local bookstore in the community, Buffalo Street Books, along with a store display of young adult books focused on mental health topics.

All the leaders and members of these clubs did worry about lack of interest and attendance. And while there were events that attracted fewer participants, most of them had robust turnouts and ran out of room, which illustrates that these clubs fulfill an important need. What's more, with the college transition being a very stressful one for students, a baseline of mental wellness education helps students make that step with more confidence. At Nobles, NHT has inspired offshoot support groups, such as the Affinity Group for students who need more specific support around mental health, as well as a parent group for those who have children living with mental illness.

A basic outline of events throughout the school year and mental health week to spark ideas can be found in Chapter 12, Worksheet 12: Sample Schedule of Student Mental Wellness Events/Ideas. Ideas include fun events like a Waffle Sundae Breakfast, Test Strategy Event, Club Mental Health Fair, and scheduled speakers who spoke about tips on managing test anxiety. Events were promoted with onsite posters, announcements, newsletters, emails, school messaging systems, and social media platforms.

Students and faculty who decide to start a mental wellness club can partner with a local mental health organization for guidance and support such as locally based mental health nonprofits or local chapters of the American Foundation of Suicide Prevention (AFSP.org), Mental Health America (MHA.org), National Alliance of Mental Illness (NAMI.org), or other local nonprofits. If your students don't want to freelance it, there are organizations that do provide the framework for student wellness clubs; see the next section for a list of these nonprofits.

Organizations Supporting School Mental Wellness Club Initiatives

"A school club was started by a student who was motivated by one of our foundation's speaker events at the high school and it was called Stigma Free HSE [Hamilton Southeastern High School]. The mission of the club was to educate students and the school community about mental health, advocate for those who can't, and be a resource for those who need support. They have since joined Bring Change to Mind [BC2M, BringChange2Mind.org] organization and have had great success with their leadership and curriculum of materials.

I have seen incredible things when youth/students get involved and do projects and/or programs in the schools and community around mental health. In my opinion, students should get some sort of training in school as they are the on the front line as first responders since most of the time students will go to their peers first when they are struggling. My foundation has helped fund the club activities when needed. Both [local] high schools have a Stress-Free room—a safe place to go for youth to get away from daily stresses—no phones allowed! These rooms have been beneficial to students as many have shared that they don't feel like they have a safe place in the school where they can go when they are struggling. Also a great meeting place for support groups."

Mike Riekhof (He/Him/His), Survivor of Suicide Loss,
Founder of The Peyton Riekhof Foundation, Fishers, Indiana

School groups who might be overwhelmed by starting a group from scratch can tap into existing mental wellness club curriculums generated by national nonprofit organizations. These are well-thought-out curriculums with online toolkits that include ideas, support, campaigns, resources, and website logins for wellness club leaders, and most are at no cost.

Some national organizations that promote peer-led club and wellness culture through their nonprofit missions include:

- *Our Minds Matter* (MindingYourMind.org) through Minding Your Mind nonprofit. For club information, look for "Our Minds Matter."
- *Bring Change 2 Mind*, (BringChange2Mind.org) a mental health awareness organization. For club information, look for High School Program and then "Starting your own club."
- *The Youth Wellness Council (YWC)* (WCClubs.org), a high school leadership program of the Mental Wellness Center. For club information, look for "Wellness Connection."
- *NAMI on Campus Clubs* (NAMI.org) are student-led clubs that tackle mental health issues at high schools and on college campuses. For club information, look for "NAMI on Campus - High School."
- *Erika's Lighthouse* (ErikasLighthouse.org), a winner of the 2020 Community Builder Award from the Child Mind Institute as part of its annual Change Maker Awards, has an initiative for student-led clubs. Look for "Teen Empowerment Club."
- *GSA Network,* formerly known as Gay Straight Alliance, now *Genders & Sexualities Alliance* (GSANetwork.org) These student-run clubs are geared specifically to unite LGBTQ+ and allied youth to build community and organize around issues impacting them in their schools and

communities. We list them here due to LGBTQ+ youth being a higher suicide probability. Having a GSA can have a positive and lasting effect on student wellness, protect students from harassment based on sexual orientation or gender identity, and long-term it can improve school climates for all students. Look for "Start your GSA" or "Register your GSA."

These organizations provide resources and support in terms of programs, campaigns, videos, and initiatives for high schools, many of which can be promoted through emotional wellness clubs:

- *JED Foundation* (JEDFoundation.org) and *Active Minds* (ActiveMinds.org) started with a focus on university-level mental health and suicide prevention, but given their success these organizations are starting to provide resources and support for high schools.
- *NAMI.org* has local chapters in every state with resources and programs for schools including a speaker program.
- *AFSP.org* has local chapters in every state and frequently runs or partners with other organizations on campaigns aimed at youth.

In addition to national organizations, there are many regional, chapter, and local mental health organizations and state government initiatives that have programs like the Peer-to-Peer Depression Awareness Campaign in Michigan (DepressionCenter.org) and The Peyton Riekhof Foundation (ThePeytonRiekhofFoundation.com) in Indiana, which supports school wellness club initiatives with funding and more. Johnny's Ambassadors (johnnysambassadors.org) in Colorado offers education on marijuana-induced psychosis. Lock & Talk (lockandtalk.org) in Virginia focuses on limiting access to lethal means for persons with suicidal thoughts by providing free safety devices to secure firearms and medications as well as educational materials and guidelines about storing and securing means. Youth MOVE (Motivating Others through Voices of Experience) through NAMI Virginia (NAMIVirginia.org/youth-move-virginia/) is a platform for young people to share their story and inspire others. These initiatives can be promoted through the clubs to build awareness of their messages. See what resources you have in your state.

Framework and Guidelines for Speaking, Panel Events, Videos, and News

Trigger warning: Method mentioned in examples of what not to say when telling a story about suicide.

Many student wellness clubs schedule speakers, have speaker panels, and make videos starring students who have lived experience with a mental illness, trauma, suicide attempt, or as a suicide loss survivor. Featuring students who have fought back and found a path to emotional healing can be transformational experiences for both the speakers and the audience. Oftentimes they are the most powerful events for stimulating conversation on difficult topics and inspiring those who are hurting to fight for themselves and reach out for support. Mental wellness clubs, sponsors, school counselors, teachers, and leaders should familiarize themselves with guidelines for storytelling and messaging on topics related to suicide.

A story starts with a struggle or hardship. Then the audience wants to know how that individual got through it—the help they received and the strategies that were used to find healing. And finally, a message of hope that the speaker wants to leave with the audience. If you were to share a document with recommendations for potential speakers to write their story for review prior to presentation, focus on **Story Guidelines**. (See also Chapter 12, Worksheet 15: Guidelines for Telling Your Story.)

Storytelling Guidelines

Storytellers should avoid graphic details of a suicide or suicide attempt and include these themes, known as the four Hs:

HARDSHIP

Your story

HELP

What helped you through the crisis

HEALING

How you healed

HOPE

Why you have hope

The Framework for Successful Messaging[3] is a research-based resource that outlines four critical issues to consider when messaging to the public about suicide: strategy, positive narrative, safety, and guidelines. We've listed seven points here and included examples. The idea is not to homogenize a person's story or project but to help make your wellness group events, videos, promotions, presentations, and newsletters more effective. This outline can feel overwhelming but these guidelines revolve around promoting themes that inspire those 4 Hs of hardship, help seeking, healing, and hope.

1. **Strategy** involves planning and focusing messages so they are as effective as possible. For better results, start by deciding **why** you're messaging, **who** you want to reach, and **what** you want the audience to do[4] after hearing the message.

   For example, if you did a poster campaign on the crisis text line:

   - Your "why" would be to provide a resource for students.

   - Your "who" would be to reach those who might be struggling before it becomes an emergency event.

   - Your "what" would be that you want them to text 741-741 for support and help. And given that the goal is to have people contact the number on the poster, it needs to be a large element that stands out, also referred to as a Call to Action.

2. **Safety**[5] is avoiding content that is unsafe or undermines prevention. For this section, we'll use examples of headlines since that's an easy way to express the concept of the guideline in a single sentence of what *not* to say.

   What content is unsafe? Increased risk is associated with:

   - Repeated, prominent, or sensational coverage. *Skyrocketing* is sensational.

   - Example of what *not* to say: "Skyrocketing Suicide Deaths Stun the School."

   Details about suicide method or location.

   - Example of what *not* to say: "School in Shock After Student Shoots Himself," "Highland Station RR Tracks Site of Sixth Suicide this Year."

   Portraying suicide as a common or acceptable response to adversity.

   - Example of what *not* to say: "Student Overwhelmed with Schoolwork Kills Himself."

Glamorizing or romanticizing suicide.

- Example of what *not* to say: "Diving Star Takes Final Half Gainer off Suicide Bridge."

Presenting simplistic explanations for suicide.

- Example of what *not* to say: "Student Suicides Because of Bullying."

Including personal details that encourage identification with the person who died.

- Example of what *not* to say: "Lonely and Depressed, Anna Jones Left a Stack of Suicide Notes."

Avoid details of or about a suicide note. Avoid sharing overly graphic details of self-harm or methods of suicide or suicide attempt in a speech.

- Examples of what *not* to say: "And there I sat with a belt around my neck. . . ." Or "I tasted the barrel of the gun. . . ." Or "I entered the bathroom and the bathtub was full of blood. . . ." Or "I dragged the sharp razor along my skin in cross hatches and when it bled, I felt elated. . . ."

- If a suicide attempt survivor speaker is in a wheelchair as a result of her attempt, mention of a firearm is part of that story and cannot be left out. However, mention of method should be brief. "I found my Dad's gun and woke up in a hospital paralyzed from the waist down." And it should be balanced with narratives like "I wish I had asked for help before it got that bad," or "I'm grateful to be here now and am glad that I lived because. . ." If the person telling the story found a body, they could say, "I did find my sister in the bathroom and I needed trauma therapy to manage the pain of that discovery," or "It was so traumatic finding my sister, I wish I would have gotten help with that at the time." In short, no story about suicide needs to be sensationalized or include graphic detail because it can be triggering to an adolescent population. On the other hand, no one wants to leave out a critical piece of a story that ends up coming across as a coverup.

3. **Positive Narrative**[6] means ensuring that the collective voice of the story is "promoting the positive" in the form of actions, solutions, successes, or resources. This doesn't mean saying to a group of students that everyone must deny difficult feelings and always "look at the bright side."

- There are actions that people can take to help prevent suicide.

- Prevention works.

- Resilience and recovery are not only possible but probable.
- Effective programs and services exist.
- Help is available.
- Examples: "I found a support group through NAMI that made all the difference in my recovery." "It was awful and seemed hopeless while I was going through it but I'm so glad I worked through it and feel stronger today because of my experience." "It's because my brother didn't listen when I told him not to tell anyone I wanted to die. He did tell and that's why I'm alive today." "I reached out to my favorite teacher and she connected me to the counseling team. And that's how my healing started."

Timing

While loss survivors' grief journeys vary, a good rule of thumb for suicide loss survivors who come to the school to tell their story would be two years after the tragedy.

For students who've struggled and want to tell their story, look for signs that they are through the worst of it and have found healing. If a student is still in a place where they are overly angry or resentful, they may need more time to process.

Support

Have a CSR (Community Support Resource) on site. Every talk about suicide or mental illness should include at least one or two counselors, professionals trained in ASIST, or qualified individuals from community organizations who are on site in case a student needs support. They should be introduced at the start of the event and familiar faces are always best.

Have students interview the counseling team. These students could then present the results of their inquiry to the student body to raise awareness of the available resources on campus and how to seek help in their school.

Hand out resources. This is an opportunity to educate and promote help-seeking behavior and raise awareness of the resources available in your community. Print out cards with resource numbers and ask mental health agencies and nonprofits to supply information or giveaways to hand out—rubber bracelets, wallet cards, pins, literature.

Offer a trigger warning. Example of a topic sensitivity script read by a host or emcee:

> "Coming up next is [speaker name], who will be speaking on his story as a suicide loss survivor [or other topic]. This is an emotionally sensitive topic and we want to keep you safe and hope you will practice good self-care. If you need to leave the room, signal to our Community Support Representative, Connie, with a thumbs-up thumbs-up, meaning, 'I'm headed to the restroom,' or 'I'm headed into the hallway because I can't be parted with my Instagram feed for a whole hour.' Thumbs-down Thumbs-down or no sign at all means that you need support. So don't be surprised if you see someone behind you asking how you are feeling. (Resources such as the suicide prevention lifeline and crisis text line should be visible on a slide.)

Use the Right Language

- Avoid saying "committed suicide" but instead say "died by suicide," "ended his life," "took his life," "killed herself."

- Avoid saying "successful suicide" or "unsuccessful suicide." If someone died it is a suicide. If they didn't it was a suicide attempt. It doesn't need qualifiers.

- Avoid saying "completed suicide." It's either a suicide or an attempted suicide.

- Avoid saying "drug addict" and instead say "person with addiction" or "person with substance use disorder." Same goes for someone living with depression.

Story Guidelines[7]

Use the best practices on this outline for narratives that include suicide and focus on these bullet points for creating a story that will be shared in public with students.

- **Describe who you are**, what you do, and a bit about yourself.
- **Share your experience of crisis.** What happened before you received the help you needed? Think about the most important thing you'd like your listener to know. Keep this section brief.
- **Share what helped you.** Describe how you got through crisis and found help and hope, or what more would have helped you. This step is

important, as it illustrates the value of support and provides resources or actions others can take.

- **Share your experience of recovery.** How has this experience changed you for the better? What kind of support helped you? Share how you maintain recovery and share your hope for others.

- **Share resources**. Every talk about suicide or mental illness should also have resources at the start to encourage people to reach out. That can be in the form of a slide and cards to hand out that promote help-seeking behavior.

After Telling Your Story

- Be prepared that others will reach out and tell you their story.
- Be ready with resources or point out the resource table.
- Use self-care practices and your support network if you feel overwhelmed.

If you are a suicide loss or attempt survivor planning to tell your story, further direction is available in these guides found online: Special Considerations for Telling Your Own Story: Best Practices for Presentations by Suicide Loss and Suicide Attempt Survivors (Suicidology.org), Storytelling for Suicide Prevention Checklist (SuicidePreventionLifeline.org), and Speaking Out About Suicide (AFSP.org).

Funding for Your Mental Wellness Club

While student wellness clubs are not costly ventures, having some funds helps cover the costs of materials and speakers. If your school doesn't give your club a budget, students can fundraise, apply for a grant, or appeal to places of worship, the PTA, a local nonprofit, or local community-based civic clubs like Assistance League, Rotary, Lions Clubs, or Kiwanis Clubs, or fraternities like Moose Lodge. Community service clubs like Rotary will often donate to support initiatives for their local schools. Most of these civic groups meet weekly, have many local chapters, and exist only to serve causes in their communities. Students and teachers can schedule a presentation to a community club and follow up by filling out a form to request funds. Student presentations to these clubs are very effective and you can expect checks from $100 to $1,000 or more depending on the ask. So go to the meeting with a schedule and a plan, expected outcomes, and a budget on executing the initiatives. There is nothing more rewarding than seeing students take leadership roles, raise money, develop ideas and execute them, put together panels, tell their stories, and organize walks to support a cause.

There are many ideas in this chapter and this book on creating a foundation of student wellness that translates to a culture of suicide prevention. If leadership is not yet on board with a school program or gatekeeper education, seek training for yourself such as QPR, safeTALK, Start, or Kognito ($0–$35), described in more detail in the previous chapter, and then integrate some of the classroom strategies you've read about here. Try one of the quizzes in the worksheet section, use an icebreaker, start Mondays with a mindfulness exercise to improve student focus, have a mental health check-in on Fridays, post a crisis line 8.5-by-11-inch printable poster for your classroom walls, and take any opportunity to facilitate problem solving. Start with one idea and see how it goes. If that doesn't resonate with your class, try another. The idea is to shift your teaching style to one that includes integrating and modeling social emotional strategies to your students.

"We've had teachers pick up the book [*DBT Skills in Schools*] and say, you know, I'm going to do this in my history class because I have several kids who are struggling and are off task and I'm yelling at them. And it's not good for the kids, it's not good for me, and it's not good for the entire class to see that. So they've picked it up and they've started teaching it. And they've dropped their referrals and disciplinary issues in their class to zero and the other teachers are like, 'How are you doing that?' I would start with mindfulness. Teach your kids that there's a pause between having an urge to do something and actually doing it. You can have an emotion or a thought to do something. You don't automatically have to do something just because you have that thought."

James Mazza, PhD (He/Him/His), Professor, University of Washington, Author of
DBT Skills in Schools

You can be one of those school champions, as James Mazza has stated. Otherwise school becomes a kind of mill where you put kids on a conveyor belt. They get math, calculus, Spanish, and language arts, and by the time they're done, we haven't prepared them for being an adult, which means they can't interact, deal with crisis, speak in public, or ask for what they need. This translates to struggles with relationships, the disruption of which is a key trigger in a constellation of other issues that results in substance misuse and suicide. The sacredness of the interpersonal relationship still exists in schools. It's one of the few places it does. We're counting on you to cultivate that, to allow other voices to be heard, and to build the trusted relationships that kids will remember for a lifetime.

NOTES

1. Our Minds Matter Flyer. MindingYourMind.org
2. AFSP.org
3. Action Alliance Framework for Successful Messaging. http://suicidepreventionmessaging.org/
4. Ibid.
5. Ibid.
6. Action Alliance Framework for Successful Messaging. http://suicidepreventionmessaging.org/
7. Suicide Prevention Lifeline: Storytelling for Suicide Prevention Checklist. https://suicidepreventionlifeline.org/storytelling-for-suicide-prevention-checklist/

Chapter 7
Intervention: They've Told You They're Thinking of Suicide. What Now?

Trigger Warning: Suicide method mentioned

"So what happens is that the school really becomes the home base of where they can talk about [suicide]. And that's what we've really worked hard to create in our school, is a place that kids feel safe sharing these feelings. I was walking down the hall last year and I saw this little sticker. It must have been two inches of a sticker, and it said, 'Feeling suicidal? Go to Jessica's office.' I was like, 'Wow, all these kids are really speaking to each other, you know?'"

Jessica Chock-Goldman, LCSW (She/Her/Hers), Doctoral Candidate, School Social Worker, Stuyvesant High School in Manhattan, New York

Teachers can come in contact with a student in distress in several ways. A student might deliver a wish to die as a joke, or an offhand remark. They might tell outright, hint at it, or a friend of theirs might deliver the message on behalf of a student they are worried about, or you could overhear a conversation about a post on social media that has friends concerned. A student may start by telling you an inventory of problems they are facing all at once and your gut-feeling alarm begs you to pay attention. Often students don't tell you directly but leave hints in the papers they write and the pictures they draw. It could be a doodle on a folder, a poem thrown in the trash, or an obsessive and cryptic conversation with a student about celebrities who've died young. If it's a paper or drawing, you can turn that over to the school counselor and offer to be a partner in a conversation with the student. That all depends on the protocol you have at your school. The key is that once you see something, the time to say something is immediately, not next week.

No matter how you hear it and no matter how it's delivered, talk of suicide has to be taken seriously because this is life or death. Students who are considering suicide rarely say things like, "I need to tell you, a trusted adult, that I am thinking of killing myself by asphyxiation tonight at 7 p.m. when my parents will be leaving for a night out." It would be nice if it was always that straightforward. And even when kids do confess outright, they are often seen as not being serious. Although the comments are usually vague, the suicidal person often thinks their hints are as obvious as a flashing neon sign. But what's obvious to them will not be picked up by someone who doesn't know the signs. (See Figure 7.1.)

"if ppl can't see it through me then they must not care bc its so obvious + even if i tell ppl what would that change? They would just be in my business for no reason."
Jay, teenager who left a comment on the Emotionally Naked blog after searching on Google for a way to die

---

Not all students say something but instead offer clues with their behavior. If you notice a dramatic shift in mood or a behavior that is alarming, your wise mind will say, "I need to find out more," at the same time your fearful brain offers up an escape clause by trying to convince you, "Everything is fine. It's just preteen angst." This is a point when you can collaborate with a coworker who also teaches that student and find out what they think so you can compare notes. Having your concerns validated will often give you the courage to push forward, even if the student pushes back.

"One of my colleagues was working with a student who had cut herself before. It was after hours and there was hardly anybody left in the building. This colleague of mine did everything right. She texted me because she didn't feel like [the student] would be safe if we let her go home. And so between the two of us, one of us stayed with her and the colleague told the student, 'I'm concerned for you and we need to bring in a professional or we need to let the administration know.' The student, you know, was a little bit upset that that had to happen, but also didn't bolt and knew that it came from a place of concern."

Leigh Rysko (They/Them/Theirs), Spanish Teacher and World Languages Department Chair, Kansas Public High School

Figure 7.1 Some students will doodle dark thoughts in notebooks or the margins of papers. One young adult described how she drew a picture of herself drowning at age 14 as she wrestled with thoughts of suicide. Her teacher found the drawing in the trash and alerted the school counseling team.

You are not expected to fix a person's suicidal thoughts but to listen with empathy, stay with the student, and connect this child or teacher with the right person for help and assessment. This chapter offers information on what suicidal students may be thinking and how their minds work so you can approach the conversation from a place of compassion and understanding of what's going on in their heads. It is designed to empower you to press forward, to ask the right questions, and to give those who are trained a refresher and those who are untrained some talking points and guidance on how to respond when a student says yes to the question "Are you thinking of suicide?" This will always be an uncomfortable conversation, so go ahead and set the expectation that you'll feel that way since you'll need to override the impulse to leave it up to someone else or dismiss it because you think it's being too nosy. You may even feel unqualified to do this. Just know that even the most seasoned suicide interventionist feels that moment of fear when it comes to the subject of someone taking their life.

"I knew I had to start learning a lot more to teach psychology than just be interested in it. We didn't have the Internet back in those days [1983], so I was in *Reader's Guide to Periodical Literature* looking up articles on suicide because I saw that there was a just a tiny little blip on the curriculum, that said, 'Suicide.' I didn't know anything about suicide. But I remembered the gentleman who lived in the same apartment complex as me [who had attempted]. So in this article I read it said that if you're dealing with youth as a teacher, and a child comes to you and says he's suicidal, you take them seriously, but you don't try to be Sigmund Freud. You get them help. You know, you get somebody who can intercede. That made sense. Well, I had my class. . .and I went over the basic things on the blackboard and did handouts from the mimeograph machine about what do you do, what are the warning signs. And I'd say most parents weren't happy that I was doing this. Some administrators were saying, 'No. If you talk about this, more kids are going to do it.' And I said, 'Listen, it's on the curriculum. School board says we have to do this. So I'm going to do it until they tell me no.' But I also kind of felt that there was a need because I didn't see kids dying by suicide, but kids were hurting just from comments they would make.

So I did my little class and at the end of it, I told the kids, 'If a friend of yours tells you that they're going to hurt themselves or they're contemplating suicide, you can't be sworn to secrecy. You have to tell somebody. Don't take it on yourself. You've got to be a friend. You've got to tell a parent. You've got to tell a trusted adult—somebody—because, you know, it needs to be done.' A week later, a little bit before 8:00 in the morning, a young lady comes into my classroom. I didn't know her. But she throws a piece of paper on my desk and walks out. I look at it. And it was a suicide note that her locker partner had written that said she was going to suicide. She was going to drink and then drive her car into a stone bridge so her parents would be spared the idea that their daughter died by suicide, that, you know, it would go down as drunk driving. Now, the girl I didn't know heard about it from a girl at the lunch table who was in my class. Wow. And the thing that she took from that was if, 'Somebody tells you, you have to do something.' So this girl who I didn't know got the note and brought it to me. I was the only person she could think of. We were able to get the girl help. She didn't kill herself. She was very angry at me that day. But anger wears off. She's still alive. And I used to get Christmas cards from her."

Sean Reilly (He/Him/His), Retired Teacher, Kansas Attorney
General Suicide Coalition Task Force, The One Heart Project

Information on the topics of mental health and suicide will reach the ears of those who are thinking of suicide or those with a friend who is because their minds are consumed with what to do about it. We can't leave kids out there with this burden all alone. The more people think about their secrets, the more ashamed, isolated, and inauthentic they feel, causing emotional distress undermining well-being.[1] We need to invite them to share these secrets by having uncomfortable conversations. You can't always fix it, but listening can help youth feel heard at a point when they are having a rough time getting out of their own heads.

KIDS WANT TO TELL

"Number one [from our protocol] is to listen and show compassion. You know if that student is sharing [thoughts of suicide] with you, they would hopefully, in theory, share some more. So try to get as much information out of them and also absolutely bring in someone who's trained to deal with that. So we have a school psychologist, we have social workers."

Leigh Rysko (They/Them/Theirs), Spanish Teacher and
World Languages Department Chair, Kansas Public School

In an environment where no one is talking about these subjects, students will defer to Dr. Google to find answers. We need conversations on issues students wrestle with to be happening in our schools, and resources available on the walls of the halls in which they walk, on the virtual calls in which they participate, in bulletins, libraries, newsletters, social media spaces, and on school websites. Their parents also need to be receiving tips on talking to teens about mental health, anxiety reduction tips, coping, and parenting strategies.

Source: Crisis Text Line. Crisis Text Line, 741-741, does Texting Triage by answering the highest-risk texts first.

From school library computers to mobile phones using the school ISP (Internet Service Provider), young people access the web and look up how to write suicide notes, how to tell someone they are thinking of suicide, how to help a friend who is cutting, what are signs of depression, and specific methods on how to kill themselves. Or they search for videos on YouTube that offer step-by-step instructions on how to kill themselves in a specific way. And these macabre resources do exist. When they can't tell someone they know face-to-face or even by text, these young people will leave comments to strangers on posts and videos they find in their searches. They seem more encouraged to leave their own comment if they see that there are many other comments with replies, and that someone cared enough to respond to their cry for help in what seems like a vast and uncaring world. As most trauma experts will say, all it takes is one trusted adult to improve the trajectory of a child's life.

Comments left by young people on Anne Moss Rogers's You Tube Channel on a video people find when searching for a way to kill themselves. (The video does not offer instructions but does offer resources.)

underlingGOAT: "There is no other way to end the pain and I'm tired of being alive for other people's happiness I don't trust nobody they will just laugh which makes me wanna go even more but I keep trying to push through, keep checking my phone as if I was important to somebody I have to fake so much smiles everyday so other people don't feel the pain that I feel, because I know how it feels to be a piece of shit, worthless, and ignored. And I really can't take it anymore, it's too much pain♡. ✋"

DramaQueen: "i am told i have a good life.... its a lie. if i said the reason why i wanted to die they would call me a drama queen. i feel embarassed insecure and damaged. i am the odd 1 out in the family i just wish they wouldnt see me as a useless fatty because thats what im known as. . .i dont want to be in this family nor world/ gooodbye :/"

Alexis: "I left a suicide note but i dont now if i should do it please help please. I am only 11 is a girl i live in north Carolina and im getting bullied so much at school so i started cutting my wrist everyday i want to live but it hurts getting bullied everyday what can i do."

(Note: Alexis left her name and used her middle school email in the comment section that can only be viewed by admin. Anne Moss was able to call the school counselor in North Carolina and let them know this student was at risk.)

With a suicide, we often ask why that person didn't tell someone they were in so much pain or wanted to die. However, despite definitive declarations of a wish to die, those who hear them are either unaware of the significance of these warnings or do not know how to respond to them. In interviews of significant others following the suicide attempt of a loved one despite clear and explicit statements of intent to suicide, family members and significant others were reluctant to act, and in some cases immobilized.[2] The burden of rescue or fixing the problem may have been perceived as so overwhelming that the person shut down. The most common response to a clear suicidal declaration by significant others in all groups studied was "almost total silence—a verbal vacuum," followed by reports of increased tension, anxiety, evasiveness, and in some cases anger and aggression.[3] If the most common reaction to a direct statement of intent to suicide is silence, irritation, anger, or dismissal, then the use of evasive language as a yell for help is understandable. There is often fear by suicidal persons regarding how people will respond to their declaration. Withdrawal of love, rejection, looking weak, being humiliated, letting parents and loved ones down, and other negative reactions are reasons why young people who suffer are afraid to tell or don't seek help.

The following are some comments and cries for help by teenagers on articles written on the Emotionally Naked blog, the YouTube Channel, or in response to an article on The Mighty called "How to Tell a Parent You Are Thinking of Suicide" by Anne Moss Rogers. These emphasize the importance of having a conduit through which students can reach out at the school. By supporting conversation on sensitive topics, those who are at risk can use direct language. Sometimes a parent is not the best person to tell. And even when the parent should know and is very involved, the child might need someone else to tell so the threat to life is taken seriously or when there is fear of how parents will react, which is a barrier to seeking help.

Jenna: "Hi I'm 13 years old and I keep hearing voices in my head. And they keep saying I should kill myself. I AM NOT JOKING! I'm really worried I'll cave in and kill myself! My parents don't know. I'm afraid they would freak out. I'm also worried that I'm not getting good enough grades. A few kids said I would fail everything and I ran into the bathroom and started panicking and I got a pen and started cutting my arm open. I was so worried I had lost my mind and stopped and stayed there for the rest of the day. please please please believe me. I told a teacher but I didn't tell him I was hurting myself, he told my parents but they can't help me because I don't want to worry them. I keep dreaming I'm falling through a red void and a man screams at me to kill myself. I am in need of a lot more help than anyone realizes and I don't know when I've been more worried. Please you got to help me! I don't know if I can take it much longer!"

Zane (12): "I've tried dropping subtle hints to try to get my parents to notice; I've looked up topics related to suicide on their electronics, and I try to sneak facts about depression into conversation. My hope is that they'll notice that what I research and talk about isn't normal, and that I won't be able to lie if they ask me up front."

Kim: "I have been thinking about suicide. I have told my friend but I don't really get to see them anymore. I am not going to tell my parents because I am afraid that they will tell their friends because they tell their friends everything. Their friends are my friends parents. I don't want everyone knowing. I am kind of scared to actually do it because I am afraid that the physical pain will be worse than the mental pain. The only thing I really have to kill myself is kitchen knives. I would stab myself in the heart if I knew there wouldn't be any pain but there is. Is it possible to smother yourself? I really just want to die. Can anyone help me?"

The following dialog is a series of comments posted in response to an article Anne Moss Rogers wrote for The Mighty, "For the Teen Contemplating Suicide and Looking for the Strength to Reach Out." Many students are afraid of the reaction a parent might have and, given how important this relationship is to their overall emotional well-being, they are not willing to confess directly to a parent but instead would rather tell someone at school. This conversation illustrates the level of trust this student had in his favorite teacher.

MIKE: I don't know how to tell my parents or anyone else for that matter. I was actually looking for tips on how to tell parents when I found this website. should I tell my favorite teacher and tell him to contact my parents instead? I just don't feel comfortable talking to someone on the phone either. I also have a little brother and I am worried about how he would react if I told them. Please contact me again. I am really worried. Ps I am sorry for your son.

ANNE MOSS: That is a great idea to tell a teacher. Ask them [the teacher] to contact your school counselor and then your parents. Please share this article with your teacher so he knows to be very clear and say the word "suicide." To us parents, it's hard for us to recognize that life would be so bad one of our children, he would no longer want to be in it. So having someone else tell us is fine. Brilliant idea!

MIKE: Thanks for the advice, I'm going to tell my teacher tomorrow at break time. You helped me a lot, probably more than you know and I'll hopefully stop having these nightmares soon:-) I'll let you know if anything else happens. -Thanks!

ANNE MOSS: Thank you so much for coming back, letting me know, and keeping in touch. Most the time I don't get that and I really appreciate it. And I want you to know, I am going to share that idea with others, too. And you get credit.

MIKE: Thank you so much! I've told someone and I started getting the help I need. You literally saved my life!

Different cultures and religious groups treat the subject of suicide differently. When some students do tell their parents, the responses have not always been ideal. Not because parents are bad people, but often because it's hard for them to imagine things for their child would be so bad they'd take their own life. It's not an easy confession to take seriously or know what to do with when a child does tell. In some cultures, families are dishonored if a child has these thoughts, makes an attempt, or dies by suicide, so their instinct is to punish and shame the child back in line, which is a dangerous and life-threatening response to a vulnerable teen. There are, of course, situations where a parent is not the person to tell as that could further endanger a child's well-being, such as in cases where there is physical or sexual abuse occurring in the home or nonacceptance by the family for a LGBTQ student.

The following are real responses teenagers have reported after telling a parent about their suicidal thoughts. Again, this emphasizes the importance of the school being a safe space for students to share their thoughts of suicide and a protocol to manage the confession in a sensitive and empathetic way. These are from messages sent and comments posted on the Emotionally Naked blog, the affiliated YouTube Channel, or in response to an article on The Mighty called "How to Tell a Parent You Are Thinking of Suicide." While there are many instances where teens who did tell a parent got the help they needed, many got responses like this:

"Telling my mom just made things worse. She told me to 'quit threatening her with that.'"

"I told my dad and he said I should Just pray on it."

"I really feel like telling my mom because we are so close but the last time I told her she got mad and said that killing yourself is for cowards"

"Hi! I'm 14 and I want to tell my mom but I know she'll send me to a mental hospital. she'll twist around on herself asking, 'am I not good enough? I have given you everything! You stupid girl! (She won't [accept] me as boy.)"

"My mom said, 'Suicide is selfish. You need to toughen up.'"

"My dad said, 'How could you think of suicide? You are so lucky and have so much.'"

"I told my mom and sister and they both said I was drama queen."

"My mom said I was just trying to get attention."

"When I told my mum she said I am always thinking of myself."

"My dad told me I should be happy. What do I do?"

Then there are students who are afraid to tell a parent and struggle to do so and they look for other options and trusted adults with whom they can share such sensitive confessions.

"I'm scared of being judged and yelled at. What can I do?"

"I love my parents a lot and I also don't want to tell them about my worries because they are already stressed out with a lot of other things. . . ."

"If I tell my parents. They will look at me differently. They probably won't be proud of me and right now that's all I have got."

"I have been thinking about suicide for a while, and my parents think that every time I cry, I'm faking it."

"I am suicidal but don't know how to tell my mom I'm scared and ashamed of myself. . . ."

"I'm 15 and I feel depressed all the time. I cry a lot, and I haven't told her that I have suicidal thoughts but she knows I feel depressed and she just yells at me and gets mad at me for it. she says that I'm exhausting to be around."

To prevent suicide, students need to feel supported at school, especially if they are not supported at home. That starts with trust and a frank conversation to communicate to students about how these thoughts can be addressed, the fact that resources exist, and what will happen if they use them. Because they are often desperate to tell and afraid of the next step, which is unknown to them. Teachers and educators deserve to be given talking points and training on what to say in these conversations. But even if you don't know what those are, being an empathetic listener who doesn't dole out advice or say, "You have so much to live for," which invalidates a person's feelings, is a significant part of the process. (The end of this chapter has specific response steps for counselors and teachers.) That happens in classrooms where the students have a relationship of trust with the teacher. As in the case of Mike earlier, he didn't feel comfortable telling a parent but he did have a good relationship with a teacher to whom he was willing to convey his painful secret. And educators who are on the receiving end of those confessions should feel honored that they have achieved a level of trust that a student would bare their soul. It's those relationships that make the profession of teaching so special. While you cannot promise complete confidentiality in the instances where a student is at risk for harm to themselves or others, you can promise discretion and transparency of the protocol of what will happen next. You can also express that you are willing to be a partner in the process and advocate for that student.

Creating or enhancing a student-focused school culture takes collaboration and leadership focused on the well-being of students. You wouldn't be reading this book if you were not in that category. All school counselors and teachers we interviewed emphasized the importance of communication and collaboration. This requires a team approach between school counselors, teachers, and any other administrative staff.

"We have a system in which each grade has a dean and that person is aware of all the academic, social, emotional, behavioral issues with the kids at that grade level. The deans meet every week with the counseling team. We also have a student life team and this is an interlocking, interwoven web of support where we are talking about and connecting with our students."

Jennifer Hamilton (She/Her/Hers), School Psychologist, Director of Psychology and Counseling at Noble and Greenough, Independent School, Dedham, Massachusetts

---

Jennifer tells a story about one student who had been experiencing a difficult family situation. The student had been talking to her about this issue.

First thing in the morning, she got an e-mail from the advisor who was saying he thought this student was having a very hard day and he just wanted to let her know. Throughout the day, she heard from three of this student's teachers about how subdued and quiet he was, which was not in his nature. Jennifer is quick to add that a teacher or counselor shouldn't be like a rash on the kid's skin but rather act as part of a collaboration of people who have a heightened sensitivity in regard to their students so they can understand why there are incomplete assignments or the kid can't stay awake in class.

School counselors, social workers, and psychologists often team together to meet students' needs regarding mental health. Most of the time, this group would be referred to as student services, a student wellness team, or a care team. This group then interfaces with the teachers and other staff so that an interwoven web of support can be created. You may be thinking that a dean system is OK for a 600-person school, but hardly feasible for your 3,000-plus public school. Jessica Chock-Goldman, a school counselor Stuyvesant High School in Manhattan and the only mental health professional for a school of 3,600 students with a majority population of Asian Americans, says we really need to be asking about student mental health all the time. She says most teenagers are having some sort of hiccup and their moods shift fast.

"Back when I was a young clinician, I met with a student who was 16 years old. We had a session that day and our conversation revolved around her recent college acceptance. She was so excited and told me what she wanted to study. It was all forward focus, no red flags at all even though she was a kid with an IEP [Individualized Education Plan] and on the autism spectrum. We sat and just talked about what she was going to do next year. I was working through an agency at the time and got a call later. She got into a fight with her twin sister, left school, and [killed herself]. It was such a shock. Because again, that morning we had talked about college and her future. I've done a lot of bereavement work on this and worked through it. But I have learned as a clinician, you really do need to be asking the question."

Jessica Chock-Goldman, LCSW (She/Her/Hers), Doctoral Candidate,
School Social Worker, Stuyvesant High School in Manhattan, New York

---

Most counselors report they do ask frequently, and students routinely tell them they are feeling or thinking about dying or killing themselves. Or they are concerned about a friend. We can no longer let students stew in their suicidal thoughts and not ask because we worry about lack of resources or protocol to manage it. It means we need to at least be having the conversation and educating and integrating policies and protocols to address the issue, while embedding those social emotional lessons to build coping and life skills.

_____

"You really do need to be asking all of the time. 'Are you having thoughts of suicide?' Most teenagers are having some thought of suicide. I have yet to meet a kid who, if I ask them that, they say, 'No, never.' They'll say like, 'I failed that test and I want to die.' Or they'll say, actually, 'I do think about this often.' We really do need to be asking everyone."

Jessica Chock-Goldman, LCSW (She/Her/Hers), Doctoral Candidate, School Social Worker, Stuyvesant High School in Manhattan, New York

_____

REMOVING MEANS

Trigger Warning: Suicide method mentioned briefly

_____

"Well, I had a plan already. I already knew I was gonna take a bunch of medications. I didn't know exactly what—when I first started I was like, 'I'll just take medications that I already take.' Well, so when I got out of the first hospital my mom had locked up all the medications, and so I was like, 'Okay. That's good cuz I won't be able to and stuff'. . .Then that day that I really wanted to, I—right when I left the bathroom I was like, 'Okay. I'm gonna find something. I'm gonna find something so I can kill myself.' I walked in my room and the first thing I noticed was that I had—I still had my old medications in my room cuz she didn't know I had them, so I took those."

A suicide attempt survivor on the role of access to means in her attempt

_____

If a student confesses thoughts of suicide and tells a teacher how they will carry through that action, that should be relayed to someone on the school counseling staff, a psychologist, or a school nurse, depending on your school protocol and resources. So to be clear, a teacher and student can go together to talk to the school counselor and the teacher can state something like the following to let them know how the student is planning to suicide so that the means can be removed from the home at least temporarily or stored more safely long term. You could say something like this in the presence of the school counselor and the student:

_____

"Jamal has told me that he is depressed and his parents are fighting a lot because of their divorce and this has followed the recent loss of his beloved dog, Toby. He tells me he has struggled with frequent thoughts of suicide, mainly at night, and then has trouble sleeping. He confessed that his father has a gun in his bedroom in a drawer by the bed and had planned to use that. Do I have that right, Jamal?"

The reason for including the student in the conversation is to quiet his fears that something is being said behind his back and to be respectful and transparent in the process whenever possible. If appropriate, the school counselor in this example would then talk to the parent(s) about "means safety," which involves asking the family to temporarily store firearms outside their home by having that family ask another gun owner to "babysit" the weapon or store their weapons with the police. Overall, we want to emphasize tighter and more secure safe storage. The conversation would also include removing or locking up other potentially lethal medications and chemicals. If a teen is struggling with intense thoughts of suicide and they have to hunt for a means to end their life, the impending feeling of needing to die can fade in the search process. Not having access to a means to end their life and putting more time between thought and action decreases the odds of a suicide death, as the acute risk of acting on suicidal thoughts is only minutes long.[4] A good resource for means safety is Means Matter at hsph.harvard.edu/means-matter.

WHAT TO SAY, WHAT TO DO

"I was in some state giving a talk and I said something like, 'OK. So in your school, who is the person that the kids want to talk to? Could be, you know, the lunch lady. Could be the counselor. So, who is it?' And I heard some people laughing and it turned out it was the coach. He was not in the training that I was giving, but he usually came to all of the presentations and he would just sit in the back. He was so much less threatening than the counselor person because he was the coach. And, you know, it's always stuck with me as mental health folks are important, but often they're not the ones that kids want to go see."

Jonathan B. Singer, PhD, LCSW (He/Him/His), President, American Association of Suicidology, Author of Suicide in Schools: A Practitioner's Guide to Multi-level Prevention, Assessment, Intervention, and Postvention

Addressing a student who is struggling with suicide can meet with an overwhelming fear that you'll say the wrong thing and that the student will die by suicide and you will feel responsible. However, if you don't intervene at all, there is a much higher likelihood the person will die by suicide. It's a challenge to sit with someone in their pain and *not* try to fix the problem by making suggestions or offering an example of how you resolved a similar situation. But that's what's needed. Few people feel qualified to address a suicidal person but the truth is that people are far more likely to tell someone they know who is not a mental health professional. The goal is first to listen and then connect the person with a qualified individual for an assessment.

It is far more effective to do this imperfectly and be a good, empathetic listener than it is to be a poor listener and do everything by the book. Someone who has been struggling with thoughts of suicide is more likely to trust those who care. But if you do say something you recognize as being unhelpful, you can quickly apologize: "I'm so sorry. I don't know why I said, 'You have so much to live for.' I know it invalidates your feelings. Please ignore that and keep talking. I'm listening."

Often a student will not mention suicide but will list many things that are going on in his or her life that are causing emotional stress. They may say, "I'm so worthless," which is an invitation to ask that child to have a conversation.

"It should be on teachers' minds that if a student is having a change in their academic performance, chances are they didn't get dumber since last week. So in almost every circumstance, unless they've had maybe a brain injury, if you have a B+ student who's suddenly doing C– work, chances are something is going on in their psychosocial universe. Now we're quick to say, 'Oh, go see the school counselor,' because again, people are afraid to have a personal conversation with a kid. Because they're afraid they'll be left holding some disaster. But you'd hope that they'd be prepared to have a conversation with a kid, where they say, 'You're not doing as well as you used to. What's going on? Is there some problem or something someone can be of help with?'"

Victor Schwartz, MD (He/Him/His), Former CMO of The JED Foundation,
Founder of MindStrategies Advisors, Clinical Associate Professor,
Department of Psychiatry, NYU School of Medicine

A concise list of what to do or say is summarized at the end of this chapter. For the most part, you'll be listening with empathy, which means eye contact and head nodding to show you are engaged. The most important part is that the person feels heard and often that doesn't require you to say much or ask too many questions and if you do ask questions, ask open-ended ones that require explanation. It is OK to ask if they have a plan but it's not required. If a student reaches out to you, they've made the most emotionally naked confession a person could ever make and you should be honored they saw you as a person who could be trusted with such sensitive information. So take a cleansing breath. You will be OK. Don't focus on fixing. You can't save their life but you can try to help them save their own life and keep them safe from suicide.

This is how a hypothetical abbreviated conversation between a teacher and a student might go if it's in person. As you will see, it's just a chat between a human adult who cares and a human child who is hurting and it's not something you'd need to memorize but is just an example to help you understand the flow of conversation. You don't have to ask, "Are you thinking of suicide?" but instead connect them with a counselor if it's too uncomfortable. However, we do urge you to lean in to the discomfort and try to have the conversation, and do a warm handoff once it is indicated. The following is a scenario where the student has come to a teacher in a classroom during a planning period to talk and how that educator can engage with that student to keep her safe from suicide.

CASEY:	Mrs. Reynolds, do you have a sec?
MRS. REYNOLDS:	Sure, Casey. Have a seat. What's up? Talk to me.
CASEY:	Ummmm. Well, you know my brother was killed last year in a car accident and I. . .and then my mom got cancer and I just. . .
MRS. REYNOLDS:	Wow, I knew about your brother, Casey, but your mom, I didn't know. I'm so sorry. You have a lot going on. No wonder you are in pain. Keep talking.
CASEY:	I just feel. . .I mean I can't concentrate and I don't think I can do this anymore. I mean, I don't know. . . .
MRS. REYNOLDS:	You can't do this anymore? Can you explain?
CASEY:	Yeah, like I don't care anymore or don't want to be here anymore. Everything is hard. Just getting out of bed is hard. I don't care about anything. . . .It feels dark.
MRS. REYNOLDS:	I will need to ask you a specific question because many times when someone is going through all you are going through, and they say, "I can't do this anymore," they are struggling with thoughts of suicide? Are you thinking about suicide?
CASEY:	Ummmm. . .I think. I mean I don't know. I have these dark periods and then they just go away and then I don't want to hurt myself and I feel fine. But sometimes I do want to and I don't feel like I have control, especially late at night when I can't sleep. My mom and dad would be devastated. But I feel so useless and I don't want to tell them because my parents are so worried about mom's cancer and then my brother

	just died not long ago. I can't put this on them, too. I just can't. My dad has a shotgun and I have thought about it would make the pain just stop. It won't stop sometimes. . . .
MRS. REYNOLDS:	This is serious, Casey. First, I'm honored and grateful you trust me with this. I really am. I also know what courage it took to come tell me all you have, to open yourself up like that. And to trust me with this. Thank you.
CASEY:	You don't think I'm weak?
MRS. REYNOLDS:	Not at all. It's so brave. People don't understand how hard it is to tell. But you have and I'm so very thankful. So let's you and me talk about next steps because we need to make sure you are safe from suicide. We should go talk to Mrs. Ellerbe, the school counselor. She'll know the next steps. We can walk down there together or call her together. Does that sound OK?
CASEY:	Will she call an ambulance or my parents? They just can't handle this right now.
MRS. REYNOLDS:	Your parents would not want to lose you. We can agree on that, right? And I don't know the whole process or when that happens but let's find out next steps together. We are not going to keep secrets but share with you the next steps and ask how you feel about it. And we will handle this discreetly. Let's you and me call Mrs. Ellerbe together now and let's talk to her and she'll come down or we'll go to her office. But I am going to tell her what you told me and also about the gun to keep you safe from suicide, OK? No one is angry with you at all and we are *not* calling an ambulance right now because you are with me and safe right? No limbs are falling off? You're not having a heart attack? So we don't need an ambulance. But we do need help and I'm with you on this, OK?
CASEY:	OK. But I do feel better today. . . .I mean it probably won't come back.
MRS. REYNOLDS:	You may be right. But let's be sure. We are going to tell you next steps. No secrets. Are you with me?
CASEY:	Yeah. I trust you, Mrs. Reynolds. I do.

If you have to leave for any reason, make sure there is someone who can stay with the student until they can be connected with support services. No student should be sent alone down the hall or given a phone number to call support for themselves. And follow up later with a quick check-in, which can be a simple "Hey, let me know how things are with you today," or eye contact with a head nod and a smile.

It all starts with a willingness to be uncomfortable, then by saying "Tell me more," followed by thoughtful listening, connecting, and empathizing with the person and their pain. You should express gratefulness that you were the trusted person with whom they decided to share, show partnership, and be transparent on next steps as you know them to be, connect them with support, and make sure they are not left alone. And then the next day that quick check-in to let them know you care.

> "One of the things that people say all the time which we caution against is, 'Suicide is a permanent solution to a temporary problem.' The kids hear 'permanent solution.' They don't hear a 'temporary problem.' At a time when a student is in so much pain and feeling so hopeless, we don't want to interject statements that potentially present suicide as a viable option."
>
> *Jim McCauley (He/Him/His), LICSW, Co-Founder and Associate Director of Riverside Trauma Center, Needham Heights, Massachusetts*

During any conversation, the person suffering is likely to list a whole litany of issues that can't be resolved right then, or they might even propose something that is unlikely to happen. That moment is not the time to disagree, because it's a contributing factor to what got them in that very intense moment.

So if they say something like, "My girlfriend will take me back. I'm sure she will once she sees how I've changed." We have no idea what might or might not happen. But appropriate responses would be:

> "It sounds as if you are thinking about your future, doubtful about suicide, and want to explore options. So let's discuss how to keep you safe right now."
>
> "We can't fix all those problems right now. The only one I am worried about at this moment is keeping you safe from suicide. Let's call Mr. Hamilton together."

So many people, including students with suicidal ideation and suicidal behaviors, say they use ideation as a coping strategy, leaving it as an option that gets them through moments of extreme adversity. The hope is that they don't follow through but all we can do is keep the student as safe as possible while under our watch, knowing that the effort increases the chances they'll live.

> "Thx I texted them [the Trevor Project at 648-648], I give myself 14 days before I take the discussion to take my life just to be sure I didn't waste any chance to escape from where I'm in. and like start over which I can handle my mental issues later by finding a therapy
>
> now I'm in the 8 day

I don't know why I'm saying this to u but it's just a way to do what it takes to stay safe from this world with adult think actions 'encouraging myself'. . .I don't wanna be mad or scary about it

I Kno typing this would just makes u feel bad. I'm really sorry"

Milli's response on YouTube to a video she found on
Anne Moss Rogers's channel while searching for a way to die

An appropriate response to someone in immediate crisis when they show a glimmer of willingness to get help, yet they also want to keep suicide as an option for a sense of security, is: "Suicide is final. You are expressing doubt about it and since you have those doubts today, let's move forward with the next step to getting help because you don't want to do something so final if you are not absolutely sure. So let's make that call for additional help. Agreed?"

We never want to pass judgment, say it's "wrong" to keep it as an option, especially when they are in a vulnerable state, because who are we to say this is a bad strategy? Our goal is to get them to accept help and the object is to keep your eye on the ball.

We are also conditioned by images we see in the media to look for the "sad" student, when in fact it can be the irritable, angry student who may be experiencing depression and acting out because they are in pain. Depression is expressed in many different ways, from isolation to anger and frustration. These students can often lash out with angry language because they are in pain and that's the point where educators need to take a deep breath before de-escalating a situation that can easily be contained or turned around with some empathy.

Conversation from "Itz All Good" on a YouTube video on Anne Moss Rogers's channel
that the young person landed on when searching for a way to die. (Screen name
changed to protect privacy.)

Itz All Good: 🙂 you never told me how to in many ways this is clickbait—and before you ask, I'm not depressed or anything or trying to commit Suicide I just wanted to see how to, so I can learn some actual knowledge. I did not need to see your son or have this talk like bruh thanks for the clickbait 😡 and wasting 52 seconds of my life.

Anne Moss Rogers: I am just glad you find your life valuable enough to say that 52 seconds of it was wasted. To me, that's good news. I know it didn't meet your expectations and I take full responsibility for that. I hope you are better today.

Itz All Good: Sorry I just have anger issues ;-; I didn't mean to lash out 😄.

ANNE MOSS ROGERS: Itz All Good, you know, when someone is hurting they are not always feeling like miss polly positive. If I were in the pain you were in, I'd not be very nice either. It's very thoughtful of you to apologize. But I do understand and have learned not to take it personally and am honored you did make a comment because I believe there is part of you that is really struggling to live.

Students struggling with their gender or sexual identity or those who have mothers or fathers who are abusive or neglectful may have a heightened fear of their parents finding out. Those kids need to know you understand their reservations and that the team will do whatever they have to do to maintain confidentiality in terms of gender or sexual identity, or access other services in cases where the parents are irresponsible and likely not to respond appropriately, putting that student at greater risk. Students who are in a marginalized ethnic or cultural group may not have much trust in a system that hasn't treated them fairly in the past. Understanding their fears and letting them share these with you can also be an important part of the conversation. As scary as it feels to you, the recipient of the news, it's paralyzing to the student who had to work up the courage for days, weeks, months, and even years before they told someone.

Adolescents think that the present feeling is permanent. They don't understand that feelings are temporary, but if they are in a suicidal crisis all they can think about is making the pain go away. And if they are sitting with you, the young person is not engaging in suicidal behavior, which puts time between thoughts and action, and that is lifesaving. We want to say it will get better. We want to tell them not to do it when what we really need to say is, "Tell me more," and listen with empathy without fixing. If they are telling you, they are having doubts about suicide. And since there is doubt, there is hope. So here is some guidance on what not to say and what would be better to say. You can say all the wrong things but if they feel you care, that's what matters most. Again, if you feel too uncomfortable talking with the student, then tell them that you are concerned and say, "Let's go talk to (or call) the counselor together. I'll be with you."

DON'T SAY: You have so much to live for!
INSTEAD SAY: Tell me more about how you feel.
DON'T SAY: You shouldn't feel that way. You have so much going for you.
INSTEAD SAY: How long have you been feeling this way?
DON'T SAY: Promise me you won't attempt suicide.

INSTEAD SAY:	*Please put me on your contact list if you are struggling. And while we're at it, let's put in some crisis lines now.*
DON'T SAY:	I remember when I had a breakup and I got over it. You will too. You'll find someone else.
INSTEAD SAY:	*That must be very painful to lose a relationship that you were so invested in. I know you loved them. Tell me more about how you're feeling. I can't fix it but I'm here to listen.*
DON'T SAY:	Think of what this would do to your family.
INSTEAD SAY:	*You mentioned a sister. Tell me more about her.*
DON'T SAY:	Are you just trying to get attention?
INSTEAD SAY:	*I'm here to listen. How long have you felt this way?*
DON'T SAY:	Suicide is a permanent solution for a temporary problem.
INSTEAD SAY:	*I'm so sorry you suffer these unbearable episodes. You're so brave to have endured them for so long. You got through your brother's death. Tell me how you did that.*
DON'T SAY:	You are the most popular kid in school, everyone loves you.
INSTEAD SAY:	*I hear you saying that life just doesn't seem to matter to you right now. Is that right?*
DON'T SAY:	It will get better. You'll see.
INSTEAD SAY:	*It sounds like you feel you can't live with pain this intense.*

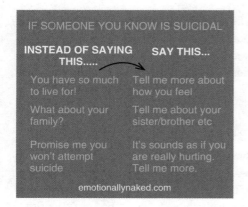

The goal is to connect a student or teacher with someone who will assess them and see what supports are needed. We need more spotters out there than we need people trained in assessment. The clues are subtle, but less so once you know what people say and how to respond, and most of all how you feel in your gut. So don't ignore it.

ASSESSING SUICIDE RISK

"I think [teachers should] be able to identify and have interpersonal conversations with their students. They don't have to be the therapist. As a matter of fact, they're not trained to be the therapist. They do have relationships with kids that a lot of our counselors don't have. So it's that relationship the adolescent sees— 'This teacher cares about me.' That allows disclosure of what's going on. And so then asking the right questions and making that referral."

James Mazza, PhD (He/Him/His), Professor, University of Washington,
Author of DBT Skills in Schools

With the exception of those who are also qualified school mental health professionals, teachers and administrators are not expected to conduct a formal suicide risk assessment. However, you should be aware of the components so you can understand what students will experience and what a protocol might look like. Whatever role you play in this process, such as referring a student to the trained in-school professional who conducts an assessment, it is vital to commit to the intervention and process, rather than worrying about or focusing on the outcome. In short, stay in the present.

In a typical suicide risk assessment conducted by a qualified mental health professional and/or school counselor, parents and youth are interviewed separately to prompt information about their current (and history of) suicidal thoughts, plans, and actions. It is critical to ask open-ended and detailed questions about suicide, including the "who, what, when, where, why, and how." If the youth reports suicidal thoughts, the assessor must then ask about the presence of a suicide plan (or multiple plans), the intent to carry out the plan, and access to the means necessary to move forward with the plan. It is important to be as specific as possible, asking information about the timing and location of the act, the lethality and availability of means, and whether there are suicides currently in preparation. Even if the youth does not endorse firearms as part of a suicide plan, it is always critical to ask about access to firearms because of the lethality of the method. In 2018, firearms accounted for 37% of suicide deaths in youth ages 10–24.[5] Because ingestion or poisoning represents a common suicide attempt method for youth, assessors must ask about access to over-the-counter medications, household cleaning supplies, and prescription medications. A separate meeting with the parents is also essential to give them information for how to keep the home environment safe for suicidal youth,[6] also known as means safety.

Whenever possible, medications that are in blister packs are preferable over pills in a bottle in any household cabinet, because the time it takes to punch out the pills puts time between thought and action, and that alone can thwart a suicide attempt simply because the suicidal intensity ended before they accessed the means.

SAFETY PLANNING

Safety planning is a collaborative process between the youth, family, and clinician that typically consists of written strategies and sources of support that the youth can use when they are experiencing a suicidal crisis. It includes six core steps:

1. Recognize warning signs of crisis.

2. Utilize coping strategies.

3. Contact social supports.

4. Enlist family members/adults to help.

5. Contact mental health providers.

6. Remove lethal means.[7]

Safety plans are not the same as no-suicide contracts. Research consistently demonstrates that no-suicide contracts are not effective, since they do not provide a reasonable and agreed-upon plan and they ask individuals to promise to keep themselves safe when they may not have the skills and resources to do so.[8] However, safety plans *are* effective. Many smartphone apps now include safety plans to facilitate ease of use and may be particularly useful to teens, given that smartphones are extensions of self in this age group.[9]

Three-Step Suicide Prevention Intervention for Teachers, Coaches, and Other School Staff

Sample conversation points if a child confesses to feeling suicidal or says yes to the question "Are you thinking of suicide?" You can skip to step 3 if you feel too uncomfortable with 1 and 2.

1. Engage in private conversation. Additional talking points/tips:

   - Say something like, "Tell me more," or "How long have you been struggling with these thoughts?"

   - Avoid saying, "You have so much to live for."

---

2. Listen with empathy, without "fixing" or offering solutions. Additional talking points/tips:

- Don't say, "You are not worthless," but instead ask, "Why do you feel worthless?"

- If they mention a loved one, instead of saying, "They would never get over losing you," say, "You mentioned you were close to your sister. Tell me more about her."

- You can ask, "Do you have a plan?" (You do not have to ask this, but you can.)

- They may list an overwhelming litany of issues. You don't have to fix or address any of them specifically. You can say, "It sounds like you have so many difficult issues all at once and could use additional support."

3. Connect the child to a school counselor/social worker and show partnership. Additional talking points/tips:

- "I can tell you are really in pain and this is serious. I'm not sure of the next step but I want to help you. Together, let's call/visit the school counselor." (If after hours, call a local/national crisis line about next steps.)

- Promise discretion but not complete confidentiality.

- Don't leave a student alone. They should not be sent anywhere unescorted.

- Ask the student if it's OK to tell the counselor what they have said to you so they feel some agency. (You will have to report it regardless.)

If there is imminent danger, such as a child holding a firearm, call 911. If a student has taken something, call poison control at (800) 222-1222.

For School Counselors: Specific Questioning for Suicide Inquiry

Ask about suicidal ideation, plans, behaviors, and intent openly and frankly:

- Have you been having thoughts about killing yourself either now or in the past?
- Do you ever feel that life isn't worth living?
- Have you ever wished you could just go to sleep and not wake up?
- Have you ever tried to hurt yourself, wishing you would die?
- Have you ever tried to kill yourself?
- What did you think would happen when you. . .(overdosed, etc.)?
- How do you feel that you are still alive after having attempted suicide?

If the youth answers yes to any of these, ask who, what, when, where, why, and how:

- What are you thinking of doing?
- When do you think you might do it?
- Where might you hurt or kill yourself?
- How might you hurt or kill yourself?
- Why do you want to kill yourself?
- Who knows about this?

Hypothetical Scenario

If a student walks into class or the school clinic and tells you they've taken a handful of pills as a suicide attempt, they need medical attention right away. It's not uncommon for someone who has made a suicide attempt to regret it right after. Even an overdose of Tylenol (generically known as acetaminophen) can be lethal or life-altering. Adolescents often attempt suicide by intentionally overdosing or poisoning with what they find at home.

Call 911 if they stop breathing, collapse, or have a seizure. These are signs of an emergency in which the victim needs emergency medical help immediately.

Call poison control at 1-800-222-1222 (US) if the person does not meet the above criteria. This connects you to your local poison center, to speak with a poison expert right away. This expert can give you advice on first aid and may save that child a visit to the emergency room.

When to call the regional poison control center:

- If there's been a poisoning and the person has NOT stopped breathing, collapsed, or had a seizure (if the victim DOES stop breathing, collapses, or has a seizure, call 911 right away).

- If you're concerned about a possible poisoning.

- If you want information or materials on poisoning.

Important reminders for calling the poison control center:

- Do not wait for the victim to look or feel sick.

- Do not treat the person yourself (especially, DO NOT treat with ipecac syrup, milk, or try and make the person throw up).

- Make sure to have the container of the product you think caused the poisoning nearby. The label has important information.

- Be ready (if you can) to tell the expert on the phone:

  - The exposed person's age and weight

  - Known health conditions or problems

  - The product involved

  - How the product contacted the person (for example, by mouth, by inhaling, through the skin, or through the eyes)

  - How long ago the poison contacted the person

  - What first aid has already been given

  - Whether the person has vomited

  - Your exact location and how long it would take you to get to a hospital

Poison Control, Text: Poison to 484848, **Call:** 1-800-222-1222

Source: Poison.org.

NOTES

1. The Problem with Keeping a Secret by Michael Slepian, Sanford C. Bernstein & Co. Associate Professor of Leadership and Ethics at Columbia Business School. He studies the psychological effects of secrecy, the development and formation of trust, and person perception. https://www.spsp.org/news-center/blog/slepian-keeping-secrets
2. Wolk-Wasserman, D. (1986). Suicidal communications of persons attempting suicide and responses of significant others. *Acta Psychiatrica Scandinavica.* 73: 481–499. https://www.qprinstitute.com/uploads/QPR%20Theory%20Paper.pdf
3. Ibid.
4. Hawton, K. (2007). Restricting access to methods of suicide. *Crisis* 28(S1): 4–9.
5. Centers for Disease Control and Prevention, National Center for Injury Prevention and Control. (2020). *Web-based Injury Statistics Query and Reporting System (WISQARS)* (Fatal Injury Reports, 1999–2018, for National, Regional, and States). Available at www.cdc.gov/injury/wisqars. Accessed June 10, 2020.
6. https://www.ccsme.org/wp-content/uploads/2017/01/Suicide-Proofing-Your-Home-Brochure-English.pdf
7. Stanley, B., and Brown, G. K. (2012). Safety planning intervention: a brief intervention to mitigate suicide risk. *Cognitive and Behavioral Practice* 19(2): 256–264.
8. Wortzel, H. S., Matarazzo, B., & Homaifar, B. (2013). A model for therapeutic risk management of the suicidal patient. *Journal of Psychiatric Practice* 19(4): 323–326.
9. Melia, R., Francis, K., Hickey, E., Bogue, J., Duggan, J., O'Sullivan, M., and Young, K. (2020). Mobile Health Technology Interventions for Suicide Prevention: Systematic Review. *JMIR MHealth and UHealth* 8(1), e12516.

Chapter 8
Reintegrating a Student into School After a Suicide Attempt or Family Loss

"When we dig into the data, the truth is that the vast majority of people who struggle with feeling suicidal do not go on to die by suicide—that recovery and resiliency, connection and hope are not only possible, they're probable. We really want to tell those stories of strength and recovery and resiliency and help normalize those pathways towards knowing we can get through it, and we can get better."

Scott LoMurray (He/Him/His), Executive Director, Sources of Strength

Students who have survived a suicide attempt may feel dismayed, ashamed, exhausted, overwhelmed, and embarrassed. Many kids simply cannot make sense of what drove them to attempt in the first place. They often want to get out of the treatment center but dread the awkwardness of the return to home and school. The student might wonder how they are going to respond to why they were out for a week or more, or if they will face a wall silence if no one asks and people act like nothing happened. Add to all that the overwhelming amount of missed work, which generates a healthy dose of folder fear—the tsunami of makeup work plus the due dates of real-time assignments. One teen suicide attempt survivor described the combination of stressors that led to her suicide attempt:

"I had just gotten back into school, and everything was so stressful and there's so much work. I was really anxious about everything. I was so behind in everything. It was all so much for me, it just pushed me over the edge."

Consider, too, that some teens get little support at home. The teen might be pressured by parents about missed assignments or dropping grades, yelled at because the family was shamed by the act, or victim of the family's conflicting emotions that reinforce the teen's own feelings of unworthiness. Within that family, there may be underlying cultural issues or gender identity conflicts, denial that it ever happened, family members with substance misuse problems, and other related trauma. They may engage in scapegoating, shifting all the blame onto the school.

Then there are the parents experiencing emotional chaos following the near-death experience of their child who may go into hyperdrive protection mode, which creates an atmosphere of high anxiety. Petrified of losing their child to suicide, these parents may overreact, hovering over the adolescent, camping out beside them in sleeping bags on suicide watch, making them feel smothered, fragile, and helpless. All of this can complicate the reentry, making it crucial that school feel like a safe space.

Appropriate management of the reentry process following an attempt is an essential part of suicide prevention. So here we will address strategies for minimizing the risk, which is higher following a stay in the hospital.[1] And while you might not be the one spearheading this process, it's good to know the basic guidelines and what role you will play since the child will be in your class, although you may not be aware of where they were. This process is likely to vary in every state and school district, and although necessary for the continuity of care, it can be complicated to obtain appropriate information in order to assist the student. In these cases, the school counselor should pursue securing a signed release from parents or guardians to communicate with the discharge team, which can be the hospital or the student's therapist.

Tip

Use these excellent guides on transitioning students back into school:

HEARD *Alliance Toolkit for Mental Health Promotion and Suicide Prevention* pdf, found at heardalliance.org, has some great reentry guidelines and worksheets for school counselors as part of the guide.

Issues and Options Surrounding a Student's Return to School Following a Suicide-related Absence pdf, found at SPRC.org, by Hazelden, creator of Lifelines, gives a three-page overview of the reentry process.

TRANSITION FROM THE HOSPITAL SETTING

If possible, and with permission from the parents, it can be helpful in facilitating the reentry if someone from the school such as the school counselor visits the student in the hospital or at home prior to their return to school,. This provides a bridge back to normalcy, which the student is likely to crave if the school experience has been positive. It's also an opportunity to connect with the family and provide resource information on how they can find support, such as NAMI Family Support Group or a NAMI Family-to-Family Class (NAMI. org) about living with loved ones with mental illness or other resources in the community. Families often think it's just the student's recovery but it's important for them to understand it's theirs, too. Everyone has to adapt, shift, find support, and make changes.

Prior to the student's return, a reentry meeting should be held with the student, parent(s), school nurse, counselor, and any key administrators that are allowed to be in the meeting and have permission. The goal of this meeting should be to create a plan to address expectations for attendance and academics, as well as help-seeking for mental health concerns should they arise in the school setting, and a general discussion with the student about how the school can support their mental health in an ongoing, effective manner. (Reentry is addressed in Chapter 5 in the section "Example Protocol."

"The highest risk is actually after hospitalization for kids, especially with our families and also our school due to the high academic standards. They have so much work they have to make up and they feel totally overwhelmed. So, I try to work with the teachers to make sure to minimize how much work they have to do, to give them a longer extended timeline. We have a post-hospitalization plan in our school where we change the workload. The kids are asked to come to my office every day to do a check-in with me. It may just be like, 'Hey, I'm fine,' or, 'I'm feeling crappy.' It doesn't have to be a therapy session. I like the check-in. I like the eye contact. And just knowing that they are there. And then the other thing that I feel so strongly about is to make sure parents aren't the first people on the safety plan. This is for many reasons, one of which is that our families are just starting to learn what mental health means so we need others more well versed in suicide prevention and mental health to be primary on the safety plan."

Jessica Chock-Goldman, LCSW (She/Her/Hers), Doctoral Candidate,
School Social Worker, Stuyvesant High School in Manhattan, New York

---

Meeting with parents about their child prior to the student's return to school is integral to creating an individualized reentry plan (IRP) and the decisions concerning needed supports and the student's schedule. Educators can help returning students by directly involving them in planning for their return to school. This participation helps the student to regain some sense of control in a stressful situation.

The school counselor should consult with the student to discuss what support they feel is needed to make a more successful transition. What would that student like to say to friends and peers about what happened? By meeting with the student prior to their return, the counselor can help the student plan what to say and offer examples of what people in similar situations have said in the past, alleviating some of the student's stress.

It helps to understand the risk factors that make this young person more or less likely to consider or attempt suicide and the protective factors that will reduce the risk. This should guide what kind of supports are needed to bolster the protective factors of that student and how to engage the teachers, while maintaining confidentiality in that process.

Students Identify Their "Trusted Adult"

Who are trusted adults in your school?

- "Teacher [I'm] close with, a counselor, maybe a dean."
- "Teacher who's had an impact on me."
- "Would go to a coach."
- "Had something happen in my family, kept it to myself, teacher noticed something was wrong, 'poured everything out,' I trusted him."
- "Go to people who I spend the most time with."

Source: Comments from several teens during SOS Signs of Suicide Youth Focus Group for reviewing new video content.

Key Aspects of Reentry Meeting

Often after a student has been in a psychiatric hospital, they feel stripped of their freedom and treated like a young child. That treatment might extend to their home situation, too. Finding the balance between providing support and giving some space and freedom is challenging but important.

- When possible and advisable, parents should be involved in the reentry process from the beginning. This includes signing release of information forms for the school counselor to speak with the student's outside clinician and review their safety plan.

- Classroom teachers do need to know whether the student is on a full or partial study load and be updated on the student's progress in general. They do not need clinical information or a detailed history. Discussion of the case among personnel directly involved in supporting the student should be specifically related to the student's treatment and support needs, and discussion of the student among other staff should be strictly on a "need to know" basis (i.e. information directly related to what staff has to know in order to work with the student). Having a plan will provide a sense of consistency and stability for all parties and have a positive impact on the student's ability to cope.[2]

- Students need the freedom to express the range of emotions that are experienced when integrating back into the school community and must have a protocol in place of a supervised area where they can go in the event that they are feeling too distressed to be in class. Like Jessica mentioned in her comment, she had students just do a daily check-in. She wanted to be able to put her eyes on the student. In Chapter 6, Mike Riekhof mentioned that his nonprofit had funded a Stress-Free room—a supervised safe place to go for youth to get away from daily stresses.

- Teachers must know and understand the protocols put in place to support the student and ensure their safety. At the same time, teachers must be mindful of the student's confidentiality and honor their privacy.

Peer Connections and Support

At some boarding schools, particularly therapeutic boarding schools, when students return from a hospital stay at a psychiatric facility, they are connected with another student. This is sometimes called "shadowing" and it's similar to how medical schools pair experienced physicians with medical students. In short, it's pairing a person with a buddy to help them transition more smoothly and feel supported. Those asked to shadow are caring and empathetic young people who've found stability after their own crisis to provide peer support. Alternatives or additional support could include a school-based support group, peer helpers program, or a friend. If the culture at the school has been diffi-cult, school staff and parents might decide to arrange for a transfer to another school if recommended.

RETURNING TO SCHOOL AFTER SUICIDE LOSS

> ## Tip
>
> *Children, Teens and Suicide Loss* cowritten by the Dougy Center, the National Center for Grieving Children and Families, in partnership with the American Foundation of Suicide Prevention (AFSP). This is available as a book you can purchase online for a few dollars, at your local chapter of AFSP, or as a free downloadable pdf online.
>
> This is an excellent tool and one of the best and most concise guides to give to a family who has suffered a suicide loss. It offers easy-to-read tips for parents on what to say, transitioning back to school, and how to manage the loss with their children of all ages. Find it at Dougy.org, AFSP.org, or call your local AFSP chapter.

Teens who lose a parent or sibling to suicide struggle with how the death changes their identity, and how they think of themselves and their family. They are now "that kid whose brother killed himself" or "the kid whose mother died by suicide," which is a difficult storyline to incorporate into one's autobiogra-phy. A loss by suicide often challenges a teen's assumptions about life and how the world works. Many report realizing, for the first time, that life is not pre-dictable or fair.[3] In a school paper, 14-year-old New Jersey middle school stu-dent Kiernan Gallagher described how she felt going back to school after her father's death by suicide:

"I didn't return to school for about three weeks and returning was like being held underwater. When my dad first passed away, I didn't want the sun to rise. I didn't want my favorite song to play. I didn't want to look at the stars—I didn't even want to eat. I didn't want to do anything because I lost my dad, my hero, my best friend, and so much more all in one. So going into school—a place which feels like a prison—was not fun. Upon walking in school, I genuinely believed I was going to be okay. I wouldn't shed tears, I would answer questions strongly, I would get my work done. I thought people would be there for me: I would have people to talk to.

I was entirely wrong. I sobbed, couldn't stay in class, and when people asked questions, I only had the strength to answer some. Everyone's faces were turned towards me but would turn away the moment I looked back in their direction. I didn't have many people to talk to other than some adults who were at least able to admit they had no words.

My day of return felt like everything was in slow motion. Opening my locker and seeing a handprint of heat left behind because my body temperature was spiking. Tears welling up forever, but not letting them fall until my sight was blocked. Imagine how things will be for me now from here on out at school; although I can lock the emotions up, sometimes, they can't be hidden.

People may see me laughing, smiling, and being 'happy,' but what you see isn't all there. You can see me laughing, smiling, carrying on conversations. . . . But you can't see the tears I've held back; the monstrous tears that claw at me and take over me. You can't see my brokenness, my heartache, the things I cover up, the things I never share, my regrets. When people fill in the blanks with their own ignorant stories, they bury him and our family over and over again. You can't see how much I wish my dad was here, using the mop as a microphone to sing as he made all of us help him clean the house. Although you can't see it, it's there. I promise.

The night my dad passed away—September 25, 2019—and all the memories and conversations before it play over and over again in my head, like a broken record. I now lack focus at school, and in general, get lost in my thoughts. Oftentimes, people will tell me they don't want to bring it up because they don't want to remind me about it. Trust me when I say I haven't forgotten; and that I'm not going to. There is a part of me that exists only in that moment, when an officer said, 'Sean has died.' I will never forget the police sirens, the ambulance sirens, my mom's screams, not being allowed at my house, the goodbye that I didn't know was goodbye. . . . There is so much I will never forget about my dad's death; it is a scar as permanent as a tattoo. But, I will also never forget how great of a person my dad was."

Excerpt from "My father died by suicide four months ago" by Kiernan Gallagher, 14, written for a school project and then submitted and published on the blog Emotionally Naked. Reprinted here with permission from Kiernan and her mother, Dawn.

Bereaved Teens and Preteens

Friends and family of a bereaved teenager struggle with:

- **Whether to talk about the person who died or mention the cause of death.** Loved ones think they are reminding the person of their loss or might make it worse, although the bereaved never forget.

- **Listening with empathy.** Friends and family are frustrated that they can't fix the pain or make things better and try to say something upbeat when all they need to do is listen and be there.

- **Sitting with someone in their pain.** Sometimes a movie and the company of friends and family is enough, but loved ones aren't sure of that. They feel nothing they do is enough.

- **Being uncomfortable.** A loss by suicide is overwhelming to everyone, including friends, family, and loved ones. Sitting with a bereaved teen feels awkward and uncomfortable and the fear of saying the wrong thing is paralyzing. There is temptation to whisper the cause of death, which is something that doesn't happen with other causes of death.

While losing a close loved one to any cause of death is difficult, losing one to suicide carries with it some additional confusion, secrecy, and shame. If it's a parent who died, the child may have lost the center of their universe, the one person they thought would always be there for them. Sometimes a child feels at fault, wonders why their love wasn't enough, or that their parent didn't love them enough to stick around. The most distinguishing and difficult aspect of a suicide loss compared with other causes of death is the "perceived intentionality" of the death, and the related "perceived responsibility" for the death. Survivors as well as others perceive suicide as a choice when it's more like the person was "driven" to a death by suicide and it wasn't necessarily an act over which the deceased had control at that moment.[4] Although suicide is something of a trance-like episode of someone who wants to end excruciating pain, that journey through the "coulda, woulda, shouldas" for survivors can be unbearable. The fact that suicide is preventable makes it even more difficult after a loved one ends their life. The bereaved teen may worry others will die or that their grief is less important than their parent's. If it's a sibling the child might be also overwhelmed by the parent's grief, or feel responsible for "looking strong" at home so as not to upset their parents or have them worry about them. They can also suffer survivor guilt for being the one still alive or responsible for carrying an additional burden of their parent's hopes and dreams.

Upon returning to school, the stigma around this loss leaves friends speechless and the young person feeling more isolated, making the process especially stressful. Peers might ask questions, or go silent. They may ask questions that are disrespectful or hurtful. Grief this monumental can't be fixed. And being a child from a family who has suffered a suicide death puts that child at risk for suicide, substance misuse, self-harm, and more. How this transition is handled could be pivotal to preventing those outcomes even years or decades later.

In an effort to make the transition a little easier, see Chapter 12, Worksheet 8, Managing a Loss by Suicide for Middle and High School Students, as well as one that offers guidance to help you plan for the student's return, Worksheet 7, How Educators can Help Youth Bereaved by Suicide.

First, it helps if one teacher, school counselor, school nurse, or other staff representative has a conversation with the student to express condolences and share the guide *Children, Teens and Suicide Loss* from AFSP and the Dougy Center (AFSP.org and Dougy.org) with the parents, bookmarking the section about returning to school. You can also share the worksheet to help guide a conversation and encourage practicing how to respond to the question "What happened?" or "How did your parent/sibling die?" It's recommended that two people from the school visit: the school counselor or principal, and a teacher or coach the student knows. The presence of a someone they know, usually a teacher or coach, creates a relationship bridge from the student to the counselor if they don't already know each other.

What Does the Teen Want to Say?

Regardless of whether the student chooses to share at school or isn't ready to do so, educators and parents can help them formulate answers and practice what to say, which will alleviate stress. However, the parent might not be up to it. Given social media and digital devices, keeping the cause of death secret is rarely possible because word has likely traveled and peers are already aware. There may be an investigation or delay in the coroner's report but regardless, the worksheet will help a student who has suffered an important loss.

Here are examples of how to answer the question "What happened?" or "How did your dad/brother/sister/mom die?"

- "My mom ended her life."
- "My brother took his life."
- "Daddy died from depression."
- "My dad killed himself."
- "My sister died last week and that is all I want to say right now."
- "I really don't want to talk about it."
- "We don't know yet."[5]

Although there is no wrong answer, the child should avoid graphic descriptions of the death, the method, or use the phrase "committed suicide" at school. The response is fluid, meaning how one answers can change based on who has asked, where the bereaved student is, or the mood the student is in.

Given the awkwardness and dread the bereaved student feels, and the fear and confusion other students also feel in response to a loss so great, having a close friend meet and go over what that student wants or doesn't want to talk about and planning the return to school is helpful. This would be a peer ambassador who is supported and coached by a school counselor or social worker.

Does the student want a friend or friends to walk in with that first day back? That first week back? Are they OK with people asking about the person they lost? What would they like to talk about and what would they rather not talk about right now? The student ambassador can use Worksheet 8: Managing a Loss by Suicide for Middle and High School Students (see Chapter 12). The bereaved teen is likely to be in shock and feel confused, but by presenting this early enough before their return, they'll have time to process and think about the answers.

There should be a process that the bereaved student comes by once a day and eventually once a week to check in and let the designated teacher or school counselor know how things are going. A student ambassador should be in daily contact with the bereaved student, much like an old-fashioned buddy system, and also follow a schedule to check in with the adult advocate. Overall, this creates a system of support for the bereaved student.

If schools can make returning to school after a loss by suicide more bearable to students, this benefits everyone involved and fosters a culture of connection, caring, and support. Kiernan's heartfelt narrative about her back-to-school experience after her father's death by suicide could have been easier. It's a credit to her own strength as well as her mother's that she was able to express herself so eloquently in her writing and use that as an outlet to manage her grief. Reading a book about the subject of student suicide shouldn't be without rewards and stories of perseverance, so we'll share with you what Kiernan said at graduation to all of her classmates:

"As co-president of Ocean Township Intermediate School's student council in 2020, I delivered a graduation speech. I mentioned how the year presented challenges for everyone, and closed with a quote from my father: 'Do good things, I know you will.' My dad always expected me to work hard and, quite literally, do good things, so my moment at graduation was one I knew he was proud of. Not only was he proud of me as he watched over, but I was proud of myself because I was able to push through everything and be there to deliver a speech I did amazing on."

Kiernan Gallagher, 14, Middle School Student, Ocean, New Jersey.
Reprinted with permission from Kiernan and her mother, Dawn.

NOTES

1. Hunt, I. M., Kapur, N., Webb, R., et al. (2009). Suicide in recently discharged psychiatric patients: A case-control study. *Psychological Medicine.* 39(3): 443–449. doi:10.1017/S0033291708003644. Knesper, D. J. (2011). Continuity of Care for Suicide Prevention and Research: Suicide Attempts and Suicide Deaths Subsequent to Discharge from the Emergency Department or Psychiatry Inpatient Unit. https://www.sprc.org/sites/default/files/migrate/library/continuityofcare.pdf.
2. HEARD Alliance Toolkit for Mental Health Promotion and Suicide Prevention. heardalliance.org
3. Returning to School After a Suicide Loss: For Teens, by Dr. Pamela Gabbay, childhood bereavement consultant. AFSP.org
4. Jordan J. R. (2020). Lessons learned: Forty years of clinical work with suicide loss survivors. *Frontiers in Psychology* 11, 766. https://doi.org/10.3389/fpsyg.2020.00766
5. Children, Teens and Suicide Loss, co-written by the Dougy Center, the National Center for Grieving Children and Families, in partnership with the American Foundation of Suicide Prevention (AFSP). Dougy.org

Chapter 9
Postvention: After a Student or Teacher Suicide

"When we announced this young lady's death, you could see in the faces of her friends; they just knew that it had been a suicide. What happened in the hours that followed is that students started writing on sticky notes and posting them all over the school. The notes said things like 'You're not alone,' 'You are loved,' 'Reach out if you're struggling.' And suddenly within a couple of days, the whole school was just plastered with these sticky notes. It was kind of amazing. It all came from the kids; it was their way of supporting one another."

Jennifer Hamilton (She/Her/Hers), School Psychologist, Director of Psychology and Counseling at Noble and Greenough, Independent School, Dedham, Massachusetts

Because grief increases risk for suicide, particularly in an adolescent population, having an evidence-based postvention guide such as *After a School Suicide: A Toolkit for Schools* on hand is critical and is available as a free download.[1] It has scripts that can be used for announcements or emails and offers step-by-step guidance on how a school moves forward after a suicide loss, from handling media attention to hosting a parent meeting. In addition, *Support for Suicidal Individuals on Social and Digital Media* is a toolkit available from SuicidePreventionLifeline.org.

After a school suicide, whether it's a student or faculty member, emotions are high and tangled, the atmosphere confusing and chaotic, which makes managing the crisis difficult. Administrators fear liability, suicide contagion, and negative publicity, in addition to sadness, helplessness, and shock. Counselors feel they failed their job; teachers feel guilty for having missed signs of tragic unhappiness.

For some students who have also struggled, they think, "If they can do it, I should, too. Then all my pain will be gone." Other students blame themselves for having missed signs of a peer who was struggling. How could despair that monumental go unnoticed? And how does the school move forward and what is the right thing to do? The first step is creating a school culture that allows for the conversation about grief and suicide to happen in a thoughtful, sensitive, and empathetic way.

While this chapter is a guide on the follow-up after a suicide event, this is not a one-size-fits-all. For example, if you have a culture that is very sensitive to suicide, you might need specific cultural guidance on what postvention should look like and how to edit the guidelines to suit that population. If you serve a population where traditions on grief vary, ask the family about their cultures and traditions around grief.

Postvention Goals

- Reduce the likelihood of contagion by identifying other kids at risk
- Stabilize the environment: help teachers get back to their job of teaching and students back to their job of learning
- Facilitate healthy grieving

Source: Jim McCauley, Riverside Trauma Center, Needham Heights, Massachusetts.

"A suicide death is also a traumatic event. And that always complicates things for everyone because you're dealing with both grief and trauma. In schools, that's dicey because you're trying to figure out how to support kids who have lost a good friend, and at the same time you're trying to support other kids that may have a trauma history of their own. They may have heard some gruesome stories about how the student died, or they have been hospitalized for suicidal behaviors and now they're all stirred up and thinking about their own life and what's going to happen to them. And you know, 'If this worked for this student then maybe it'll work for me.' So that contagion you hear people talk about which is about 2–5% of kids in that 15- to 24-year-old age group is what we always worry about. So when I go into a school, we're trying to reduce the likelihood of contagion, and we're trying to stabilize the environment—get teachers back to their job of teaching and kids back to their job of learning, and then also trying to find a way to facilitate healthy grieving."

Jim McCauley (He/Him/His), LICSW, Co-Founder and Associate Director of Riverside Trauma Center, Needham Heights, Massachusetts

Well-thought-out postvention is prevention. Put simply, leaders who can effectively respond to loss survivors can lessen the likelihood of future suicides.

Resources for Native Americans

For Native Americans, educators can reach out to SPRC.org (Suicide Prevention Resource Center) and use the contact form for guidance on postvention for specific tribes since traditions and cultures vary widely.

Source: Shelby Rowe (She/Her/Hers), Co-Chair, Indigenous Peoples Committee, American Association of Suicidology (AAS).

James Biela, LCSW, is an Itinerant School Social Worker whose population is Alaskan native students, and the potential for contagion is high in his state. To get to the village schools in Alaska, he travels by bush plane, sleeps in the school on a cot, cooks there, and meets with students in the school store or sometimes in a maintenance closet. When he went out to Toksook Bay, Alaska, he noted a lot of cases of complicated grief because so many village members were dealing with suicide, after suicide, after suicide. This can and has triggered a high rate of contagion among young people. So a suicide up in Chevak can have an effect in Bethel, which is 115 miles away. He and his team get to know who the family members are and how they are all connected. To prevent copycat suicides after a death by suicide, he immediately reaches out to trusted adults in the village like an old-fashioned phone tree so they can intervene and support family members and friends who could be at risk. In school districts, there is a similar protocol. If your school has suffered a student suicide, then other schools in that district should be notified right away because it can affect the emotional wellness of students in those connected schools, and educators need to be on alert.

Initially, trauma experts advise reaching out to gather people together that have had the same experience—that close set of friends—and support them separately. The next focus is to look at every class that student attended and reach out there too, offering support and at least having a conversation in those classrooms. According to experts at Riverside Trauma Center, a large school with 1500–2000 kids might have anywhere from 5% to 10% of the kids who need support either because they're grieving or because they're vulnerable.

Although there is always a lot of focus and fear regarding contagion, Jim McCauley points out that his team is also very concerned about cohorts. So it's not just that two- to four-week period after that is a concern; it's that class of students as they move through their school years that may be vulnerable to suicide at some point in the near future.

"There was a local school that had a sophomore girl who died by suicide. When they were seniors, two kids from that same [sophomore] class died by suicide. Then [those kids] all went off to college and there were four more [from that class who died by suicide]. There were a total of seven deaths from that class before they finished college. So it's that cohort experience that also worries us."

Jim McCauley (He/Him/His), LICSW, Co-Founder and Associate
Director of Riverside Trauma Center, Needham Heights, Massachusetts

---

Why is it that kids from the same class of the student who died by suicide will, years later, take their own life? What makes them a higher risk? Nobody knows exactly what the dynamic is that leads to these protracted tragedies, but Jim thinks it could be that the students exposed to it see it as another tool in their toolbox for solving pain. It's possible that there are simply more kids in a single class who are more susceptible to suicide in the first place, those who've had moments where they've thought they couldn't go on, and these are the kids who, years later, see suicide as an option when life gets rough.

From studies, we know talking about suicide doesn't give teens the idea to kill themselves. And experiencing an actual suicide at a school may not either, but rather makes it more of a viable option that they could act on years later. Most people who attempt suicide and survive tell us they'd had thoughts for months and even years, as early as five to eight years old.

While the potential suicide of close friends is a valid concern, those who are experienced in the aftermath of a suicide feel the danger is on the next outer layer, those kids who are deeply empathetic who knew the person who died but maybe not all that well.

"In the aftermath of three deaths, in a local school community there were a lot of kids who were seen by the emergency services team but about 20 of the 25 students seen did not know the student who died well if at all. And they were almost overly empathic about wondering what it was that the student was experiencing in those last final hours of his life. 'I wonder where they are now?' 'Where did they end up?' 'Was anybody helping them?' 'They must have been in so much pain,' and just getting into sort of existential issues about what happened to the student. They were not close friends and that's the other thing that we always find, too, is that we are not talking about the close inner circle of friends of the student who died, we're talking about sort of that next outer layer, kids that may have been in the class with them when they were freshmen. Maybe they were on the baseball team together. But that next outer circle of kids, I think is sort of what's also worrisome to us. It's just my speculation but I think this issue of these sort of super empathic kids—that have been struggling themselves for a long time. They're vulnerable."

Jim McCauley (He/Him/His), LICSW, Co-Founder and Associate Director of Riverside Trauma Center, Needham Heights, Massachusetts

---

As harsh as it may sound, if it does happen, working to make it a teachable moment is what will help prevent future suicides. Because if your school community has not experienced any student deaths for a decade and then there is a suicide, parents will come to your mental health educational presentations and assemblies. Prior to that, most of those events attract 20 parents out of a 1,000-plus student population. We want to note here that in most cases there should be a delay before suicide prevention education is introduced after a suicide.

Tip

A Sample Agenda for Parent Meeting is a framework included in the free pdf download **After a Suicide: A Toolkit for Schools.**

This guide suggests, in an effort to contain strong emotions, that the parent meeting should ideally be broken into two parts. During the first part, presented by school staff, the focus should be on dissemination of general information to parents, without opening the meeting to discussion. During the second part, have parents meet in small groups with trained crisis counselors for questions and discussion.

Source: After a Suicide: A Toolkit for Schools, 2nd ed., written in 2018 by the American Foundation for Suicide Prevention (AFSP) and the Suicide Prevention Resource Center (SPRC), Education Development Center (EDC).

The following is a brief outline to offer an overall view of how postvention events should unfold. These steps might need to happen simultaneously or be adjusted. When a death occurs, activate the school's crisis team and plan to address the loss. Identify and coordinate with other schools that can be impacted.[2,3]

1. First, verify the information from family members, guardian, or local authorities.

2. Next, determine what information the family is willing to have disclosed (or what information has already been released publicly from a reliable

source). See the script in this chapter and in Chapter 12, Worksheet 14: Script for Asking Parents' Permission to Disclose a Suicide Death.

3. Review/download "Reporting on Suicide" from ReportingonSuicide. org so that any media releases have the right language, tone, and listed resources.

4. Once the death has been verified, meet with advisory groups if appropriate, and notify the school staff and students.

5. Consult with the family about memorials. The person designated as the liaison with the family needs to be prepared to explain the memorialization policy to the family while respecting their wishes as well as the grieving traditions associated with their culture and religion.

6. Solicit ideas to memorialize the deceased in positive ways that celebrate life, and do not put other students at risk or contribute to the emotional crisis. Know the sensitivities for your school population and consult with the family before implementing any of the following ideas:

    • Invite students to write personal and lasting remembrances in a memory book or on index cards located in the counseling office, which will ultimately be given to the family. This can include a story or a memory of that student.

    • Encourage students to engage in service projects, such as organizing a community service day, sponsoring behavioral health awareness programs, or becoming involved in a peer counseling program.

    • Invite students to make donations to the library or to a scholarship fund in memory of the deceased.

    • Do a volunteer day that reflects the deceased loved one's personality. For example, if the person loved dogs, dedicate a Saturday or after-school activity to supporting the cause by having an adoption event. Or have therapy dogs come into the school.

7. Be prepared to address the unique aspects of a suicide death:

    • Use the opportunity to educate students, families, and the community about a death by suicide. (Not suicide prevention education but more suicide grief education. Suicide prevention education should happen later.)

    • Monitor social media sites for signs of risk to other students.

    • Emphasize events that celebrate life and community.

COMMUNICATION WITH THE IMPACTED FAMILY

While the first item on this guidelines list says, "Verify the information from family members, guardian, or local authorities," this step involves more than a confirmation of a death. Jim McCauley of Riverside Trauma Center says there should be an empathetic response from the school to the family as soon as they know and without delay to express condolences. The representatives who meet with parent(s) or guardian(s) could be faced with great despair or with anger and accusations, so sending someone who is compassionate but also armed with strategies to deescalate the latter helps. The purpose of the visit is to express condolences for a devastating loss, find out how the school can support the family, and to obtain permission to disclose the cause of death. No matter how it goes, and it's often without fiery incidents, it could be important later for the school to be able to say they did reach out to express their sympathies, and emotions were still too raw for meaningful conversation at that time. For the safety of other students, barring any particular specific cultural modifications, the delegates from the school should seek parental permission to release the cause of death.

"Parents don't have to disclose that it's a suicide death. But there are reasons it's really valuable to let the school community know that a student died by suicide so that we can directly address this issue when we're working with a large group of grieving students and identify other kids who might be at risk, therefore preventing more teen suicides."

Jonathan B Singer, PhD, LCSW (He/Him/His), President, American Association of Suicidology, author of Suicide in Schools: A Practitioner's Guide to Multi-level Prevention, Assessment, Intervention, and Postvention

---

When dealing with this kind of crisis, the school representatives who will be making the home visit should find out more about the family so they know how to go about obtaining permission to disclose the cause of death once it is known. What has been the relationship between the school and this family? What are their demographics? What kind of cultural, religious, or ethnic traditions might this family have? Are there other members of the family at area schools and, if so, which ones?

Visitation: Postvention Recommendations

- Two people should visit the family of the child lost to suicide immediately after getting the news and at least one of them should be a school administrator, who goes with someone the family knows like a favorite teacher or coach. (The administrator should be the principal or assistant superintendent, not the superintendent, because you want to be able to say that you need to take any requests back for approval in the case of a request that is hard to fulfill.) While it is unusual for school administrators to visit the home right after hearing about a student's death, it's a mistake not to. School administrators may get advice from lawyers that the family may sue. But not visiting immediately only increases animosity (if there is any). Having a familiar friendly face like the favorite teacher or coach will help make the visit less awkward and more meaningful.

- Sometimes parents have been fighting for years with schools about a better education plan (504 or IEP, etc.). There may have been a history of bullying complaints or some other issue and it is still recommended that this admin/teacher team visit the family. You may get the door slammed in your face but the family won't be able to tell the press they "never heard from the school" if it comes to that.

- Note that sometimes the family will make difficult requests of the school. "We want to hold the funeral in the school auditorium," or "We would like to build a memorial in front of the school," and so on, so the administrators can always say they don't have that authority and will have to take the request back to the superintendent or school committee. This is why the superintendent does *not* go and why the school should have a policy for commemoration because it gives you a framework to refer to and allows for more consistent memorialization.

Thank you to Jim McCauley, LICSW, Riverside Trauma Center,
the source of these guidelines.

———————————

So how does someone go in and ask for permission to disclose the cause of death of a child who just died by suicide? Isn't that awkward? Just like there is no one-size-fits-all for postvention, there is no one perfect script. There would most certainly be back-and-forth conversation when at the home and it is unlikely to be as linear as this script. However, the template below (also included in Chapter 12 as Worksheet 14: Script for Asking Parents' Permission to Disclose a Suicide Death) gives you something to work with. It's designed for an in-person visit, and not a letter or email. If you can't visit, then certainly a telephone call is the next best thing.

"I am deeply sorry to hear about your daughter's death. Please know that the school community is mourning with you and that includes me. Is there anything we can do to help right now? Any resources you need?

I know this is a difficult topic and I have to ask you an important question. We have heard this was a suicide. If that's true, and because we don't want other teens to see suicide as a solution, would you be willing to grant us permission to disclose the cause of death with the goal of preventing further loss of life? We ask this because we know that sensitive, respectful conversation and education on the subject encourages other students who are struggling with thoughts of suicide to ask for help. Keeping silent, on the other hand, means those students are less likely to come forward and are at heightened risk. As you might imagine, any time a teenager passes away prematurely, his or her peers inquire about the cause of death. With a family's permission, we would typically share that information with the community, and we don't want to treat your daughter's death differently. Silence implies shame and we want to make sure that students understand that there is no shame in mental health challenges. Suicide is a serious public health threat to our young people and we want to do all that we can to support those who are struggling in getting the help they need and deserve. Thank you so much for your openness. Please know that we will continue to be here to support your family in the weeks and months to come and beyond."

Thank you to Jennifer Hamilton, School Psychologist at Noble and Greenough School, and Jim McCauley, LICSW, from Riverside Trauma Center for feedback and editing of this script.

After a Suicide Death: Sample Email

Example of written communication to the school community and parents in the event of a suspected suicide when the cause of death is not yet obtained or disclosed.

I am so sorry to tell you all that one of our students, [NAME], has died. The cause of death has not yet been determined.

We are aware that there has been some talk that this might have been a suicide death. Rumors may begin to come out, but please don't spread them. They may turn out to be untrue and can be deeply hurtful and unfair to [NAME] and [HIS/HER/THEIR] family and friends. I'm going to do my best to give you the most accurate information as soon as I know it.

Since the subject has been raised, I do want to take this chance to remind you that suicide, when it does occur, is very complicated. No one single thing causes it. But in many cases, a mental health condition is part of it, and these conditions are treatable. It's really important if you're not feeling well in any way to reach out for help. Suicide does not have to be the only option.

Each of us will react to [NAME]'s death in our own way, and we need to be respectful of each other. Right now, I'm feeling very sad, and many of you may feel sad too. Others may feel anger or confusion. It's okay to feel whatever emotions you might be feeling. Some of us may have known [NAME] well, and some of us may not. But either way, we may have strong feelings. You might find it difficult to concentrate on schoolwork for a little while. On the other hand, you might find that focusing on school helps take your mind off what has happened. Either is okay.

I want you to know that your teachers and I are here for you. We also have counselors here to help us all understand what happened. If you'd like to talk to one of them, just let me or one of your teachers know, or you can seek out the counselors in [NOTE SPECIFIC LOCATION] between classes or during your lunch. We are all here for you. We are all in this together, and the school staff will do whatever we can to help you get through this.

Source: American Foundation for Suicide Prevention (AFSP) and the Suicide Prevention Resource Center (SPRC), Education Development Center (EDC). (2018). *After a Suicide: A Toolkit for Schools,* 2nd ed.

But what if the parent doesn't offer permission?

When suicide is not mentioned, it doesn't mean all efforts cease. For one, students are likely to ask their teachers, or rather accuse them and the school of not being open or honest about what happened.

"[When cause of death is not disclosed], the kids will say 'The school is not being honest with us about what happened, [or] 'The school is lying to us,' and we say, 'The school has been in touch with the parents and the parents are not acknowledging how their son died. And so, we have to respect their wishes.' We tell the superintendent, and the principal, 'You can't put anything in writing about how the student died, but we can certainly have those conversations in the classroom.' We can say, 'So the parents are not saying how their son died. But you know what you have heard, and what you think and how does that change your reaction if you think that he died by suicide?' So you could still have that conversation."

Jim McCauley (He/Him/His), LICSW, Co-Founder and Associate Director of Riverside Trauma Center, Needham Heights, Massachusetts

The conversation right after a suicide centers more around connection, mental health, supporting students, identifying other students at risk, and coping strategies for grief. While the topic of suicide is discussed, it's not the time for an exhaustive conversation on warning signs or risk factors, or prevention presentations to students because it can make people feel more guilty. However, it is important that teachers understand the risk factors and protocol because this is the time when more students are at risk and we need those observing eyes. While the guidelines in this chapter work for the majority of the schools in the US, and avoiding the subject of suicide can be detrimental, there are schools with more concentrated ethnic populations where postvention will look very different. Nora is a ninth-grade dean at an East Coast high school, but prior to her position there she was an administrator at a small school where 99% of the attendees were students of color from a specific immigrant ethnic population. She said they relied on postvention trauma consultants that adapted to the particular needs of that school and student population.

"I think it is important to understand community and the culture of community when a school goes through a loss. Sending a trauma expert who is embedded in the community where the school is located and who is a relational person that students can see themselves in makes all the difference. Earlier in my career I was in an urban public school. Riverside Trauma sent a counselor of color to our school (which was 99% students of color) and there was an immediate level of trust. Our trauma counselor was anti-vigils, anti-commemoration. He was worried about copycat syndrome, particularly in our community. And he was concerned about the glorification of suicide. He emphasized the importance of celebrating life— whether it be an annual softball game or gathering, celebrating the person rather than the event was essential. In this case, commemoration should not revolve around specific dates or events, but more about celebrating life."

Nora (She/Her/Hers), Ninth-Grade Dean, East Coast High School

In instances where your school might have a concentration of a specific ethnic group, the *After a Suicide Toolkit* (2nd ed.) recommends finding a "culture broker," someone who can edit postvention guidelines for a specific ethnic population. SPRC.org is also a resource for culture-specific postvention suggestions. A suicide death creates a lot of fear—fear of doing or saying the wrong thing. What it comes down to really is understanding the framework of what is recommended, knowing your population, and having a commemoration policy with culture-specific guidelines.

Some schools have been or may be advised by lawyers not to visit or reach out to the family, which would be a huge error because nothing angers shattered parents more than blackout silence after their child's suicide. That tactic never goes well, and with a suicide death a school district's fear of being sued or accused can drive their decision to go quiet. But if a parent's cries or accusations are met with silence, emotions can erupt faster than dry brush catches fire on a hot summer day in California.

Take the case of a young freshman named Phoebe Prince from South Hadley High School who died by suicide on January 14, 2010. The school acted on internal advice not to go out to the family and share sympathies for fear of a lawsuit. The mother and the sister were interviewed on national programs and the child was pictured on the cover of *Newsweek* more than once as the face of a child who was bullied to death and a school who said and did nothing even in the aftermath. It all unfolded when social media was just emerging and schools were distancing themselves from this new media by saying, "What happens online, away from school, is not our problem." The case resulted in the school getting hate mail from places as far as Paris and South Africa and students who went on spring break in Italy had Italian police yelling at them because they were wearing South Hadley sweatshirts. They got so many hate calls that it actually shut down their phone system.

In a landmark case that divided the town, the district attorney charged six students in connection with the bullying Prince endured. The South Hadley superintendent and the high school principal retired the following year; the school committee chair stepped down; and in late 2010, the Prince family settled a lawsuit against the school district for $225,000.[4] In an effort to avoid a lawsuit, they had likely inspired one with their silence.

If a representative from the school does reach out to parents and accusations are made, it's best to hear the parent out and then the school should bring in trauma consultants who specialize in suicide postvention as soon as possible to stabilize the situation so the school is not branded as "uncaring" and others are not further traumatized by negative events following the suicide. Trauma consultants are not lawyers or spin doctors for the media. Their focus is to provide guidance in a crisis for the health and well-being of a grieving school community by helping manage the aftershocks of a tragedy to prevent further trauma and loss of life. No matter what population you serve, all postvention efforts should lead with empathy because a death by suicide is a devastating loss to a family and school community.

PROTOCOL AND MAINTAINING STRUCTURE

After a suicide is also a time when the school administration would rely on the crisis protocol of who does what (e.g. PREPaRE). And if your school doesn't have one, the *After a Suicide: A Toolkit for Schools* (2nd ed.) does offer a framework. It's always easier to manage a crisis with a structure in place than to try and improvise in the moment when everyone is in shock and thinking brains have taken flight in the wake of emotional chaos. For example, if two different counselors call the parents following the death of a child by suicide with the same goal of expressing condolences and obtaining permission to disclose the cause of death, it makes the school appear insensitive, unprepared, and unable to manage the situation for the health and safety of its students. Besides that, it adds confusion at an already difficult time. Keep in mind that right after a death, you may not have all the answers. For example, the coroner might not have determined the cause of death yet. In some cases, it might be days if there is a police investigation. However, there is always gossip about how it happened and if there is talk of suicide, then it's important to address that.

"On the morning after Paula's* death, an announcement was made by our head of school in our daily assembly. Everybody heard the same information first thing in the morning. We then broke into advisories and gave teachers and advisors some talking points so that they felt equipped to have these difficult conversations in small, familiar groups. We know that in challenging times, students want to connect with people they know and trust. If your community experiences some kind of trauma or crisis, it is so important to maintain the structure of the day as usual, with the understanding that it will most certainly not be business as usual. So we kept the structure of the regular day but took a few minutes at the start of each class to take the temperature of the kids and to allow them to talk. It was one of the really important things we did. In some cases, the lesson plan for the day just had to be set aside because the students wanted and needed to process together. Paula's death occurred a few weeks before an assessment period, and a lot of kids were saying, 'I can't take my assessments. How can I possibly move forward and do this? I can't concentrate.'

We certainly listened deeply to these concerns, but one of the things we didn't want to perpetuate was the idea that if you can't do something perfectly, you shouldn't even try. That type of black-and-white thinking is never helpful. And so we did not cancel exams. We did not cancel classes. We made it clear to students who were struggling, and to their parents, that we were not expecting them to do their tip-top best. It was just so important that they show up and try to do what they could under these difficult circumstances. . . . And that even if they were unable to do their best right now, that would be OK. We encouraged students who were having a hard time concentrating to reach out to their teachers. We made sure to convey that teachers would be flexible and understanding, which they were. But we did not put out a blanket policy of 'OK, we won't expect you to do anything,' because that would send a message of 'How can kids possibly cope?' By removing all expectations, we would be fragile-izing our students and saying we don't think they can manage when in reality we knew we would move through this painful time by supporting one another. This was the most difficult thing that many of our students (and some of our adults) ever had to manage. It was so hard. But we really wanted to say that we'd get through it together and that however we are doing will be good enough right now."

Jennifer Hamilton (She/Her/Hers), School Psychologist, Director of Psychology and Counseling at Noble and Greenough, Independent School, Dedham, Massachusetts
*Name has been changed to protect privacy.

It might seem that after a death by suicide, given how devastating the loss, classes and any scheduled tests be canceled. The school should instead focus on maintaining its regular schedule, structure, and routine.[5] That's because each student will connect differently with that student's suicide. Some students and teachers who were close to the deceased will be experiencing more profound grief, and those who had less contact or social involvement with that student will be less impacted.

"There was a day in class where the students didn't want to talk about the young man who ended his life. They had had enough and I respected that. But I had to be honest with them and through teary eyes I told them I was really struggling that day and I wasn't capable right then to do a regular class. The student who died was just one of 13 I had in that particular class that year so we had become close and that empty seat was staring back at me. We did a chemistry lab that day because they talk with each other when they work on lab. That was easier for me to handle than my being up front with all eyes focused on me on a day when my emotions were so raw. I think they needed to see that I was grieving, human and vulnerable."

Science teacher at a large public high school in the western US

While it's not business as usual, it is important to maintain some boundaries and allow students to make choices such as leaving the class or waiting after to talk to a teacher. Being together and connecting is an important part of the grieving process and school is one place, if not the only place, where this can happen consistently over a period of time. After a crisis, many schools often set up "memorial rooms" or "crying rooms" and instruct anyone who's having a hard time go to the room and stay there. If they are not well organized, sparsely staffed, or operated solely by outside counselors who are unfamiliar to the students, this can be detrimental. While these are created with good intentions, post-trauma consultants and school counselors recognize that these are situations in which students can become dysregulated. Because even kids who aren't having a hard time absorb that energy and it becomes chaotic and overall it can have an unsafe feeling. The goal is not to make teachers into grief counselors but simply provide them with the tips on how to be good and willing listeners with grieving students. This helps both students and faculty with their grief.

"You don't have to be a psychologist. You don't have to be an expert. You just have to be willing and able to sit with students in their sadness and discomfort. Not just counselors, but all of the teachers, all of the coaches, every member of the faculty—needs to be ready to listen and to be in that space with kids, because they're going to want to talk with the people they know and trust the most. The most helpful model is to ensure that everyone is getting the same information about the tragedy in the same way; and then to empower faculty, advisors, and coaches with the skills and the confidence to know that they can manage those conversations. And they can. I mean, I think they're wonderful at it."

Jennifer Hamilton (She/Her/Hers), School Psychologist, Director of Psychology and Counseling at Noble and Greenough, Independent School, Dedham, Massachusetts

It also makes sense for administrators and counselors to ask what the teachers want and need while appreciating how exceptionally difficult it is to be the one standing in front of a group of grieving students all day after a crisis.

Teachers provide a vital point of connection in the healing process after a death due to the relationships they have developed with students.

"The county has a system in place where extra counselors and psychologists are on hand to assist, usually posted in the library for students to go as needed. After Reginald's* suicide, one of my best students, they sent a counselor and psychologist directly to my classroom to talk to the whole class. This was well intended but a horrible decision. I was first to address the class and teared up as I gave them the limited information I had and discussed how there was no normal way to feel right then. The kids were not themselves and I could see they were holding back, not sure how to share their pain with strangers present. The counselor and psychologist did their best to address the class and offer their help but you could hear the crickets chirping. I asked the counselor and psychologist to sit in the hall so we could have a moment as a class and that was far more productive due to the relationships I had developed with them year long.

I knew the psychologist well and asked that when my next class met later that day, that the counselor and psychologist begin by greeting the students at the door with me as they entered but remain in the hall at first so I could open with the class more like the family we were without the outsiders, who meant well, but imposed a certain weirdness to the situation."

Mr. Nigro, High School Teacher, World History II and Economics, Chester, Virginia
*Student name has been changed to protect privacy.

Lack of consistency in routines or structure in the day may heighten feelings of being out of control and unable to cope. James Biela points out several important points. One is that the "Quiet Room" for his Indigenous population of Alaskan natives is staffed with people they know and recognize because it's unlikely kids will bond with a stranger. Another point he makes is that kids are *escorted* to the room from their classrooms—not given a hall pass to trot down there by themselves. Jonathan B. Singer, president of the American Association of Suicidology and a consultant to schools on suicide, said it was too often that a kid at risk he was scheduled to meet with would walk in alone to the school office where he was waiting. There is too much risk that a child experiencing suicidal thoughts, trauma, or the despair of grief could take a dangerous detour.

Tammy Ozolins, a middle school teacher, also emphasized that she doesn't even let kids go alone to the nurse but always has someone escort them. "Because if a kid faints or something, at least there's another student right there that can run to get help." By escorting the student, the school is maintaining standards to keep kids safe as well as providing much needed connection at a vulnerable time for a human being who needs the support, even if no words are spoken. It's a way of saying "you matter" through action. And you can always tell your students that you are instituting that until further notice because everyone needs support in that moment in time or because it makes you feel like everyone is accounted for.

_____

"After a suicide, we set up a Quiet Room where one of the counselors will be in the room. They know who we are and we've spoken with most of these kids and families at some point. The kids who request it are escorted to the quiet room if they need a timeout from the classroom. We emphasize, 'Keep your structure going. Don't relax your structure.' I got chewed out by one teacher big time because he felt sorry for the kids and let them go on YouTube and stuff. And I found out there was a big meltdown in that classroom."

James Biela, LCSW (He/Him/His), Itinerant School Social Worker, Lower Kuskokwim School District, Bethel, Alaska

_____

James Biela works in the largest school district in the state and has a set protocol. Schools in Alaska are within small villages and he serves seven of them. He spends several days per month at one location he reaches by bush plane since there is no road system. Their team has a set protocol after a suicide loss and it starts with having a meeting with the site administrator, also known as the principal. Then they have a meeting with the site administrator and all the teachers before school to offer talking points. They visit the family, take food, and eat, with the deceased body that has been returned after embalming and laid out on the floor as per their custom. Since contagion in Alaskan Indigenous communities is high, he communicates with elders in other villages, most often by CB radio, after a student suicide. For a public school in the lower 48 states, that means communicating with nearby schools in the system because the risk of copycat suicides isn't just contained in the walls of where the student attended. James and his staff know which kids are at risk, the relatives of the child who died, and the kids who are most likely to be triggered. There is a protocol of reaching out to touch as many relatives of the deceased as possible to take the temperature of affected loved ones to prevent copycat suicides.

When he started in 2004, Alaska was the state ranked first in the nation for suicides, and he began his tenure there right after two students killed themselves. Alaska's rank dropped to number three in 2019 statistics and given his is the largest district, it's likely due to their team's efforts of educating about mental health, suicide, coping skills, and incorporating an annual ritual for grief into the community. This event is held outside school as a community event. James recognized that their area had suffered suicide after suicide, which was creating a community of unbearable despair. He declared that Kuskokwim needed to start healing and it had to be done in a way that included their customs and traditions.

So he sat with the site administrator, the student government, the high school teachers, and some high school kids and told them about International Survivors of Suicide Loss Day, which is hosted by the American Foundation of Suicide Prevention and happens all over the world in November. In this close-knit community of Alaskan villages, this was the only collective event for honoring their deceased and helping with grief. James made the commitment to doing the event culturally and traditionally in the Yupik language and he engaged the help of the students, a process that helped them put their grief into action, which supported their healing process as well as that of the community. The kids created posters by hand because they don't have a printing shop, and passed out these flyers for every household. They had a remembrance wall for that day, which included those who wanted to honor loved ones who died by other causes such as cancer. This event was the only game in town in an area where there is little behavioral health support. Normally, this is a two-hour event. The Yupik event began at noon and went until 4 p.m. They had speakers, including students, and even elders who told their stories of struggle, many of whom revealed they had had thoughts or suicide attempts, and the event ended on a message of hope and healing. Prior to the students and elders speaking, James went over their scripts because he didn't want elders saying that it was a sin, because trying to shame people out of suicide is not effective or respectful.

The event had a huge impact. The first part ended at 4 p.m. At 6 p.m., the group reconvened and sat down on the floor of the gym and had a memorial feast with Yupik food, also known in the lower 48 states as a potluck dinner. The kids served and cleaned up. Then from 7 to 9 p.m. they had traditional dance where the kids wore their formal outfits, called Kuspuk.

The population of Toksook is seven hundred people, and six hundred showed up for the event. Bingo is big in that territory and the town council shut that down, as well as the store. That's how big a deal this was. This is now an annual occurrence that continues to grow in attendance, because they need this healing event. James says, "That's how I got them to start talking about suicide." And that's how he got students involved in the local AFSP chapter, which he founded in the state of Alaska.

"I have one young man, Wilton, who's now a field advocate. He's 21 and my co-chair of the Alaska Chapter of AFSP Field Advocacy Program. He has lost so many relatives by suicide that he's one of the key players now for suicide prevention and other kids want to do it, too, because of his example. Young people listen to young people."

James Biela, LCSW (He/Him/His), Itinerant School Social Worker,
Lower Kuskokwim School District, Bethel, Alaska

While experts do not recommend large memorial events at schools after a student dies, this was an event outside the school that memorialized multiple deaths by suicide, in addition to others who had died. He recognized what his community needed and how different it is from other school communities. One of the most important aspects was how he engaged the students to put their grief into action, and in so doing helped them learn to cope with their own feelings of loss.

EDUCATOR TALKING POINTS WITH STUDENTS AFTER SUICIDE

Figure 9.1 Students may ask a lot of questions about what happens after we die. If you are unsure of a student's motive behind a particular question, comment, or conversation, ask, "What made you think of that?"

Preteens and teens often want to talk about a student who has died, reflecting a natural human desire to remember those we've lost. However, it can be challenging after a suicide for schools to strike a balance between compassionately meeting the needs of grieving students and appropriately memorializing and remembering the student who died.[6] Handling it poorly or ignoring it can bring unwanted media attention, trigger a copycat event, create friction between staff and parents, and threaten educator-student relationships at a fragile time. If the death is treated differently than others in the past, students often feel as if their friend was disregarded and forgotten. One high school student described his feelings about the school's response following a classmate's suicide:

"Following my friend's suicide, we really wanted to talk about it right after. And it was really awkward when it wasn't talked about at all. That didn't help the problem with mental health stigma and I think it just added more. So I think it was counter-productive."

_____

Students will express their grief in different ways. Kids who were less engaged with the student when they were alive might get tired of too much conversation and feel aggravated. Other students might be competitive over who was closest to the victim and argue about who knew the person best or whose grief is the worst. Comparing grief is never helpful and everyone reacts differently to it. Some will be grandiose about memorializing; others will make awkward and inappropriate jokes that might make other students mad, and still others will keep their sadness inside. Shock, anger, sadness, fear, confusion, isolation, guilt, numbness, anger, helplessness, and frustration are all normal emotions.

There will be kids who will plunge further into their own despair and be envious of the person who died because they are struggling, too, and they want to die by suicide because someone else did and all their problems are now gone. And it's these kids who are in a dangerous place and the most vulnerable to copycat suicide. By not talking about suicide after a death, educators run the risk of making students feel like it must be kept a secret and that suicide is not an OK subject to talk about. With some cultural exceptions, this can be invalidating for students, especially those who have been impacted in some way.

The kids who suffer quietly are the ones overlooked and most likely to ghost at a time when everyone else is struggling to simply make it through the day. Contagion is a real phenomenon and the best way to get in front of it is to talk about grief in a sensitive and safe way, publish resources wherever you can, support help-seeking behavior, encourage students to pay attention to their peers, and tell a trusted adult when a friend expresses a wish to die. The focus after a student death from any cause is connection, healing, and healthy coping. Asking students to show grace for where others are in the process and meet them where they are can help stabilize emotions. If they know a friend is struggling with thoughts of suicide, it's not a secret they can hold in confidence and that student needs to tell a trusted adult. This is the time to weave these specific themes into your student discussions and this is the section in which we will give you talking points, followed by some sample scripts for inspiring ideas. The most important part is that teachers be real with students.

What if you cry in front of your class? Your students might not be aware that you walk your dog, eat dinner, and live outside your classroom. And while a teacher wants to avoid losing control and dissolving into racking sobs, getting momentarily choked up is only going to make you look more human and approachable. Students want to talk to those who are genuine and care about them.

_____

> "One year we lost a student as a senior who I taught as a sophomore. When news of his death hit the school, students were in shock. He was a popular star soccer player. I had a colleague call me on my cell because a couple of his closest friends were in his classroom but were falling apart and those students asked him if they could come to my room. I said to send them and I waited in the hall. They lunged into my arms sobbing because they had been a part of my class where we developed a solid, trusting relationship. This is not to say my colleague was less capable of handling the situation. Quite the opposite. He recognized that they were reaching out for an adult whom they felt would understand their pain due to the relationship we had from our time together in class."
>
> _Mr. Nigro, High School Teacher, World History II and Economics, Chester, Virginia_

_____

Talking points here in this chapter empower teachers to lead discussions. And in the case where you might not feel you can, that's the time to ask for support from the school counseling department or a community resource. Be candid with your students, share with them that you are struggling, and that you recognized it, reached out, and asked for classroom support to lead a conversation so you could learn more, too. In that case you are being a role model for help-seeking behavior. Besides that, "I don't know" and "I'll try to find out" are perfectly suitable answers to questions of which you are unsure.

Postvention Talking Tips for Teachers

- **Do listen to students if they want to talk.** It is important for students to feel they can talk with a trusted adult about how they are feeling or what they are experiencing.[7] When students feel they've been heard and have support, they are more likely to share their struggles.

- **Identify students in need of further assessment and support** and act as a partner in discussing options for seeking further help, making students feel you have arrived at a solution together. This can be done by saying. "This is serious. What you say has me concerned. Can we talk to [school counselor's name] to see if additional support would be helpful? Let's walk down there now."

- **Do be empathetic.** Students want to be heard, which you do by demonstrating that you are listening with nonverbal clues, such as facial expression, leaning in, and shaking your head. Don't try to fix but instead ask for more information, "Why do you feel that way?" "What makes you think you are at fault?"

- **Do maintain normal routine as much as possible.** Evidence-informed guides and trauma experts have emphasized the importance of trying to maintain structure even if the lesson plan is not delivered. Teachers need it, as do the students. Having a routine provides some level of certainty and comfort, which is often temporarily lost after a traumatic event.[8] Maintaining routine also helps minimize obsessive discussions by students that can increase their distress and that of other students. Not all students are as deeply affected, depending on how well they knew the deceased.

- **Do guide a discussion about grief and the death if you can be comfortable with the uncomfortable.** If your students seem distracted and consumed by the topic of how the student died and what it means, it may be appropriate to facilitate a class discussion about what has occurred,[9] making sure that you state that whatever someone says deserves a moment of grace. Avoid any discussion of method or graphic descriptions, limit the time to about 5–10 minutes, and emphasize messages that it's important to access help and support, that thoughts of suicide are treatable, and that there are healthy coping strategies. You can allow them to talk about the person who died by sharing stories. It is important to try to dispel any rumors about the student's suicide and explain that they may increase their own distress or that of the family.

- **Do be aware of risk factors and how other students are coping.** Having a basic awareness of risk factors will assist you in being able to identify students who may be at risk.[10] If you are concerned about any students, refer them to the school care team. Very empathetic students from that next layer of acquaintances who knew of the student can possibly be at risk as well as others who have struggled emotionally before.

- **Do allow students to share their ideas for memorializing.** Ask them to write them down and share with the wellness team because students need to feel they are part of the process. Hopefully, the school has a commemoration policy that all deaths be treated with equal respect and memorializing. Please review the memorial policy before executing any ideas because some memorial ideas are not worthy precedents to set for the school, and some grandiose memorials can encourage vulnerable students to think that suicide is a solution. If their ideas are not meeting guidelines or the policy, sit down with students, hear them out, explain the dilemma and potential consequences, and strive to reach a solution that fits in the guidelines.

- **Do allow a class discussion on what to do about the "empty desk syndrome."** Since the emptiness of the deceased student's chair can be unsettling and evocative, after approximately five days or after the memorial, seat assignments may be rearranged to create a new environment. Teachers should explain in advance that the intention is to strike a balance between compassionately honoring the student who has died while at the same time returning the focus to the classroom curriculum. Students may be involved in planning how to respectfully move or remove the desk; for example, they could read a statement that emphasizes their love for their friend and their commitment to work to eradicate suicide in his or her memory.[11] If it's a class the student was part of, this can help students be part of a collective decision-making process when appropriate. One teacher of a small class asked if her students wanted to take turns at the desk and made a schedule for who would sit there that week. These students needed more time to grieve since the class had been very close; they liked the idea and it was what they needed.

- **Make sure you honor your own grief journey.** Seek support from grief groups and counselors and allow yourself to grieve, too. Students need to know you are human and it's OK if you are not having a great day and you can tell the students you are struggling.

Sample Email to School Community

"The cause of [NAME]'s death was suicide. Suicide is not caused by a single event. In many cases, the person has a mental health or substance use disorder and then other life issues occur at the same time, leading to overwhelming mental and/or physical pain, distress, and hopelessness."

Source: Doreen et al. 2018 / AFSP and Education Development Center.

WHAT TEACHERS SHOULDN'T DO OR SAY

- **Don't let students leave alone to visit the counselor or to go for extra support.** For student safety reasons, see that they are escorted.

Explain that during this time, no one should be alone and that it would lower your stress level if they used a buddy system.

- **Don't make assessments or diagnose.** This should only be done by professionals with appropriate training. When discussing a student with the wellness team, share changes in their behavior and any other observations you may have made.[12]

- **Don't allow the whole class-time discussion to be focused on suicide.** While there is clearly a reason to discuss suicide, it is important to contain this to a limited period within class time. Some students may feel the need to discuss the suicide, but there are often others who find it more distressing since not everyone would have had the same relationship with the deceased or the subject of suicide. Help the students understand that 5–10 minutes will be allocated to this discussion and that the remainder of the class time will be focused on the learning content,[13] even if you and they are not doing it well under the circumstances. Adding in time for a mindfulness activity, a mental health check-in, or some other short activity focused on self-care is also appropriate.

- **Don't allow students to stay on digital devices cruising the Internet.** Keep your classroom rule on digital devices consistent with what it has been in the past. Having the whole class engaged in videos or on social media is missing an opportunity to connect with one another, which is a healing experience and a strong protective factor.

- **Don't perpetuate myths and gossip.** Simply express that rumors can be hurtful to the family who is already suffering.

Keep in mind that with certain cultures or situations, these talking points may need to be amended to suit the population you serve.

When a Friend or Classmate Dies

When a student says, "I can't believe this happened."

Respond: "It is so shocking and that is normal when we find out someone has died. Shock is a combination of disbelief and numbness. I know I'm having trouble concentrating and understanding the 'why' behind [insert name]'s death. I know how I feel, but I'd like to know how you feel. What has your experience been like?"

SCRIPTS ON HOW TO FACILITATE CONVERSATION WITH YOUR CLASS

So how can you be there for yourself and your students after a suicide loss and still get through the day? How can you look for that student who might also be thinking of joining the one who died when your mind is blurry and untethered? What do you say or do? And if you do it all wrong, will that mean someone else will die?

Just know that silence hasn't worked because students are more likely to take their life if all the adults are being hush-hush after the suicide. Besides that, silence is what we've done for decades and it has served only to promote suicide, while deaths from other causes have decreased over the years. Stigma silences people and stirs up fear. Denial is part of its charm, judgment so crucial to its success, and shame is where it thrives. Talking about it is awkward, hard, and scary. When we speak up, stigma loses its fire and finally fades, and people are more likely to ask for help. And that's what you can do for a new generation. You can be the catalyst to starting an important conversation about preventing suicide, and it starts with your class of needy souls who want to hear from you as a human.

Focus on how the student lived, more than how he or she died. While you may not know this child's emotional history, you can emphasize the connection between suicide and those problems, such as depression or anxiety, that may not be apparent to others (or that may manifest as behavioral problems or substance misuse). In short, use this as an opportunity to educate.

Keep in mind:

- Do not force students to share their feelings with others, including their peers or out loud, if they do not feel comfortable.
- Provide students with other opportunities to share their feelings privately (e.g. papers, letters, art).
- Evaluate the emotional maturity of your class. Younger middle school students might not be developmentally ready for some of these discussions, so edit them to suit your audience.
- A bulletin board of common feelings and facts about grief can serve as a helpful guide to what is "normal."

Discussions should include:

- Identifying two adults they would talk to if they had some problem, whether related to suicide or not.

- Memories about what the deceased person liked to do and who they were.

- Reminders that they can't keep a friend's thoughts of suicide a secret but to share those discoveries with a trusted adult.

- Reminders that suicide is the result of a constellation of issues that converge all at once, not just one reason.

- Bringing their attention to crisis lines and school resources. (See Chapter 12, Worksheet 7: How Educators Can Help Youth Bereaved by Suicide, for a complete list of crisis resources.)

- A message of hope, coping strategies, and identifying sources of strength.

- That thoughts of suicide can be addressed and we can find ways to cope with them.

Sharing Stories About the Deceased Script

What has happened at our school has shocked all of us. That includes me. I hardly slept all week. How about you? (Look for head nods.) And today is a hard day for me because I am so sad about Sebastian's death.

Before I ask for your participation, I want to point out the crisis text line, which is right there on the wall. If you are struggling with thoughts of suicide or any other emotional difficulty like anxiety, I want you to let me know, or tell our school counselor, your parents, or text that crisis line, which is for any problem you are facing. And if you know of someone who is struggling, you should tell a trusted adult.

So I wanted those of you who knew Sebastian to share a memory, a brief story, a character trait, something he liked to do, or some snippet about him in remembrance. And if you wanted to write it down, we can add it to a notebook that we'll give his parents. No one is obligated, OK? We'll do this for about 10 minutes. Sound good?

Directions: Give the students who want to the opportunity to share a memory and talk about the student who died.

Feelings Check-in Script

We are going to have a short, 5- to 10-minute discussion about Carolyn's death because we are all hurting. I am hurting. To do this, we need this to be a safe space. So we are going to grant everyone in here the grace of expressing how they feel without judgment inside or outside this class, and to keep what is said in here between us. Can we agree on that? (Look for head nods.) Anger, sadness, frustration, helplessness, disbelief, and even awkward and inappropriate humor are all ways in which some of us express our grief. What's important is that we allow ourselves to feel the feelings and also allow ourselves to be distracted or even laugh.

Before I ask for your participation, I want to point out the crisis text line, which is right there on the wall. If you are struggling with thoughts of suicide or any other emotional difficulty like anxiety, I want you to let me know, or tell our school counselor, your parents, or text that crisis line, which is for any problem you are facing. And if you know of someone who is struggling, you should tell a trusted adult.

Now let's get in a big circle. Let's go around the room and have each of you share what emotions you are all feeling right now. If you wish not to share, just say "pass." Just one or two words. It's OK if you are sad. It's OK if you are angry. It's OK if you are thinking about something different than the rest of us. It's OK if you are tired of it all, too. I might ask for more detail and it's up to you whether you share that. Again, if you wish not to share, just say "pass." It is not mandatory to share. Sound OK?

Discussion points

- So I hear many of you saying that as you look back, you see signs that you missed. Let me ask you this. You know all the answers now, the outcome, and everything. Do you think it's fair that you're looking back at yourself before the death through the lens of a person who is now better educated and knows the outcome?

- Let's figure out how a change in routine, a walk around the block, or a shift in body temperature, for example, might force your brain out of that self-defeating "if only" cycle. Let's discuss some coping strategies that might make that happen (writing, painting, listening to music, exercise, spending time with family/friends).

- Can we really control what another person does?

Working Through Our Grief Script

I've not slept well since Jamal died by suicide. And I think it would be a good idea if all of us shared some ways we've been coping with all of this—with our grief. Because maybe one of your ideas will help me or someone else. And maybe mine will help you. Can we do that for 5 to 10 minutes? I think these strategies will be applicable to other situations, so this will be helpful for everyone even if you didn't know Jamal well. Because we are all affected by his death, no matter how well we knew him.

So take about two minutes and write down a few, then I'll go first, and who wants to go after me? I can't wait to hear some of your ideas and I'll write these on the whiteboard. A good coping strategy is one that can be done long term without negative consequences. I want you to recognize that you can't heal if you can't feel and that all feelings are temporary. But you are allowed to laugh and find distraction, too. So what are some good coping strategies to manage the grief? It can be writing or art or running. . . .You have two minutes to make the best list you can.

Sample coping strategies:

- Finding support from another person or group
- Writing
- Mindful exercises/meditation
- "Not OK" app
- Sleep
- Acts of kindness and giving back
- Exercise
- Connecting with each other
- Talking it out
- Listening to each other
- Making something creative
- Talking about the person/telling stories
- Embracing faith
- Start the day reflecting on something you are grateful for
- Breathing exercises

- Forgiving yourself
- Self-care (examples: meeting up with a friend to ride bikes)
- Listening to music
- Writing or playing music
- Making a plan for days that may be hard
- Talking with friends
- Starting a mental wellness group
- Giving yourself permission to laugh or have fun
- Starting a fundraiser for a nonprofit that matches what he loved (SPCA if the student loved dogs, for example, or have an Out of the Darkness walk to raise funds for suicide prevention)

Sometimes students will say something like "retail therapy" is a good strategy. Keep asking them questions until they recognize that over time this strategy can be a problem because they can't pay for food due to having spent it all on stuff to make themselves feel better. Before class ends, ask them to think about which of these strategies they'd use to manage a difficult situation and to think of two trusted adults they'd talk to, one at school and one outside of school, if they were feeling anxious or struggling with a problem.

Responding to Grieving Adolescents

Adults play an essential role in supporting grieving youth, but well-intentioned adults can also say things that are not helpful in supporting loss. Resist trying to cheer them up or being all lollipop positive, which can come across as not genuine and being out of touch. Instead, encourage the students to talk through their feelings, allow them to cry if they want by passing them a box of tissues. The most important part is listening. The following list offers some phrases to avoid and suggestions for what to say instead to initiate conversation and get a read on whether this student needs more support.

DON'T SAY: Please don't cry! (or Don't be sad!)
INSTEAD SAY: *Tell me more about how you feel.*
DON'T SAY: I know how you feel.
INSTEAD SAY: *I know how I feel but what has this loss been like for you?*
DON'T SAY: You need to be strong.
INSTEAD SAY: *How have you felt the last few days?*

DON'T SAY: He/She/They is/are in a better place.

INSTEAD SAY: *I know you wish [name] was here. Tell me about [name].*

DON'T SAY: You should focus on all the good memories about [name].

INSTEAD SAY: *What qualities made [name] a good friend to you?*

DON'T SAY: You shouldn't blame yourself.

INSTEAD SAY: *I hear you say you think you are at fault. Tell me why you feel that way. (Then ask questions such as: So do you think you could control the actions of another?)*

DON'T SAY: It will get better. You'll see.

INSTEAD SAY: *It sounds like the grief is really raw and intense right now. Over time it does soften but tell me how you are feeling now.*

DON'T SAY: Everything has a silver lining.

INSTEAD SAY: *The emotions I see you express right now speak volumes about how much you cared about [name]. Tell me what made [name] so special.*[14]

MEMORIAL ACTIVITIES AND SUPPORT AFTER A STUDENT SUICIDE

Because adolescents are especially vulnerable to the risk of suicide contagion and in the interest of identifying a meaningful, safe approach to acknowledging the loss, schools should meet with the student's friends and coordinate with the family. The goal should be to balance the students' need to grieve with the goal of limiting the risk of suicide contagion by not glamorizing the death.[15]

Make sure to be sensitive to the cultural needs of the students and the family, and identify with students some meaningful, safe approaches to acknowledging the loss. Schools should use commemoration policies that treat all deaths with equal respect and do not single out deaths of despair such as overdose and suicide as being "shameful" and therefore unworthy of recognition. The fear of copycat suicide or lawsuits are often the reasons behind gag orders issued by schools and school districts on the subject. This rarely happens with malicious intent but it can further perpetuate the stigma from these causes of death, which can prevent schools from being able to identify those at risk who usually only come forward if there is thoughtful and sensitive conversation on the subject.

Often a memorial event that works best includes both students and adults. However, ideas created by adults are likely to work well for them but not for students. Students can choose activities that are generally more meaningful and expressive and therefore therapeutic for survivors. Planning the activities are part of the ritual of a healing process, keeping in mind the commemoration policy guidelines in Chapter 4, "Suicide-Related School Policies." However, events that give back to the community have multiple benefits, including future suicide prevention.

"So, you want to take those understandable feelings of helplessness, anger, sadness, rage, confusion and channel it somehow so that really good things can happen for the community. To be able to take those feelings and cultivate them into something productive so that you don't have posttraumatic stress, but post traumatic growth."

Jennifer Hamilton (She/Her/Hers), School Psychologist, Director of Psychology and Counseling at Noble and Greenough, Independent School, Dedham, Massachusetts

---

Since students do use social media to commemorate and memorialize, someone at the school should be designated to oversee those pages and look for signs of other students who may be struggling. Talking to the students and asking them to monitor the mood on these channels to protect the health and well-being of their friends and asking them to report to a faculty member is an effective way to monitor students who might not be doing well. The object is not to police the site but to maintain a level of general awareness. Ask students to bring to an adult's attention any worrisome, destructive posts, such as suicidal or homicidal intentions or critical comments about the deceased.[16]

Sample Idea/Checklist for School Postvention Efforts:

- Student-led "sticky note" initiative for support (u matter, you can sit with me, etc.)
- Interactive "gratitude" board put up in front lobby
- One-hour faculty suicide prevention workshop (understanding and being sensitive to the fact that this can trigger feelings of guilt)
- Posters in the hall with resources like crisis text line
- Bulletin board with education and stories on emotions pertaining to grief
- Bulletin board, announcements, newsletter with tips on managing the pain of grief and what to expect
- Describe action plan for structure and support in coming days and beyond

- Small group meeting with trained adult for those who were close and need more support inclusive of those who feel profoundly affected
- After-school discussion group hosted by community resource person, counselor, trained teacher and offered for students to discuss how they are coping with their grief
- Activity that involves showing students where they can get help
- Presentation to students to specifically address signs of depression, anxiety, eating disorders, substance misuse, self-harm behavior, and what to do for a friend
- Email with tips sent to students following assembly to offer resources for suicide prevention or grief
- Email with tips sent to parents to prompt a discussion of grief
- Reach out to teachers and get their help identifying students who might be at risk
- Have teachers monitor their coworkers for stress and offer staff self-care tips
- List compiled of students who will receive increased focus/counseling, as well as identified members of the counseling team to meet with those students
- Work with students to organize a memorial within the guidelines
- Give students an opportunity to write notes to the student/faculty member who died to put in a notebook for the family
- Communicate with the families of the deceased about parents attending wake/funeral with their students
- Newsletter articles to parents about mental health, healthy grieving, suicide, and suicide prevention
- Email home to address parent concern around exams to reiterate concept of maintaining structure and fostering resilience, even though it's not business as usual
- Contact local nonprofit on mental health, trauma, and/or grief
- Advisor check-in about student's death upon return from break
- Mindfulness group (e.g. Mindful Jenga session)
- Resource cards given to all students with suicide warning signs and crisis numbers

- Send out end-of-year email to parents, students, and faculty with information about resources for mental health
- Mental wellness group—start one and give it a name
- Integrate one mindful activity in class so students are exposed at least two a week
- Monday mental health check-in: 5–10 minutes
- Idea sharing on coping with grief: 5–10 minutes
- "Dogs and Donuts": therapy dogs on campus during assessments for stress-reduction
- No HW weekends to lower stress
- Student wellness survey to gather data on stress, sleep, well-being, etc.

Thank you to Jennifer Hamilton, School Psychologist, who shared her postvention list and ideas from other teachers and counselors who were interviewed. A sample postvention timeline is included in the After a Suicide Toolkit for Schools, *2nd ed., found online.*

THE EMPTY DESK SYNDROME AND TAKING CARE OF YOU

"When I went back to the room where I taught at the end of the summer, I just sat in the desk Michael had sat prior to his suicide. That was his spot. I'm not sure I can go back to that classroom again."

Doris (She/Her/Hers), Science Teacher, Colorado Public School

Teachers and other educators are not immune to the grief of a suicide loss. And often they are so engaged with connecting with parents and students, their own needs go unmet. Everyone, including teachers, is tempted to numb their feelings because when people are traumatized, it's natural to want to escape the pain by grabbing hold of something that feels good even if it's temporary—alcohol, drugs, food, gambling, shopping sprees. As we know, these are not healthy antidotes, and numbing emotional pain prevents healing and leaves people stuck in the grief process. That's why getting support is important not only for students but for educators, too. There is no special escape hatch to get out from under the weight and shock of a student or teacher suicide loss. And the coulda, woulda, shouldas and what-ifs are part of the process. Everyone feels responsible and this can lead to what is called the ripple effect. Over time, logic will reconcile your guilt and the blame voices will quiet down. You will understand that you don't have control over another human being. And what was once overwhelming guilt will soften to a painful sting of regret, at which point you'll remind yourself of your humanity.

"Given that I've been through five student deaths in the last five years, three of which were suicides, I looked for some long-term grief support on my own. Using alcohol to cope just isn't a good strategy. I connected with MindPeace Miracles and am using mindfulness and a tapping strategy to manage the memories and it's helping."

Teacher in the Midwest at a public high school

Your pain has a purpose of helping you heal and there are ways to manage it in a healthy way and work through it even if they're not as much fun as eating a pint of chocolate chip ice cream or drinking a pitcher of sangria. Supporting and listening to each other and talking about it, however simplistic it might sound, does work. Writing works. Finding extra support through a group or a counselor helps. Giving back certainly does, and finding ways to help your school be more prepared for future crises or rally for teacher training on suicide prevention are ideal ways to put your grief into action once you are ready to do so.

We are dedicating a section here to the empty desk syndrome and that specifically speaks to the teachers and students who have to stare at the vacant space after a student death. This was a profound part of every teacher interview for this book. And while there are guidelines outlined for this—namely, five days before you reassign the space—many have adjusted the rules to the needs of their class. Decorating the space like a float in a Macy's parade wouldn't be recommended because that would glorify the death, but there are other ways to manage that pain that don't feel like you are erasing a memory too quickly.

"The year Reginald* died, he was enrolled in two of my 10th-grade classes (World History II and Economics). He was an incredibly bright student who demonstrated a genuine zeal for knowledge and an understanding of the facts. He was an otherwise quiet student who would interact with classmates when necessary for group assignments, but usually preferred to work alone. I received a phone call from my administration on the first day of spring break to notify me of his death by suicide the previous night. I felt pain, shock, and confusion. I saw no typical indicators or warning signs that he was in distress and I felt as though I should have been able to pick up on something and did not. That pain still haunts me. There was nothing that could be done to help me prepare for my incoming class and the issue of Reginald's empty desk. I addressed the class and teared up as I gave them the limited information I had and discussed how there was no normal way to feel right then. This particular class responded with an open discussion and decided, as a class, that Reginald's desk would remain unassigned for the duration of the year (they were accustomed to a new seating chart every 9 weeks but insisted his seat stay his).

I've been teaching 21 years, all at the same school. My advice is that if a school loses a student and it is well enough into the school year for teachers to have developed relationships with their students, defer to them as to how to handle the empty desk syndrome. Of all the things teachers have to deal with, the empty desk is by far the worst. Giving back has helped me the most and I do this by consoling students and families during times of loss."

Mr. Nigro, High School Teacher, World History II and Economics, Chester, Virginia
*Student name has been changed to protect privacy.

————————————

Sheila McElwee, a chemistry teacher from Noble and Greenough School, grieved together with her students. Their class was small and all of the students were close. After the death of a female student who had been part of this class, she knew they needed more healing, as did she. She set the expectation that it was OK not to be OK and did daily mental health check-ins after the young lady's suicide and she expressed that she simply couldn't stare at the empty desk, so they devised another approach.

————————————

"In terms of how the death occurred, we still had the aftermath of the death, the empty chair. The one thing I absolutely did not want was the empty chair syndrome. We were an AP class of 13 who'd gotten to know each other really well. So when my class came the day after, we gathered outside in the hall to commemorate her and tell stories. We huddled and put our arms around each other. Everybody was in tears. We all shared a memory of Paula*—what we loved about her. And I said, 'We're going to be together this year and the spirit of Paula is going to be in our classroom all year. All this positive spirit that we just talked about did not die. Her body died, but all our love for her didn't die. And that's one of the things you're going to learn, that love goes much beyond the physical body, the love you feel for her is going to stay with you.' I asked them not to be afraid of the spaces we shared with Paula. I told them I was going to go first, and hoped they would follow, and we were all going to sit in her chair if they were so moved.

So we held hands as a human chain. And I said, 'Is there somebody that would be willing to be the first to follow me?' Her closest friend did. So I went and I sat in her chair for a minute and I touched her desk and I said, 'I love you, Paula. Your spirit will always be here.' And then her best friend, a young man, sat and touched the desk and kissed it. Everybody went through and did what they felt was right and then we went to the lab spaces. The kids were like, 'You know, I remember when we did this, or did that.' They would recall things and then we talked about how it was going to be really hard. But, you know, we were going to go on and we were going to share our experiences and we were going to huddle daily at first. So every day [in November] until Christmas break, we had the huddle before class. Then after Christmas break, we made the decision to have the huddle on Fridays. And after spring break we huddled only on special occasions like her birthday, which was coming up. So I kind of left it up to the kids to weigh in on that. But Paula was a definite presence and I tried to allow for her presence. They were really good about that and they'd come in and I'd say, 'Who's going to sit with Paula today?' They also took turns wearing her goggles or her lab apron, which had been custom made for her since she was so small. And we smiled when the tallest person in the class took his turn wearing her apron."

Sheila McElwee (She/Her/Hers), Chemistry Teacher, Noble and Greenough,
Independent School, Dedham, Massachusetts
*Student name has been changed to protect privacy.

Sheila knew what her class needed, which was different than what other teachers and classes did due to the closeness of this group, and she honored that with positive reinforcement of how life goes on while incorporating memories of Paula and acknowledging that it would take her class longer to heal.

With virtual learning, there is no empty desk. Kids who are struggling often "ghost" prior to their final act by not showing themselves or their picture onscreen, or don't show up for class altogether. This evokes a strange feeling for teachers and the class after the suicide because it's as if the student vanished before the suicide, making everyone feel responsible for not having noticed or taken action. If that student's block was there with a name and no photo prior to the suicide, afterwards the software doesn't hold space for it but instead rearranges the participants onscreen. To those who are grieving, this feels like that child's memory is erased too quickly before they've even gotten their arms around the loss. Teachers and students have described that experience as strange and eerie and it's OK to acknowledge that and talk about it with the class.

What if the suicide happens at school and an educator or student finds the body? No one in this situation should feel like the "brave thing to do" is to suffer in silence. Because no one is supposed to do this alone. Anyone in that situation should speak with a mental health professional, and that should be part of your school protocol so there is no pushback or argument on the topic. Discovering a body is a trauma, no matter what the age or cause of death. A crisis like a school suicide often triggers cases of post-traumatic stress disorder and early intervention is key to minimizing and managing the reoccurring images of the final scenery that can disrupt sleep, relationships, and overall functioning, and drive people to misuse substances to control the onslaught of flashbacks.

"You know, the adult who found the student who killed himself in that classroom left at the end of that school year. It was really hard for him to be in that in the building. He was so traumatized because of the sight of that student meeting such a graphic and devastating end."

Teacher at a small public community school in New England

Summary Postvention for Educators

- Download the guide *After a School Suicide: A Toolkit for Schools*, 2nd ed. (easy to find on Google, and free).

- Follow protocol on who does what.

- A favorite teacher or coach should be one of the people who calls the family to express condolences and can be a person who can help the parents understand the significance of sharing the cause of death to save lives and prevent copycat deaths.

- Maintain as much structure as possible, understanding that it won't be business as usual even if you don't do the lesson plan. Structure is important.

- Provide teachers with talking points about suicide and grief.

- Ask classroom teachers if they want support.

- Do not send kids to unsupervised "crying rooms" with strangers but instead escort them to "quiet rooms" staffed with people they know, if they express the desire. Allow them to talk in small groups with teachers if they are comfortable, giving the exercise a time limit of about 5–10 minutes.

- Be as vigilant as possible to spot students at risk and encourage classmates to watch out for each other.

NOTES

1. American Foundation for Suicide Prevention (AFSP) and the Suicide Prevention Resource Center (SPRC), Education Development Center (EDC). (2018). *After a Suicide: A Toolkit for Schools,* 2nd ed.
2. National Suicide Prevention Lifeline (toolkit for media releases). https://suicidepreventionlifeline.org/media-resources/
3. American Foundation for Suicide Prevention (AFSP) and the Suicide Prevention Resource Center (SPRC), Education Development Center (EDC). (2018). *After a Suicide: A Toolkit for Schools,* 2nd ed.
4. Giacobbe, A. The tragic, enduring legacy of Phoebe Prince. *Boston* magazine. (1/21/2020). https://www.bostonmagazine.com/education/2020/01/21/phoebe-prince-bullying/
5. American Foundation for Suicide Prevention (AFSP) and the Suicide Prevention Resource Center (SPRC), Education Development Center (EDC). (2018). *After a Suicide: A Toolkit for Schools,* 2nd ed.
6. Coalition to Support Grieving Students, Commemoration and Memorialization video. https://grievingstudents.org/module-section/commemoration-and-memorialization/
7. Tips for Teachers Following a Suicide, Headspace.org.au
8. Ibid.
9. Ibid.
10. Ibid.
11. American Foundation for Suicide Prevention (AFSP) and the Suicide Prevention Resource Center (SPRC), Education Development Center (EDC). (2018). *After a Suicide: A Toolkit for Schools,* 2nd ed.
12. Tips for Teachers Following a Suicide. Headspace.org.au
13. Ibid.
14. The Good Grief Program, Boston Medical Center. BMC.org
15. Joshi, S. V, Ojakian, M., Lenoir, L., Lopez, J. K-12 Toolkit for Mental Health Promotion and Suicide Prevention. https://www.heardalliance.org/help-toolkit/
16. Coalition to Support Grieving Students, Commemoration and Memorialization video. https://grievingstudents.org/module-section/commemoration-and-memorialization/

Chapter 10
How Students
Move Forward After
a Suicidal Crisis

"If I had to choose a phrase that encapsulates my story and the pain and suffering I've experienced, it would be: 'collateral beauty.'"

Young adult with lived experience, name withheld for privacy,
comment from the Emotionally Naked blog

Those cut marks, dark moments, and suicide attempts are a person's battle scars. That agony has a purpose. It's not always clear in that moment but later becomes part of the tapestry of someone's life—one in which they endured, persevered, survived, and moved forward again. And when you observe a student's journey to healing, you can encourage the process by pointing out the progress you've noticed and know that you were part of that story and maybe even the inspiration behind it. The truth is that while teen suicide attempts have increased and a lot more students think of suicide as an option, it's far more likely someone with these thoughts will live. And with awareness and the confidence to intervene, teachers and students can demote suicide's rank as a cause of death at middle and high schools.

However, there are times when even our best efforts are not enough to keep someone alive. As a high school principal in the southeast put it, "We can't let our guard down. We have to be vigilant if that child has been at risk before." In that case, there was a student who had struggled, been supported by the school staff, and was on a healing track. In a turn of events that shocked his parents and the school community, he took his life. Intervention usually works, but in rare cases a relapse in recovery can result in someone ending their life, which is heartbreaking to everyone who thought the teen had moved out of the danger zone. However, had there been no intervention at all, the chance of that child finding a path to recovery would have been remote. We can't avoid intervening out of fear of what might happen. While "no deaths this school year," is good news, it's not a ratings-grabbing headline you're likely to find in the media.

A sudden sense of calm and happiness after being depressed for a long time can be a warning sign. And it might not be. The key word here is "sudden" and we don't always know for sure but here is the difference. Moving forward after an emotional or suicidal crisis takes time, includes relapses, and that nonlinear path often evolves into a passion for helping others. It's when you witness gradual change and improvement over time, when you see someone use healthy coping strategies or taking a leadership role in advocating for mental health, that you can feel that student is using personal pain for the purpose of his or her own healing and that of others. Not that there is any time we can be completely sure, but we must learn to celebrate those moments without projecting future doomsday scenarios and cannibalizing our own sense of hope. Here's how some adolescents who have moved forward after a mental health crisis or a suicide attempt describe it:

"Personally, like I definitely got interested in mental health because I had my own personal mental health struggles. Also, a girl in my grade took her life my sophomore year, and I'd say that was definitely the catalyst for starting a [mental wellness] group. However, I definitely wouldn't have started it if I hadn't had my own struggles. So, I think it was sort of a combination of the two. And I remember the way that my struggle kind of happened was, like I had a hard time and then obviously it wasn't permanent—like I wasn't permanently happy after but like there is definitely a big change over a couple of years and I got better. So, after that, I was definitely feeling like maybe I want to do something for mental health in the future. And then when the girl took her life, I sort of realized I could use what I'd gone through to do something more in the moment."

Desmond Herzfelder (He/Him/His), Student Mental Wellness Club Founder, Psychology Major at Harvard University, Graduate of Noble and Greenough School, Independent School, Dedham, Massachusetts

"Many years ago, I was in danger of taking my life. Looking back, I am of course glad that I stuck around even though there has been pain since. I'm not sure what will help people survive such feelings, but I think having a supportive community resource like this one means a lot."

Young adult, name withheld for privacy, comment from the Emotionally Naked blog

"Hi, my name is David.* Charles and I were at [boarding] school together. He always looked after me and had my back. Charles saved me from killing myself one night in the dorm along with another person. After I came back from the hospital he was my shadow and made all the time in the world for me. I just wanted to say I'm so sorry and he was one of the most caring supportive people I've met. If it wasn't for him. I wouldn't be here. Me and my family are so grateful. I am. Thank you."

David, 18, suicide attempt survivor, in a note he sent to Anne Moss Rogers after her son Charles's suicide

* Name has been changed to protect privacy.

HOW DID THESE TEENS MOVE OUT OF A SELF-DEFEATING CYCLE?

When asking young adults how they navigated through their dark periods in middle and high school, they've offered specific coping strategies and support that helped propel them forward in a meaningful way. In no case was breaking out of this period of darkness easy or fast. It took perseverance, therapy and medication in some cases, nurturing from trusted adults, a safe space at school, and a lot of work on the part of the student and those supporting them.

Beauregard is a middle child in a family of five kids—four boys, one girl—and he attended a very traditional all-male private school in the eastern region of the US. He loves his family but describes them as conventional, even austere, especially his mother, and admitted that members of his family were and still are emotionally unavailable. During his freshman year in high school, he accidentally discovered that his father was having an extramarital affair and he connected with the school's social worker and they brought his mother in some time later with his permission. At that point, relationships with both his parents eroded and he reached out to his older brothers. They became angry with him for sharing the information about their father's affair and distanced themselves. Beauregard's support needs with the school counselor increased and then shifted from his father's infidelity to his sexuality the following year.

"Around tenth grade, I started questioning my sexuality and being at an all-boys school and having older brothers, it was something that was very painful. I warmed up to the idea of [joining] an afternoon group with a few other kids. It was an affinity group to talk about that sort of thing. And then existing at this school where no kid had ever come out in like 100 years. . .oh my gosh—so much pressure to balance, like our image and sort of the standards that I had to fill of my brothers' being there and being athletes. I mean it was, as you would expect, like I was having such an identity crisis. Like everything seemed fake."

Beauregard, graduate of an all-boys private day school in eastern United States

---

He became intensely uncomfortable with his identity and reacted by taking classes and modeling himself like his brothers, while he invested in friendships from which he was not benefiting when his carefully disguised life collapsed one afternoon. A full-on panic attack triggered intense feelings. He hated the direction in which his life was going and didn't want to exist anymore, so he reached back out to the school counselor with whom he'd built a relationship and told her how he was feeling, and she admitted him to an inpatient facility. He knew things had to change after that, and even though he continued to compare himself to his peers and his brothers for many months, he also leaned into his friendships with his affinity group. Self-hate and confusion eventually evolved into his becoming more comfortable with himself.

"I knew things had to change. So after my inpatient stay, it was a pivotal moment. But it wasn't like, 'Okay I'm better now.' It was a long journey, a year at least of conversations and struggle. So yeah, I got out of it. When I came back for senior year, I remember we had a class retreat at a camp and then one night we were supposed to draw out a timeline of our life. And I remember telling my group what it was like to be in an inpatient facility—which was huge step for me."

So what helped Beauregard move from self-hatred to acceptance?

- A supportive relationship with an adult at school (school counselor)
- A confidential affinity group of other LGBTQ kids
- Running
- Music

- Having friends who were/are supportive
- A good therapist
- Mentoring a younger member of the affinity group

Aurora Wulff, the young lady who started a student mental wellness group in Ithaca High School in New York leaned into her relationships for support.

"My friends are probably the biggest thing that helped me get through hard times. They have always been so supportive and there for me no matter what. The same for my college friends as well as my support system—friends, teachers, counselors, family, and my Active Minds Wellness Group. Running, hiking, knitting, journaling, yoga, mantras, and therapy were other coping mechanisms."

What helped Aurora work through her senior year depression to find emotional wellness?

- Friends, teachers, school counselor, family
- Active Minds (the wellness group she started at Ithaca High School)
- Running and hiking
- Knitting
- Journaling
- Yoga and mantras
- Therapy

Dese'Rae L. Stage, a suicide attempt survivor, suicide loss survivor, and founder of livethroughthis.org, said that as a young queer person in the late '90s, the kind of picture that was painted for her was that she would never get married or have a family. And due to the heightened number of hate crimes at the time, she was sure she'd be murdered. As a teen, she had insufficient adult support and struggled through high school, college, and beyond before landing in a good place later in life, now married with two children.

Her coping strategies for thoughts of suicide as a teen included a lot of creative pursuits and a controversial one, cutting.

- Writing
- Listening to music
- Playing music
- Photography

Desmond Herzfelder, the young man who started a student mental wellness group with his friend Michaela at Noble and Greenough School in Massachusetts, shares a whole strategy he used to manage his years of depression in middle and early high school:

_____

"I used to blame transitioning schools, my academic intensity, my family, and more for my depression. Eventually, I realized that it was my own habits that were creating darkness in my life. By focusing on changing how I think and behave, I slowly became a person who reacted more positively to the problems around me. Over time, these new habits became my new default, and they produced a stark and beautiful change in my personality and mindset."

_____

Habits that I worked to change (the habit I aimed for, and how I practiced it):

- Becoming less perfectionist and more self-compassionate.

  Congratulating myself and internally repeating thoughts of self-love.

- Becoming less competitive and goal-oriented.

  Talking less about competitions and success, doing more of the things I enjoyed.

- Becoming more confident and comfortable.

  I practiced speaking up, speaking my mind, embarrassing myself, and not caring what others think.

- Spending more time with friends.

  I actively reached out to people and scheduled more time with them.

- Sharing my feelings.

  I practiced by scheduling moments for me to share deep thoughts, such as "At dinner tonight, I'm going to share this _____."

- Improving general negativity.

  Practicing positive reactions and the best-case scenario internally, and repeating them every time I caught myself with a negative thought, starting the day by thinking about what I was excited about.

- Spending time on the activities I enjoyed.

  I slowly began to schedule more activities into my days/weeks that I actually enjoyed.

- More exercise and more outdoors.

  I scheduled time to exercise and do something active more and more often.

- Thinking more about other people.

  I practiced this by expressing gratitude and exercising acts of kindness.

- Improving sleep.

  I aimed to be in bed at specific times, having a good bedtime routine (like talking with family/friends, then having a positive journaling session before going to bed). I established a routine for when sleep was rocky and hard to find.

- Acknowledging spiraling anxiety.

  I used meditation, a healthy bedtime routine (better sleep), and a "when thoughts get bad" list of items that would distract me, as well as a go-to list of people to talk to.[1]

While Desmond cited the preceding list as the most important strategies for changing his habits in order to escape and manage his depression, he recognized the importance of having a plan to get through the really dark and dangerous times, which included calling a friend or a hotline. And he had activities to distract himself because he understood that the anxiety that was driving his despair was temporary and he'd watch a favorite TV show, meditate, work out, or prepare food. Mental techniques, like practicing gratitude, thinking about the best-case scenarios, reminding himself the morning would come, and reflecting on positive moments were helpful. And Desmond recognized that there were days when depression would still roll in like a slow-moving fog, smother his motivation, and sit on his self-esteem like an comfortable old sofa.

"I'd like to mention that despite this nice-looking list of strategies, there were so many days when I did not have the effort to make any of the changes I set out to do. I would watch my meals go by, my classes end, my reminders go off in one way or another, and I stare at my little notes and my 'efforts,' and do nothing. Depression is hard. Unbelievably hard. So my last piece of advice would be to forgive yourself. For falling down, for being depressed in the first place, and for not always being able to move forward. Just keep prioritizing your happiness, and doing your best. ☺."

His biggest regret? Not reaching out sooner. As teenagers, none of them relied on only one strategy but utilized several. And the three of the four who had at least one trusted adult and a peer support group at school found their way out of hopelessness much faster.

Enduring life's tragedies does have its rewards and that comes in the form of a renewed ability to cope with adversity and a sense of pride in that accomplishment. With each calamity someone faces, the initial feeling of shock is similar, but with each experience, recovery happens faster. Humility and resilience are the side effects. People build their emotional muscle by picking themselves up from a face plant in a bed of thorns, applying a bandage to the hurt, and moving forward if there is a trusted and caring adult in their life. In short, the pain we endure and work through are the building blocks to emotional healing. And students can get there if our teachers have educated eyes and ears to listen to them, offer a place of connection and expression, spot those at risk, help them find resources, and finally inspire and support them when they want to take that next step in their healing journey—giving back.

"People always ask me why I do what I do. How I can work with kids who are suicidal every day? This is why. Because one day you see a kid you worked with walk across that stage at graduation after all he went through and then they send you something like this."

Jessica Chock-Goldman, LCSW (She/Her/Hers), Doctoral Candidate, School Social Worker, Stuyvesant High School in Manhattan, New York

---

"Thank you for being there for me throughout my four years at High School. My stay could not have been better without you. Thank you for getting me into therapy, for checking in on me constantly, and being there to help me when I needed it the most. I now know how to move through tough times and make it through stronger. I cannot say thank you enough for all the memories and support you've given me, and from the bottom of my heart, thank you for everything. . . .I look forward to coming back for visits in the future."

Note from a Stuyvesant High School graduate

NOTE

1. Excerpt from "Concrete strategies that helped me work through my teen depression" by Desmond Herzfelder, from The Emotionally Naked Blog.

Chapter 11
Resources

Resources are always changing, so in addition to the ones listed here, we also have a web page where we will be offering more resources, ideas, books to read, and programs worth implementing. For access, visit the following website to download the pdf that will include these resources as well as those you will find in Chapter 12, "Quizzes, Worksheets, Handouts, Guides, and Scripts."

wiley.com/go/emotionallynaked

Password is: 988preventsuicide

COMPREHENSIVE SUICIDE-RELATED SCHOOL-BASED MODELS AND TOOLKITS

- **Model School District Policy on Suicide Prevention: Model Language, Commentary and Resources** (pdf)

  From the American Foundation for Suicide Prevention, American School Counselor Association, National Association of School Psychologists, and The Trevor Project (2019)

  TheTrevorProject.org, AFSP.org

- **After a Suicide: A Toolkit for Schools,** Second Edition (pdf)

  American Foundation for Suicide Prevention (AFSP) and the Suicide Prevention Resource Center (SPRC), Education Development Center (EDC), (2018)

  SPRC.org, AFSP.org

- **HEARD Alliance Toolkit for Mental Health Promotion and Suicide** (pdf)

  Great worksheets and flow charts included for suicide prevention

  HeardAlliance.org

- **Issues and Options Surrounding a Student's Return to School Following a Suicide-Related Absence** (pdf)

  A 3-page guide from Hazelden Foundation's Lifelines and available on Society for the Prevention of Teen Suicide website

  SPTSusa.org

- **Understanding and Addressing the Mental Health of High School Students** (pdf)

  JED Foundation research report in partnership with Fluent Research

  JEDFoundation.org/high-school-research/

- **Tips for teachers following a suicide** (pdf)

  Tips to assist teachers in discussing suicide with students and also in knowing when to refer a student to a school well-being staff member for further support

  HeadSpace.org.au

- **Guide to Being an Ally to Transgender and Nonbinary Youth** (pdf)

  11-page guide for youth leaders, parents, and educators

  TheTrevorProject.org

- **Recommended Guidelines on Commemoration of Students at Time of Graduation** (pdf)

  This 2-page guide outlines considerations and recommendations related to the reading of names at graduation ceremonies, awarding posthumous diplomas, and posting of photographs or tributes in school yearbooks pertaining to members of the school community who died. It can be found on the National Center for School Crisis and Bereavement website.

  SchoolCrisisCenter.org

- **Support for Suicidal Individuals on Social and Digital Media** (pdf)

    This free toolkit, developed by the National Suicide Prevention Lifeline, helps digital community managers and social media platforms establish safety policies for helping individuals in suicidal crisis.

    SuicidePreventionLifeline.org

- **How to Use Social Media for Suicide Prevention User Guide** (pdf)

    This guide, developed by the nonprofit Suicide Is Preventable, focuses on how to use social media effectively and safely to promote suicide prevention. Case studies and examples are included.

    EmmResourceCenter.org

- **Riverside Trauma Center Postvention Guidelines** (pdf)

    These guidelines include a discussion of how to balance the need for commemoration activities while still addressing the need to reduce the possible contagion effect, and address the need to provide some trauma response in organizations that have experienced multiple deaths or in situations where someone has witnessed the suicide or death scene.

    SPRC.org

SUICIDE-RELATED FACT SHEETS

- **Risk and Protective Factors in Racial/Ethnic Populations in the U.S.** (pdf)

    Search for the title on the Suicide Prevention Resource Center.

    SPRC.org

- **National Survey on LGBTQ Mental Health**

    Research Brief: LGBTQ & Gender-Affirming Spaces, December 2020

    TheTrevorProject.org/survey-2020

BEST PRACTICES FOR STORYTELLING AND REPORTING ON SUICIDE

- **Storytelling for Suicide Prevention Checklist**

    Suicide Prevention Lifeline and Vibrant Emotional Health

SuicidePreventionLifeline.org/storytelling-for-suicide-prevention-checklist

- **Special considerations for telling your own story: Best practices for presentations by suicide loss and suicide attempt survivors**

  American Association of Suicidology (AAS)

  Suicidology.org

- **Speaking Out About Suicide**

  A one-page guide on telling your story.

  AFSP.org

- **Action Alliance Framework for Successful Messaging**

  SuicidePreventionMessaging.org

- **Reporting on Suicide** (pdf)

  The do's and don'ts of what media should report following a suicide

  ReportingOnSuicide.org/recommendations

- **Suicide Reporting Recommendations**

  American Association of Suicidology (AAS)

  Suicidology.org

RECOMMENDED WEBSITES

For students struggling with suicidal thoughts

- NowMattersNow.org
- LiveThroughThis.org

For parents of students struggling with suicidal thoughts

- SuicideIsDifferent.org

For grieving students and schools

- **Coalition to Support Grieving Students**

  Commemoration and Memorialization Video (good video on memorials and youth)

  GrievingStudents.org

- **The Grieving Student: A Teacher's Guide**

  Products.BrookesPublishing.com

- **Good Grief Program at Boston Medical Center**

  The Good Grief Program provides support to children and families after a child has experienced a significant loss.

  Good-Grief.org

- **Dougy Center for Grieving Children and Families**

  The Dougy Center offer free resources for children and families who are grieving, including toolkits for schools. It also has a database for locating grief support for youth.

  Dougy.org

- **Talking with Children About Traumatic Events**

  Tips for talking with children when they have witnessed or heard about traumatic events (pdf)

  RiversideTraumaCenter.org

For students going through a life transition

- **McClain College Mental Health Program,** Stephanie Pinder-Amaker

  Transitions from high school to college can be traumatic. This guide offers ways to prepare students for that change.

  McleanHospital.org/treatment/cmhp, mcleancmhp@partners.org

Education on the relationship between marijuana and suicide

- **Johnny's Ambassadors**

  On-demand recordings of Expert Webinar Series

  JohnnysAmbassadors.org/recorded-webinars

Student-driven mental health education resources

- **Get SchoolEd Tour**

  45-minute high-energy webinar that educates students about mental health and the network of care that surrounds them

  GetSchoolEdTour.com

- **Youth Move National**

  A youth-driven, chapter-based organization dedicated to improving services and systems that support positive growth and development by uniting the voices of individuals with lived experience, including mental health, juvenile justice, education, and child welfare.

  YouthMoveNational.org

- **Screenager's Movie**

  An award-winning documentary on mental health in the digital age.

  ScreenagersMovie.com

Diversity and inclusion resources

- **The Trevor Project**

  For LGBTQ Students; includes TrevorChat, TrevorText, TrevorSpace (private discussion forum), Trevor Support Center, training for teachers and parents and more

  TheTrevorProject.org

- **Trans Lifeline**

  Run by and for trans people, this website provides peer support for the transgender community.

  Translifeline.org

- **Gender Spectrum**

  For educators who want to create a gender support plan.

  GenderSpectrum.org

- **Bureau of Indian Education**

  The BIE mission is to provide quality education opportunities from early childhood through life in accordance with a tribe's needs for cultural and economic well-being, in keeping with the wide diversity of Indian tribes and Alaska Native villages as distinct cultural and governmental entities.

BIE.edu

- **Indian Health Service**

  The Indian Health Service, a government agency within the Department of Health and Human Services, is responsible for providing federal health services to American Indians and Alaska Natives.

  IHS.gov

- **Suicide Prevention Resource Center**

  Provides suicide prevention resources and resources specific to cultural and ethnic groups. Use the SPRC contact form for cultural assistance.

  SPRC.org

- **IllumiNative**

  Created and led by Native peoples, IllumiNative is a nonprofit initiative designed to increase the visibility of and challenge the negative narrative about Native Nations and peoples in American society.

  IllumiNatives.org

- **WeRNative**

  This website explores the history and historical trauma of Native Americans from first contact, to government policies of assimilation, relocation and genocide, to the process of nation building, and revitalizing native languages.

  WeRNative.org

- **People with Physical Health Problems or Disabilities**

  Resources for students with autism, traumatic brain injury, epilepsy, physical illness or disability, and more.

  https://sprc.org/populations/people-physical-health-problems-or-disabilities

- **Mental Health and Wellness for Students of Color: A new kind of college-readiness**

  YouTube Video: youtu.be/UkK39QXcVCQ

- **Mix It Up at Lunch Day**

  This is an initiative to inspire kids to make new friends by sitting at a different lunch table in the cafeteria to help students break out of their "comfort zones" and explore new ways of relating to and getting to know the people around us.

  LearningforJustice.org/mix-it-up

EDUCATOR/GATEKEEPER TRAINING PROGRAMS MENTIONED IN THE BOOK

- **QPR Institute**

  QPR: Question, Persuade, Refer

  QPR: Question, Persuade, Refer for School Health Professionals

  QPR: For Sports (Coaches and staff)

  QPRinstitute.com

- **LivingWorks**

  Start Online Training

  safeTALK: Suicide Alertness for Everyone

  ASIST: Applied Suicide Intervention Skills Training

  LivingWorks.net

- **Kognito**

  At-Risk for High School Educators

  At-Risk for Middle School Educators

  Friend2Friend: SEL for Students

  Kognito.com

- **The Trevor Project**

  Trainings for Youth-Serving Professionals

    Trevor CARE Training

    Trevor Ally Training

  TheTrevorProject.org

UNIVERSAL SCHOOL-BASED SUICIDE PREVENTION PROGRAMS MENTIONED IN THE BOOK

- **Mindwise Innovations**

  SOS Signs of Suicide

  SOS Signs of Suicide Second ACT (transition for high school seniors)

  SOSSignsofSuicide.org

- **Sources of Strength**

  SourcesOfStrength.org

- **JED Foundation**

  JED High School

  JEDFoundation.org/jed-high-school

- **Hazelden Publishing**

  Lifelines: A Comprehensive Suicide Awareness and Responsiveness Program for Teens

  - Lifelines: Prevention

  - Lifelines: Intervention

  - Lifelines: Postvention

  Hazelden.org

- **Hope Squad**

  HopeSquad.com

- **CAST**

  Coping and Support Training

  ReconnectingYouth.com

- **American Indian Life Skills (AILS)**

  SPRC.org

CRISIS AND MENTAL HEALTH TRAINING PROGRAMS MENTIONED IN THE BOOK

- **PREPaRE School Crisis Prevention and Intervention Training Curriculum**

  From the National Association of School Psychologists

  NASPonline.org

- **Mental Health Training Programs**

  From the National Council for Behavioral Health and Born This Way Foundation

  Youth Mental Health First Aid

  Teen Mental Health First Aid

  MentalHealthFirstAid.org

- **More Than Sad: Mental Health Education**

  From American Foundation of Suicide Prevention

  More Than Sad: Mental Health Education for Educators

  More Than Sad: Mental Health Education for Parents, (available in English and Spanish)

  AFSP.org

PROGRAMS THAT BOLSTER PROTECTIVE FACTORS FOR AT-RISK YOUTH

- **CASEL**

  The Collaborative for Academic, Social, and Emotional Learning provides a systematic framework for identifying and evaluating the quality of SEL programs, especially those with potential for broad dissemination to schools across the United States. The CASEL guide also shares best-practice guidelines for school teams on how to select and implement SEL programs and recommends future priorities. CASEL's guide can be found for free on their website.

  CASEL.org/guide

- **DBT STEPS-A**

  SEL Program by Mazza Consulting

  MazzaConsulting.com/dbt-steps-a
- **The Emerson Model**

  By Sean Reilly in partnership with Jim Clark of The One Heart Project of Kansas City

  OneHeart.com (use the contact form)

NONPROFITS AND GOVERNMENT AGENCIES

- **Suicide Prevention Resource Center**

  The Suicide Prevention Resource Center (SPRC) is the only federally supported resource center devoted to advancing the implementation of the National Strategy for Suicide Prevention. SPRC is funded by the U.S. Department of Health and Human Services' Substance Abuse and Mental Health Services Administration (SAMHSA).

  SPRC.org
- **Action Alliance for Suicide Prevention**

  The National Action Alliance for Suicide Prevention (Action Alliance) is the nation's public-private partnership for suicide prevention. The Action Alliance works with more than 250 national partners to advance the National Strategy for Suicide Prevention. Current priority areas include transforming health systems, transforming communities, and changing the conversation.

  TheActionAlliance.org
- **American Foundation for Suicide Prevention (AFSP)**

  AFSP is a nonprofit health organization that gives those affected by suicide a nationwide community empowered by research, education, and advocacy to take action against this leading cause of death. AFSP funds scientific research, educates the public, advocates for public policies around mental health and suicide prevention, and supports survivors of suicide loss and those affected by suicide.

  AFSP.org

- **Child Mind Institute**

  The Child Mind Institute is an independent, national nonprofit dedicated to transforming the lives of children and families struggling with mental health and learning disorders. ChildMind offers some of the best and most relevant blog content of any youth mental organization, including an informative newsletter for subscribers.

  ChildMind.org

- **Jason Foundation**

  The Jason Foundation, Inc. (JFI) is a nonprofit dedicated to the prevention of the "silent epidemic" of youth suicide through educational and awareness programs that equip young people, educators/youth workers, and parents with the tools and resources to help identify and assist at-risk youth. In memory of Jason Flatt, the Jason Flatt Act was first passed in Tennessee and has been supported by the state's Department of Education and Teacher's Association. The Act, which has passed in a number of other states, mandates suicide prevention training for educators.

  JasonFoundation.com

- **JED Foundation**

  JED started with a focus on college campuses and now offers resources to high schools to improve mental health and prepare students for the transition to college and adult life. JED offers a wraparound high school program for suicide prevention, awareness campaign materials, advising and consultation, and training opportunities to protect the emotional well-being of students. (What We Do > For High Schools)

  JEDfoundation.org

- **Minding Your Mind**

  Minding Your Mind's (MYM) primary objective is to provide mental health education to adolescents, teens, and young adults and to their parents, teachers, and school administrators. They have a list of young speakers who speak at schools.

  MindingYourMind.org

- **Stanley H. King Institute**

  The Stanley H. King Institute offers a model of teaching counseling and listening skills to teachers, advisors, administrators, and other school personnel. The goal is not to train professional counselors, but to help teachers strengthen and deepen their relationships with students.

  SHKingInstitute.org

- **Indian Health Service**

  IHS mission is to raise the physical, mental, social, and spiritual health of American Indians and Alaska Natives to the highest level through healthy communities and quality healthcare systems through strong partnerships and culturally responsive practices.

  IHS.gov

- **Louder Than a Bomb**

  Cultivating artistic voices, critical thinkers and civically engaged youth, Louder Than a Bomb (a nonprofit founded in 2001) hosts an annual youth poetry slam in Chicago every spring.

  YoungChicagoAuthors.org/louder-than-a-bomb

RECOMMENDED SUICIDE-RELATED BOOKS FOR SCHOOLS

- **DBT Skills in Schools: Skills Training for Emotional Problem Solving for Adolescents (DBT STEPS-A)**

  by James J. Mazza, Elizabeth T. Dexter-Mazza, Alec L. Miller, Heather E. Murphy, Jill H. Rathus

  Designed for general education students, Dialectical Behavior Therapy (DBT) skills have been demonstrated to be effective in helping adolescents manage difficult emotional situations, cope with stress, and make better decisions. From leading experts in DBT and school-based interventions, this unique manual offers the first nonclinical application of DBT skills. The book presents an innovative social emotional learning (SEL) curriculum designed to be taught at the universal level in grades 6–12.

- **Suicide in Schools: A Practitioner's Guide to Multi-level Prevention, Assessment, Intervention, and Postvention**

  by Terri A. Erbacher, Jonathan B. Singer, Scott Poland

  Suicide in Schools provides school-based mental health professionals with practical, easy-to-use guidance on developing and implementing effective suicide prevention, assessment, intervention, and postvention strategies. Utilizing a multi-level systems approach, this book includes step-by-step guidelines for developing crisis teams and prevention programs, assessing and intervening with suicidal youth, and working with families and community organizations during and after a suicidal crisis.

Chapter 12

Quizzes, Worksheets, Handouts, Guides, and Scripts

The following are resources that can be used to educate students, help you know what to say in certain situations, and provide checklists and guides. You might ask why there isn't a worksheet for every section of the book; the answer is that there are existing evidence-informed guides created by reputable suicide prevention nonprofits and those are listed in Chapter 11, "Resources." To download these resources in a pdf, go to:

wiley.com/go/emotionallynaked
Password is: 988preventsuicide

WORKSHEET 1: HOW TO TELL SOMEONE YOU ARE THINKING OF SUICIDE

US National Suicide Prevention Lifeline: 1-800-273-8255 (By July 26, 2022, it will be simplified to the 3-digit crisis number, 988.)

Crisis Text Line 741-741 (US and Canada)
US Crisis Line for LGBTQ Youth, The Trevor Project, 1-866-488-7386
US Crisis Text Line for LGBTQ Youth, The Trevor Project, 678-678
Trans Lifeline 1-877-565-8860

It's hard to know what to say or to whom. You may even think you've been leaving clues that are flashing neon signs and no one is picking up on them. This might make you think people don't care. However, what you may think is obvious sometimes isn't evident to others. They may be missing what you are wanting to say, so here are some pointers and directions on how you can tell someone so it's clear, so you can get the help you deserve and those who love you get to keep you in their life.

For those of you reading this to help a friend who is thinking of suicide, thank you. Please tell a trusted adult about your friend to keep them safe from suicide.

Your Fears

Will the person you tell freak out? Will they think of you as weak or selfish? Will they believe you? Will they think you aren't serious?

That's why you want to choose the right trusted adult to confide in (see the section below on how to choose the right person). If they don't understand at first, it may be because they can't believe your life would be so bad that you'd want to end it. They don't understand those feelings—how persistent, invasive, scary, convincing, and life-threatening they are. So that's why you have to be very direct and bare your soul.

It can be scary and uncomfortable sharing your thoughts of suicide with another person. But the alternative is that you might die if you don't. And you have sunsets to see, people to fall in love with, and lives to save with your story.

So keep reading.

Make the decision to tell

You picked this up. You are reading it now. You can do this for yourself or for your friend. I know you have the courage because you have endured and fought these thoughts. You've managed to live through those episodes and you know how difficult that was. You did that; you can do this. Telling a trusted adult is how you can ask someone to help you save your own life.

Who should you tell?

Choose a trusted adult who is compassionate.

You want someone who is:

- Not likely to judge you
- A good listener, not a lecturer
- Not likely to gossip or spread rumors
- Compassionate and thoughtful

The person you choose could be a teacher, school counselor, parent, aunt, uncle, minister, doctor, coach, therapist, school nurse, coworker or a Godparent. If you tell a friend who is also a teen, you need to go with that person to tell a trusted adult.

You can also tell a stranger at a crisis line. (See the crisis lines at the top of the page.) Make a list or mental note of one to three people you would tell. And then commit to telling that person you chose.

How should you tell?

It's hard to know what to say. If you do tell someone, will they think you are joking? That's why you should be very direct. This is just a conversation that comes from your heart.

Don't use phrases like, "I want to hurt myself." You must be clear because the human you are talking to might not take it as seriously. And this is serious. It's life or death.

Say something like:

- "I have something very important to tell you. This is not a joke. Can you listen? I have been thinking of killing myself and I need help. When I have these thoughts, I feel like I don't have control. I don't understand these feelings of suicide and they scare me."
- Add your own personal struggles. Be open and heartfelt.
- You can tell someone in person, in a message, on a phone call, or write it in a note and hand it to that person while you are there.

How will the person you tell react?

The person you choose to tell may say something like, "You have so much to live for!" Or "You shouldn't feel that way." It's not the right thing to say, but be patient with them. It's a reactionary statement and at first they may be in denial.

The person you tell might feel scared because this is so serious. But once they absorb the news, most people feel honored that someone trusted them with such personal information. And they feel thankful they could help you. (If they aren't helpful, or make disparaging remarks, move on to the next person you thought to tell.)

You can call a local crisis line together. You can go tell someone together. You can ask someone to tell another trusted adult on your behalf. If it doesn't go well with the first person you tell, please don't give up.

Asking for help is a sign of courage. One day in the future, your story could be another person's survival guide.

Suggested Apps: My3, Not OK, Safety Plan

WORKSHEET 2: CREATING A SAFE DIGITAL LEARNING ENVIRONMENT

"Our public high school uses Gaggle Safety Management (Gaggle.net) to sweep the Google Drive of every student. Quite a few school divisions are using this now but many use it only during school hours and on school days. Our school district uses this tool 24/7, 365 days a year. For example, as a support person on call, I may receive a phone call at 1:00 a.m. that a student has written a suicide note on a Google Document, which our students frequently use for chatting, particularly when they've lost their phones. Sometimes students will also put a concerning remark or 'plan' on their Google Calendar. Gaggle can pick that up as well. Once we get a call, our mental health team reaches out to the family and/or calls for a welfare check. We also follow up with the student personally on the next school day. Gaggle is discussed with students and parents and explained in our Student Handbook so they are aware of this supervision."

School psychologist for large public school division on the East Coast

Gaggle also flags other harmful content before it's posted, including drug and alcohol use, intentions of violence, sexual content, self-harm, pornography and child pornography, bullying, and more.

Gaggle works on these digital learning environments:

- Google for Educators
- Office 365
- Canvas

Gaggle scans

- Chats
- Links to websites
- Documents and online file storage
- Attachments and images
- Outbound and inbound email

The video about what it does and the videos from how school districts are using it for their digital environments are excellent and have helped educators prevent tragedy and other potential incendiary incidents.

WORKSHEET 3: STUDENT WELLNESS SURVEYS

You can do this survey through your school computer program platform to send to all students to help you triage students in need of additional support to prevent suicide and unhealthy coping strategies. Include crisis lines and resources.

Thank you to Jessica Chock-Goldman, LCSW, DSW Candidate, NYU Silver School of Social Work, and to Joseph Feola, EdS, LPC (NJ), NCC, ACS, both School Social Workers at Stuyvesant High School, Manhattan, New York, who developed the following two mental health student surveys for their public high school.

Student Wellness Survey for Distance Learning

On a scale of 1–5, how do you feel being home (depressed, anxious, lonely, etc.)?

Choose one:

1	2	3	4	5
The worst				The best

Are you currently receiving mental health services? Yes/No

Would you like a referral for mental health services? Yes/No

Only your school counselor and [insert one other if needed] will see it. Not teachers, or other students!

Student Wellness Survey for In-Person Learning

On a scale of 1–5, how do you feel today (depressed, anxious, lonely, etc.)?

Choose one:

1	2	3	4	5
The worst				The best

Are you currently receiving mental health services? Yes/No

Would you like a referral for mental health services? Yes/No

Only your school counselor and [insert one other if needed] will see it. Not teachers, or other students!

Thank you to Tammy Ozolins, who developed the following survey.

Middle School Mental Health Survey for Students

Answer Yes/No

1. Have you gotten nervous about taking a test or quiz? Yes/No

2. Do you get nervous or anxious about meeting new people or being in a new situation? Yes/No

3. Do you know the difference between being sad versus depressed? Yes/No

4. Do you know what the word "stigma" means? Yes/No

5. Do you know anyone with a mental illness? Yes/No

WORKSHEET 4: TRUE OR FALSE SUICIDE PREVENTION QUIZ

1. It's dangerous to ask a depressed person, "Are you thinking of suicide?"

True   False

2. A person who is popular and makes good grades is unlikely to die by suicide.

True   False

3. People who want to die by suicide and tell a trusted adult are taking a courageous step.

True   False

4. Those who threaten or joke about suicide are just trying to "get attention."

True   False

5. If someone tells you they are thinking of suicide and asks you to keep it a secret, you need to tell a trusted adult anyway.

True   False

6. Suicide is preventable and treatable.

True   False

7. People who are thinking of suicide usually look sad.

True   False

8. Usually, people who are thinking about suicide don't want to talk about it or tell anyone.

True   False

9. Bullying is the reason people die by suicide.

True   False

10. People who attempt suicide or die by suicide usually talk about it first.

True   False

11. Finally, on a scale of 1–10, with 1 being completely hopeless and 10 extremely hopeful, rate how do you feel right now?

1	2	3	4	5	6	7	8	9	10
Completely Hopeless									Extremely Hopeful

WORKSHEET 5: TRUE OR FALSE SUICIDE PREVENTION QUIZ: ANSWER KEY

1. It's dangerous to ask a depressed person, "Are you thinking of suicide?"

True   **False**

Asking someone if they're suicidal will never give them the idea. Doing so can be the first step in helping them to choose to live. Most suicidal people are relieved when asked. This has been supported by multiple studies.

2. A person who is popular and makes good grades is unlikely to die by suicide.

True   **False**

Even people who appear to "have it all" can feel despair and hopelessness and die by suicide. Suicide is not a weakness but instead can be a response to underlying mental illness, trauma, societal and social issues, and a constellation of other problems that happen all at once in someone's life and leave them feeling hopeless. People can learn to work through problems and those who have at one time felt hopeless can go on to live happy and fulfilling lives because emotions are temporary and life is constantly changing.

3. People who want to die by suicide and tell a trusted adult are taking a courageous step.

True   False

Telling someone about your dark feelings of suicide is one of the most courageous things a person can do because it's hard to be that vulnerable and not know how the other person will react or what they might say. That's why every person should think of two trusted adults they'd go to—one in school, one outside of school—if they were struggling with a problem or feeling very stressed.

4. Those who threaten or joke about suicide are just trying to "get attention."

True **False**

Those thinking about suicide often mask their despair with a smile. That's why it's hard to look at someone and know. That's why you ask, "Are you thinking of suicide?"

5. If someone tells you they are thinking of suicide and asks you to keep it a secret, you need to tell a trusted adult anyway.

True False

You can promise to be discreet but never promise complete confidentiality. Will your friend be mad? The person might be angry but usually not forever. It's better to have a friend mad and alive than dead. And you can always say, "I'd rather you were alive and mad than not with us here on earth at all. I'm worried and I care about you and I hope you will understand that. If not right now, maybe you will understand later."

6. Suicide is preventable and treatable.

True False

There are prevention programs, therapies, medications, and self-care steps that can prevent suicide. Many times suicidal thoughts are a part of mental illnesses such as depression. By treating the underlying causes, most people can reduce or eliminate thoughts of suicide.

7. People who are thinking of suicide usually look sad.

True **False**

They can look sad, be irritable, angry, and even look very happy. If something a friend has done or said has left you with a feeling that something is not right, you should ask, "Are you thinking of suicide?" Then listen with empathy and connect them with a trusted adult. Sometimes people start to drink and drug too much, drive too fast, and take unnecessary risks. So while they aren't saying they are suicidal, their actions indicate something is wrong.

8. Usually, people who are thinking about suicide don't want to talk about it or tell anyone.

True **False**

Most who have feelings of suicide are scared. They want to tell because they don't understand the episodes where their brain is lying to them and making them feel worthless.

9. Bullying is the reason people die by suicide.

True   **False**

No one dies by suicide for one reason only. It is usually for many reasons, including an underlying mental health issue like depression or trauma. It's the result of many issues, including family history, health history, and the person's environment. So bullying can be a contributing factor to suicide but it's never the only reason.

10. People who attempt suicide or die by suicide usually talk about it first.

True   False

It's true that people say it in their own way. To that person, it might seem like it's a blinking neon sign and they are leaving clues. But many of us don't pick up on the clues because we are not educated about suicide. People say, "I can't do this anymore," "What's the use?" or "There's no point going on any-more." Through words or action (drinking and drugging too much, for example), most leave some clue of their intentions to someone before they attempt.

11. Finally, on a scale of 1–10, with 1 being completely hopeless and 10 extremely hopeful, rate how do you feel right now?

1	2	3	4	5	6	7	8	9	10
Completely Hopeless									Extremely Hopeful

WORKSHEET 6: SAMPLE CONFIDENTIALITY POLICY FOR STUDENTS

Thank you to Jennifer Hamilton, School Psychologist, Director of Psychology and Counseling at Noble and Greenough School, Independent School, Dedham, Massachusetts for sharing this policy language.

[Name of School] counselors are available to talk with you about any issue you might be dealing with. All conversations are completely confidential unless we have concerns about safety—for example, if someone is threatening or harming you, if you express suicidal intentions, or if you are talking about harming yourself or another person. In such cases, you can trust that your information will be handled with the utmost discretion, and the goal will always be to ensure that you have the support you need to be safe and well.

Students can confidentially talk about feelings of sadness or anxiety, share personal information, and so on, without worrying that teachers, parents, guardians, colleges, or the like will be informed. If a student is having intense thoughts or feelings and is feeling hesitant about coming to talk with a counselor for fear that their information will not be held in confidence, we encourage you to come and share whatever you feel comfortable sharing. We most certainly want to support you and hope that you will grow to trust that talking about those deeper feelings can lead to the greater support that you deserve.

WORKSHEET 7: HOW EDUCATORS CAN HELP YOUTH BEREAVED BY SUICIDE

For teenagers, routines and boundaries can provide a sense of safety and security during uncertain times. They may test and fight such boundaries, but ultimately most find comfort in knowing someone is paying attention to their lives and looking out for them.[1] They also need to know that people may say the wrong thing and understand that what they say usually comes from a place of love.

Teachable moment: Take this opportunity to educate people that we don't use the term "committed suicide." That's because suicide is not a crime but a public health issue. It was a crime in England in the 1400s, which is where the "committed" phrase originated. Appropriate phrases include:

Died by suicide

Ended his/her/their life

Killed himself/herself/themselves

Suggested Planning Checklist for a Bereaved Student's Return to School

- ☐ Talk with teachers about decreasing the student's workload
- ☐ Visit/meet with the family and share a copy of *Children, Teens and Suicide Loss* from Dougy.org or AFSP.org. (You can get this from a local AFSP chapter, order online, or download and print from online, about 40 pages.)

☐ Talk to the student about how they might answer questions from their peers at school.

☐ Create a check-in schedule. (Students drops by to check in daily the first two weeks, etc.)

☐ Coordinate with the student to choose a student ambassador for support upon their return.

☐ Coordinate with student/family regarding their wish to walk into school with a friend or group of friends.

☐ Identify two adults this student trusts—one inside school, one outside school—that the student will/can talk to in both good times and bad (e.g. school counselor, coach, teacher).

☐ Create a communication plan between parents, teachers, you, and the student.

☐ Make a "difficult day" plan. (Certain days are hard, e.g. birthdays, holidays.)

☐ Create a check-in plan. (For the first few weeks and months, some youth need to check in with family.)

☐ Give the student the *Managing a Loss by Suicide for Middle and High School Students Pledge and Worksheet.*

☐ Decide on a adult-monitored safe space the student can go when distressed.

What Does the Student Want to Say?

Given social media and mobile phones, it's unlikely this cause of death will remain secret. The school representative can work with the student, or the parent can. Regardless of how they choose to share at school or if they aren't ready to, discuss how they will respond to questions their peers have. Also find out whether the family has particular religious or cultural grief practices.

Provide examples of how to answer the question "What happened?" or "How did your dad/brother/sister/mom die?" There is no wrong answer. (Avoid graphic descriptions of the final scenery, the method, and the phrase "committed suicide.")

- My dad killed himself.
- My mom ended her life.
- My brother took his life.

Daddy died from depression.

My sister died last week and that is all I want to say right now.

I really don't want to talk about it.[1]

Brainstorm coping tools for when things are tough or for the "difficult day" plan.

- ☐ What coping skills might this student utilize?
- ☐ Finding refuge in the nurse's clinic, school counselor's office, library, or other supervised quiet spaces on campus
- ☐ Writing (blog posts, journal writing, music, poetry, letters to the deceased, English paper assignments)
- ☐ Other creative expression (artwork, drawing)
- ☐ Exercise (vigorous exercise helps in extreme moments)
- ☐ Shifting body temperature (e.g. washing face in cold water, taking cold drink of water, applying ice to parts of body)
- ☐ Listening to music
- ☐ Mindfulness practices (Headspace or Calm apps)
- ☐ Not OK app to check in with friends
- ☐ Talking about it
- ☐ Faith strategies
- ☐ Support groups or individual counseling
- ☐ Creating memorials like photo albums, posting pictures on social media in remembrance

Suicide Loss Grief Support: Where to Find It

- American Foundation of Suicide Prevention Suicide loss support group locator: AFSP.org/find-a-support-group
- GriefShare Group Locator: Use the Chapter Locator for general grief and loss: www.GriefShare.org/findagroup
- The Dougy Center: Dougy.org, Grief support for children and families
- Alliance of Hope for Suicide Loss Survivors: AllianceofHope.org (Community Forum) Online groups, forums, and more

USA Hotlines and Crisis Lines

- National Suicide Prevention Lifeline 1-800-273-8255 (On July 26, 2022, this number will be three digits: 988)
- National Suicide Prevention Lifeline (Spanish) 1-888-628-9454
- National Suicide Prevention Lifeline (Options for Deaf and Hard of Hearing) 1-800-799-4889
- Crisis Text Line, text HELP to 741-741
- Crisis Line for LGBTQ Youth, The Trevor Project 1-866-488-7386
- Crisis Text Line for LGBTQ Youth, The Trevor Project 678-678
- TrevorSpace Private Forum: TrevorSpace.org
- Trans Lifeline 1-877-565-8860
- USA Peer-to-Peer warm lines listed by state: WarmLine.org (not a crisis resource)
- USA Veteran's Services 1-800-273-8255, press 1
- USA Veteran's Text Line, send HELP to 838-255
- National Graduate Student Crisis Hotline 1-877-472-3457
- National Sexual Assault Hotline 1-800-656-4673
- Child Abuse Hotline 1-800-422-4453
- National Human Trafficking Hotline 1-888-373-7888

Apps

- *Not OK:* Sets up a group of friends to reach out to on hard days
- *My 3:* Identify and list contacts of 3 people to contact when feeling suicidal
- *Safety Plan:* Develop and enter a suicide safety plan
- *Headspace:* Mindfulness
- *Calm:* Mindfulness and meditation skills and activities

WORKSHEET 8: MANAGING A LOSS BY SUICIDE FOR MIDDLE AND HIGH SCHOOL STUDENTS

Pledge

I will survive even though I'm not sure how yet. Because as bad as it is now, it will never be as bad as getting the news. If I can survive that, I can survive anything.

1. I, the grieving person, know that friends are afraid of saying the wrong thing but I'm going to understand that what others say, even if it's not perfect, comes from a place of love. If the situation were reversed, I might not know the right thing to say either.

2. For those who say mean things, I'll take a deep breath and wonder what is happening in their life that would make them so insensitive. I will seek support from others who are more stable and supportive.

3. I also understand that friends who have not suffered this loss have limitations. They don't fully understand and their capacity to sit with me in my pain will vary, which is why I will seek additional support from a close friend, group, or counselor, because I am not meant to grieve alone.

4. I will help my friends, school peers, teachers, and family understand how to help me because they want to know and cannot read my mind.

5. I will respect where others of my family are in the grief process and not try to hide mine because they don't want me to and I know I wouldn't want them to hide theirs. We need to grieve together and talk about the person we lost.

6. I understand that my pain has a purpose and those agonizing moments are building blocks to emotional healing. It's OK to let it in, and pushing it away only makes things worse.

7. I will not allow someone else to *grief shame* me because I'm not bouncing back fast enough for them. This process takes as long as it takes.

8. I will think of two trusted adults with whom to share, one in school and one outside of school. If I am struggling or feeling suicidal, I will reach out to one of those trusted adults and talk or ask for help.

9. I won't always know the "why" behind my loved one's suicide death but I will try to learn more about suicide, so I do understand.

Friends and family will struggle with:

- **Whether to talk about the person who died or mention the cause of death.** Loved ones think they are "reminding" the person of their loss or might make it worse, although you never forget.

- **Listening with empathy.** Friends and family are frustrated that they can't fix the pain or make things better and try to say something upbeat.

- **It's uncomfortable.** A loss by suicide is overwhelming to everyone: friends, family, and loved ones. Sitting with a bereaved person feels awkward and uncomfortable and the fear of saying the wrong thing is paralyzing. There is temptation to whisper the cause of death, which is something we don't do with other causes of death.

Given social media and mobile phones, it's unlikely this cause of death will remain secret. Regardless of whether you choose to share at school or aren't ready to, you should think about how you will respond to questions your peers have. It will be less stressful if you have answers ahead of time.

Think about how to answer the question "What happened?" or "How did your dad/brother/sister/mom die?" There is no wrong answer. Do practice your answer.

- ☐ My dad killed himself.
- ☐ My mom ended her life.
- ☐ My brother took his life.
- ☐ Daddy died from depression.
- ☐ My sister died last week and that is all I want to say right now.
- ☐ I really don't want to talk about it.[2]

Name a friend who can be a student ambassador from the school with whom you can share your wishes prior to going back to school. This friend ambassador will communicate with other students, friends, and teachers what you want to say about the death and what you do or don't want to discuss. For example, you might want people to ask about what made your loved one who died special or you might not want questions at first with emotions being so raw.

Choose a friend or ask a teacher or school counselor to choose someone for you. Who are the friends from school with whom you could share your wishes?

Only one is needed. The other slots are backups.

_____

_____

_____

I would like help with:

- ☐ Getting assignments
- ☐ Altering the workload and help managing assignments because concentrating is difficult
- ☐ Getting to school
- ☐ Getting home from school
- ☐ Going back to school, I'd like a friend or group of friends who will walk in with me that first day back, or that whole first week back
- ☐ I would like calls or texts from friends
- ☐ Other things I am worried about _____

Details:

- ☐ I want family and friends to know: _____.
- ☐ I want to talk about the person who died.
- ☐ I need some space.
- ☐ I only want to talk with close friends.
- ☐ I am OK with people telling me they are sorry for my loss.
- ☐ I still want to be invited to things even though I might not go, might cancel at the last minute, or might not stay very long if I'm having a hard day.

If I am having a hard time, here's what I can do:

- ☐ Call a loved one to talk to
- ☐ Talk to someone at school: _____
- ☐ Leave class and go to a quiet place in the school like the clinic, the school counselor's office, the library, or other quiet space just to regroup
- ☐ Write, draw, or listen to music
- ☐ Things I don't want to talk about right now (know that this can change over time): _____

- ☐ Things I do want to talk about right now (know that this can change over time): _____
- ☐ I don't want to talk about my loss in these places (this may change over time): _____

I do not want to talk about my loss in these places (check all that apply):

- ☐ In class
- ☐ In the hall
- ☐ Large gatherings
- ☐ At lunch
- ☐ In private

Other _____

I do want to talk about my loss in these places (check all that apply):

- ☐ In class
- ☐ In the hall
- ☐ Large gatherings
- ☐ At lunch
- ☐ In private

Other _____

Those who have lost someone to suicide often suffer thoughts of suicide. If you are, reach out to one of your two trusted adults.

Resources you can contact:

Apps

- *Not OK:* Sets up a group of friends to reach out to on hard days
- *My 3:* Identify and list contacts of 3 people to contact when feeling suicidal

- *Safety Plan:* Develop and enter a suicide safety plan
- *Headspace, Calm:* Mindfulness and meditation skills and activities

Positive Coping Strategies

- Finding refuge in the nurse's clinic, school counselor's office, library, or other supervised quiet spaces on campus
- Writing (blog posts, journal writing, music, poetry, letters to the deceased, English paper assignments)
- Other creative expression (artwork, drawing)
- Exercise (vigorous exercise helps in extreme moments)
- Shifting body temperature (e.g. washing face in cold water, taking cold drink of water, applying ice to parts of body)
- Listening to music
- Mindfulness practices (Headspace or Calm apps)
- Not OK app to check in with friends
- Talking about it
- Faith strategies
- Support groups or individual counseling
- Creating memorials like photo albums; posting pictures on social media in remembrance
- Giving back

WORKSHEET 9: THE COPING STRATEGIES AND RESILIENCE BUILDING GAME

About a half an hour depending on class size

Supplies

1. Post-it Notes (colored ones present the most interesting visual awareness)
   Sharpies/Markers

2. A wall
3. Blackboard/whiteboard (something for the facilitator to write on)
   Lay the markers and Post-it Notes out at a table up front.

Conversation Starters

1. Start with a pledge and agreement that what's said in the room stays in the room and ask for overall respect for everyone's questions, struggles, and pathways to healing. The object is to help others feel supported, respected, and understood and students can tell others how they may have handled a similar issue.

2. Tell a story to launch this activity. The story should illustrate some way in which you, someone you know, or a past student worked through a crisis and is now managing well.

Ask students to identify unhealthy coping strategies

- Give them a few minutes to list on a sheet of paper some unhealthy coping strategies and have them think in terms of "Will long-term use of this strategy help me or hurt me?"

- Facilitate and lead a discussion, making two columns on a whiteboard or blackboard, one for unhealthy coping strategies and one for healthy coping strategies. Start with unhealthy ones. You can expand on ideas, group similar responses, and encourage conversation and examples.

- Let the students call out their unhealthy coping strategies. If you know a strategy is not healthy long term, keep asking them questions. For example, if one person thinks eating a pint of ice cream to manage anxiety is a healthy strategy, ask them, "What could happen if every day or twice a day, you ate a pint of ice cream to cope with a problem to make yourself feel better?" Let them make connections and discoveries on their own by asking questions, and typically the group will eventually categorize the skills in the correct column.

Ask students to identify healthy coping strategies

Next, have them take a minute or two to list healthy coping strategies following the same format as before. Examples of healthy and unhealthy strategies are given here.

Unhealthy coping strategies	Healthy coping activities
Self-harm/cutting	Writing
Drinking alcohol	Meditating
Drugging	Listening to music
Negative self-talk	Exercise
Retail therapy (compulsive spending)	Reading
Gambling	Working on puzzles or playing
Isolating	games
Bullying	Going for a walk
Avoidance	Going to a health club
Overeating	Relaxing in a steam room or sauna
Porn addiction	Going fishing or hunting
Promiscuity	Gardening
Smoking/vaping	Socializing with friends
Running away	Sitting outside and relaxing
	Engaging in a hobby you enjoy
	Making art

The goal is to get them to recognize which coping strategies are healthy and unhealthy for their overall wellness. Example: "What is someone who is drinking to make a problem go away doing?" Answer: Numbing the pain. "What happens when someone gets drunk when they are upset? What happens to the problem the next day? Is it solved? What could this lead to?"

"Retail therapy" is also one they often think is a healthy strategy, but spending too much on stuff means you don't have money for things like gas or college. Keep asking questions until the put it in the correct column.

Talking points for unhealthy and healthy coping strategies

1. You can't heal if you can't feel.

2. You can't control what happens but you can control how you react.

3. Reaching for a substance to solve a problem by "numbing" it robs you of the ability to develop healthy coping strategies.

Problems they've faced

1. Have students come up and write one an issue they've dealt with.

2. Share with them some example problems: parent incarcerated, divorce in your family, death of a loved one, gender identity (LGBTQ) struggles,

issues with a stutter or other disability, anxiety over tests, bullying, feeling excluded, abuse, body image issues, sexual assault/rape, depression, bipolar disorder, mom with cancer, etc.

3. Have them write one issue per Post-it Note, with a limit of 1–2 notes per student.

4. Have them post the 1 or 2 notes on the wall all together.

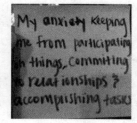

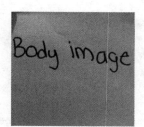

5. When they are done posting their notes on the wall, take a minute to admire the work and how many there are. Suddenly they feel and understand that they are not alone, which is more powerful than simply saying it.

6. Start reading some of them. And say something like "Wow. Two people in here are struggling with LGBTQ issues. I see that someone has a dad in jail, another two have suffered a rape or sexual assault, and several feel anxious about schoolwork and social situations."

7. Turn to your class. "Did you know your peers were struggling with such big issues? Did you know that about your classmates?"

Typically, they are pretty stunned. Ask how they feel about this. Ask them how they feel about the exercise. Has it made them more aware of others? Can we assume that sometimes when someone seems angry at you, they might just be struggling with a problem that feels really big? How can you help a friend? (listening, telling a trusted adult)

Talking points for the problem-posting portion of the exercise

1. You can't heal if you can't feel.
2. You can't control what happens but you can control how you react.
3. Feelings are not permanent and neither is a crisis. Things are always changing.
4. How others act toward you is often not personal but a result of what they are going through.
5. Minimize your exposure to toxic stress by removing yourself from the situation (abuse in the home, for example).
6. Working through problems makes you stronger.
7. Asking for help is not a weakness but a sign of strength.
8. Identify and tell a trusted adult.
9. Choose healthy coping strategies that works for you.

Before dismissal or to end the exercise

1. Ask the group to think about which of the healthy coping strategies they talked about would help them and see if anyone in the group will share which one they might try.
2. Bring their attention to the Crisis Text Line number 741-741. They can text any time of day or night and be texting with a trained counselor confidentially about any issue. Mention there are resources in the school and tell them about these.

3. Ask the group to think of two trusted adults they could go to if they needed to talk or some help—one inside school, one outside of school. "These would be the people you'd go to when you need support for a problem you are dealing with. Not just suicide. They might not be able to solve the problem, but they can listen and they might have some ideas."

WORKSHEET 10: COPING SKILLS WORKSHEET

1. Think of a difficulty you have faced in the past. Whatever it is, think back to how you got through it. How did you do it and what strategies did you use?

_____

_____

_____

_____

2. Indicate which of these coping strategies to manage emotionally difficult circumstances would be considered *healthy* or *unhealthy*? An unhealthy strategy could be one that over time could have consequences that negatively affect your health and well-being. A healthy strategy is one that can benefit you long term.

Coping Strategy

U= Unhealthy, H=Healthy. Put a U or an H in the blank below each statement.

Using drugs or alcohol to numb pain, relax, or forget something painful

_____

Writing your thoughts and feelings in a journal, blog, writing poetry, music

_____

Listening to music

_____

Eating a lot of ice cream or other food

_____

Talking about something difficult with a friend or trusted adult

_____

Using your faith to sort through a problem

_____

Volunteering or giving back

_____

Self-harm

_____

Creating artwork or other creative pursuit

_____

Using retail therapy (aka spending/shopping to feel good)

_____

Exercise and playing sports

_____

Self-criticism

_____

Fishing, hiking, camping or other outdoor activity

_____

Avoiding or isolating from friends and family (ghosting)

_____

Lead a class discussion on how they rated the strategies and why utilizing these discussion points.

1. You can't heal if you can't feel.

2. You can't control what happens but you can control how you react.

3. Feelings are not permanent and neither is a crisis. Things are always changing.

4. How others act toward you is often not personal but a result of what they are going through.

5. Minimize your exposure to toxic stress by removing yourself from the situation (abuse in the home, for example).

6. Working through problems makes you stronger.

7. Asking for help is not a weakness but a sign of strength.

8. Identify and tell a trusted adult.

9. Choose a healthy coping strategy that works for you.

WORKSHEET 11: WHAT IS YOUR PASSION?

1. If it was guaranteed that you'd be successful in whatever you chose to pursue, what would you do?

   _____

   _____

   _____

2. As a child, what did you do that you enjoyed the most?

   _____

   _____

   _____

3. I am happiest when I am. . .

   _____

   _____

   _____

4. What are your favorite topics to discuss—topics you could spend hours talking about?

   _____

   _____

   _____

5. When people ask your opinion or advice, what do they ask?

   _____

   _____

   _____

6. When you are online or in a bookstore, what makes you stop and want to read more?

   _____

   _____

   _____

7. What do you love helping people with?

_____

_____

_____

8. Is there a school assignment that you totally got into? If so, what was it?

_____

_____

_____

9. Whom do you admire and why? This can be a celebrity or a normal human.

_____

_____

_____

10. What do you enjoy doing that most people might not know about?

_____

_____

_____

WORKSHEET 12: SAMPLE SCHEDULE OF STUDENT MENTAL WELLNESS EVENTS/IDEAS

☐ Bake Sale
- Date/Time:
- Money raised:
- Hours: 5

☐ Samaritans 5k
- Date/Time:
- Money raised:
- Hours: 10

- ☐ Waffle Sundae Breakfast
  - Date/Time:
  - Hours: 5
- ☐ Work with community bookstore for a young adult mental health event
  - Date/Time:
  - Hours: 5
- ☐ Test Strategy Compilation Discussion (Midterms)
  - Date/Time:
  - Hours: 5
- ☐ Therapy Dogs Visit the School
  - Date/Time:
  - Hours: 10
- ☐ Club Mental Health Fair
  - Date/Time:
  - Hours: 5
- ☐ X Block (or panel) Discussions
  - Speaker—Social media and mental health
  - Speaker from Suicide Prevention Nonprofit—How to help a friend
  - Music therapist (Community person)—Music, mental health, and the brain
  - Hours: 5
- ☐ **Mental Health Week**
  - Date/Time:
  - Hours: 25
  - General things:
    - SOS curriculum
    - Work with library to promote specific books

- ☐ Monday:
  - Nonprofit Suicide Prevention Group Presentation
  - Compliment board
  - Balloon animals
- ☐ Tuesday:
  - Rock painting with free drinks and snacks (for rock painting ideas, check out Pinterest)
  - Pamphlets and resource cards
- ☐ Wednesday:
  - Lemonade Stand
  - Stress balls
  - Poster board with counselors
  - Celebrity quotes around the school
- ☐ Thursday:
  - Member of the club offers a personal story
  - Therapy dogs and popsicles
  - Pamphlets and resource cards
  - Club logo stress balls

Thank you to Desmond Hertzfelder and Aurora Wulff for sharing their mental wellness activities as they are reflected in this compilation schedule.

WORKSHEET 13: SCRIPT FOR RESPONDING TO STUDENTS WHO THINK INFORMATION IS BEING WITHHELD

A parent or parents may not have given permission for disclosing a suicide death. So how do you respond to students who make accusations that you or the school are holding back information or lying about a student who died by suicide? While you can't put anything in writing about how the student died, you can certainly have those much-needed conversations in the classroom.

Teachers can respond with:

"The school has been in touch with the parents and they are not acknowledging how their son died and we have to respect their wishes. It's a privacy issue but that doesn't mean we can't have a conversation about the topic of suicide in this classroom since it has come up. Because it's an important conversation to have. So, you know what you have heard and what you think, and how does that change your reaction if you think that he died by suicide?"

WORKSHEET 14: SCRIPT FOR ASKING PARENTS' PERMISSION TO DISCLOSE A SUICIDE DEATH

Below is a sample script that someone who has the task of reaching out to parents can use as a starting point.

Sample Script

"I am deeply sorry to hear about your daughter's death. Please know that the school community is mourning with you and that includes me. Is there anything we can do to help right now? Any resources you need? I know this is a difficult topic and I have to ask you an important question. We have heard this was a suicide. If that's true, and because we don't want other teens to see suicide as a solution, would you be willing to grant us permission to disclose the cause of death with the goal of preventing further loss of life? We ask this because we know that sensitive, respectful conversation and education on the subject encourages other students who are struggling with thoughts of suicide to ask for help. Keeping silent, on the other hand, means those students are less likely to come forward and are at heightened risk. As you might imagine, any time a teenager passes away prematurely, his or her peers inquire about the cause of death. With a family's permission, we would typically share that information with the community, and we don't want to treat your daughter's death differently. Silence implies shame and we want to make sure that students understand that there is no shame in mental health challenges. Suicide is a serious public health threat to our young people and we want to do all that we can to support those who are struggling in getting the help they need and deserve. Thank you so much for your openness. Please know that we will continue to be here to support your family in the weeks and months to come and beyond." This script has been reviewed and edited by:

Jim McCauley, LICSW (He/Him/His), Co-Founder and Associate Director of Riverside Trauma Center, Needham Heights, Massachusetts

---

Visitation Postvention Recommendations

Thank you to Jim McCauley, LICSW, Riverside Trauma Center, the source of these guidelines

- This is a script for an in-person visit, and not a letter or an email. If not in person, a phone call is the next best option.

- Two people should visit the family of the child lost to suicide immediately after getting the news and at least one of them should be a school administrator. This should be the principal or assistant superintendent (not the superintendent; see note below), who goes with someone the family knows, like a favorite teacher or coach. While it is unusual for school administrators to visit the home right after hearing about a student's death, it's a mistake not to. School administrators may get advice from lawyers that the family may sue. But not visiting immediately only increases animosity (if there is any).

- Sometimes parents have been fighting for years with schools about a better education plan (e.g. 504 or IEP). There may have been a history of bullying complaints or some other issue and it is still recommended that this admin/teacher team visit the family. You may get the door slammed in your face but the family won't be able to tell the press they "never heard from the school."

NOTE: There is a specific reason that the superintendent should not be one of the people to visit the family. Sometimes family will make extremely difficult requests of the school, such as "We want to hold the funeral in the school auditorium," or "We would like to build a memorial in front of the school," so the administrators can always say they don't have that authority and will have to take the request back to the superintendent and/or the school committee.

Jennifer Hamilton (She/Her/Hers), School Psychologist, Director of Psychology and Counseling at Noble and Greenough, Independent School, Dedham, Massachusetts

WORKSHEET 15: GUIDELINES FOR TELLING YOUR STORY

This is a framework for writing and telling one's story about mental health, trauma, and suicide attempt that will be shared in public with students. Use the best practices on this outline for narratives that include suicide and focus on these bullet points for creating a story that will be shared in public with students.

- **Describe who you are**, what you do, and a bit about yourself.
- **Share your experience of crisis.** What happened before you received the help you needed? Think about the most important thing you'd like your listener to know. Keep this section brief.
- **Share what helped you.** Describe how you got through crisis and found help and hope, or what more would have helped you. This step is important, as it illustrates the value of support and provides resources or actions others can take.
- **Share your experience of recovery**. How has this experience changed you for the better? What kind of support helped you? Share how you maintain recovery and share your hope for others.
- **Share resources**. Every talk about suicide or mental illness should also have resources to encourage people to reach out at the beginning. That can be in the form of a slide and cards to hand out that promote help-seeking behavior.

After you tell your story:
- Be prepared that others will reach out and tell you their story
- Be ready with resources or point out the resource table
- Use self-care practices and your support network if you feel overwhelmed

(Source: Storytelling for Suicide Prevention Checklist: SuicidePreventionLife-line.org/storytelling-for-suicide-prevention-checklist, Suicide Prevention Life-line and Vibrant Emotional Health)

4 Hs of Storytelling

Storytellers should avoid graphic details of a suicide or suicide attempt and include these themes, known as the four Hs:

HARDSHIP

Your story

HELP

What helped you through the crisis

HEALING

How you healed

HOPE

Why you have hope

SEUSS-LIKE SCRIPTS: A SERIOUS MESSAGE IN AN ENGAGING FORMAT

The following poems or scripts on the next five pages are written in the bouncy, fun cadence reminiscent of Dr. Seuss books. These work especially well in middle school but high schoolers love them, too. They deliver a serious message in a fun and playful way. Most kids have fond memories of reading or being read Seuss books as a child and this style of delivery rekindles those warm memories while delivering important messages.

When Anne Moss Rogers speaks to middle schools or high schools, she often requests that ahead of her arrival, teachers choose a student—or a group of students, who each take one paragraph—to read one or two of the scripts during a presentation. Some teens have even worn the Seuss hat and bow tie when they perform them. These scripts have been read over morning announcements, used for videos or as part of stage and virtual presentations for mental health, and posted as printouts in classrooms. How might you or your student wellness group use these? What ideas might the students have? Could they write their own scripts in a similar style to send an important message?

A fun activity would be to read the book *Oh, the Places You'll Go!* to the class and analyze it. The message is great for managing transitions in life, a time when many young people struggle.

WORKSHEET 16: BULLIES AREN'T THE BOSS OF YOU!

Some girl told you

to end it all

Then some random guy

said the same thing too

Then another wrote

something *really* mean

And you just felt

totally demeaned

Who is this dude?

Who was that chick?

Why would they say

To do such a trick?

That is so sad!

They feel so bad

So all they can do

Is pick on you

They can't tell you what to do!

Because they are not the boss of you

Put your feet in your shoes

Turn off that tech

And point yourself

In the direction you choose

You have places to go

And sunsets to see

You have no time to chat

With people like that

The answer is never to suicide

You have too much to give

To be pushed aside

There is only one you

Not three, or two

Don't cheat us out

of what you can do

WORKSHEET 17: TOODLE-OO TO TABOO

It's so taboo

Top secret

And hushed

Brushed under the rug

And cloaked in shame

Why are we stressin'

about depression

This thing in the brain

we treat with disdain

It's just a disorder

that we *can* contain

but we call it a weakness

which is inhumane

You can't get it on a plane

In a box

Or on a train

Not from cats or caffeine

Or even a trampoline

The tradition of shame

Has got to go

Be totally trashed

And completely let go

Step out of that box

Have the guts to say

That stigma sucks

And it shouldn't stay

I challenge you

And you, and you

To stop the stigma of mental illness

WORKSHEET 18: EARS FOR YOUR PEERS

If you have a friend

Who hurts every day

Can't seem to keep

Bad thoughts at bay

Maybe cutting

Or purging

Binging

Or drugging

Feeling anxious or moody

And not Howdy Doody

You can't let this drop

Or say toodle-oo

No way José

This is your job to do

So use your ears

Listen to your gut

Then stop and say

What can I do?

You don't have to fix it

But you can reach out

find a trusted adult

And let the truth come out

You can do this together

Because this is your friend

And you don't want

their life to end

I challenge you

And you, and you

To talk about depression and suicide

There is only one you

Not three, or two

Don't cheat us out of what you can do

WORKSHEET 19: I'M ROOTING FOR YOU!

You are cruising along

Doing groovy and fine

When all of a sudden

You get cut from the team

Your dog gets hit

A friend betrays

A breakup weighs.

These thoughts creep in

They tease and coerce

They make your brain think

You have no worth.

There's this thing called resilience

That helps you bounce back

It's deep down inside

Way, way in reserve.

So when people make fun

Are relentless and cruel

You need to regroup

And root for you.

It starts from within

From deep down in your toes

Bypasses your nose

To your brain it goes.

Once it gets there

You got guts and game

Gumption times ten

With get-up-and-go.

Make it come from within

Fight back and win

Because bad things that happen

Make you stronger in the end

WORKSHEET 20: DON'T BALK, DO TALK

We don't talk suicide

with neighbors or friends

Not with our parents

Or even boyfriends

Nothing triggers more fear

Everyone steers clear!

Never taking the time

Makes suicide rates climb

The morning isn't good

And neither is the evening

We don't talk on vacation.

Or in a party situation.

Not in a plane

or a train.

Not in a car

or a bus.

Not while we're running

or when we're sitting.

Not in a box.

Not with a fox.

Not in a house.

Not with a mouse.

So when is a good time?

How about now?

Talk saves lives

It saves teens

It saves wives

So make a date to talk

don't balk!

Be unique.

Have the courage to speak.

I challenge you

And you, and you

To talk about depression and suicide

NOTES

1. Children, Teens and Suicide Loss from Dougy.org or AFSP.org.
2. Ibid.

Glossary

Many, but not all, of these definitions are from the Model School Policy created by The Trevor Project, the world's largest suicide prevention and crisis intervention organization for LGBTQ (Lesbian, Gay, Bisexual, Transgender, Queer, or Questioning) young people in collaboration with the American School Counselor Association (ASCA), National Association of School Psychologists (NASP), and the American Foundation for Suicide Prevention (AFSP).

SUICIDE PREVENTION, INTERVENTION, POSTVENTION

Suicide prevention is focused on reducing risk factors for suicide and enhancing protective factors. This calls for coordinating and collaborating on a multifaceted approach with the educational system, community partners and members, government, healthcare, and policy makers. A successful response to prevention should prioritize cost-effective and evidence-based approaches that focus on student and faculty safety and wellness, education, early intervention, coordinated protocols, and consistent messaging. Combining efforts to bolster protective factors and coping skills through social emotional learning initiatives wrapped with education on suicide and mental illness creates the most effective suicide prevention environment.

The gatekeeper model of suicide prevention refers to teachers as individuals who have face-to-face contact with large numbers of community members (students) as part of their usual routine who can be trained to identify those at risk of suicide and refer them to treatment or supporting services.

There are different categories of suicide prevention programs:

- **Universal prevention programs** target an entire population to reduce risk factors or enhance protective factors.

- **Selective prevention programs** target youth who demonstrate risk factors associated with suicide, but who have not yet reported suicidal thoughts or an attempt.
- **Indicated prevention programs** are designed to intervene with youth who have already reported suicidal thoughts or an attempt.

Suicide intervention, assessment, and referral: When a student is identified by a peer, educator, or other source as potentially suicidal—i.e. verbalizes thoughts about suicide, presents overt risk factors such as agitation or intoxication, an act of self-harm occurs, or expresses or otherwise shows signs of suicidal ideation—the student shall be seen by a school-employed mental health professional, such as a school psychologist, school counselor, or school social worker, within the same school day to assess risk and facilitate referral if necessary. Educators shall also be aware of written threats and expressions about suicide and death in school assignments. Such incidences require immediate referral to the appropriate school-employed mental health professional. If there is no mental health professional available, a designated staff member (e.g. school nurse or administrator) shall address the situation according to district protocol until a mental health professional is brought in.

Suicide postvention is a crisis intervention strategy designed to assist with the grief process following suicide loss. This strategy, when used appropriately, reduces the risk of suicide contagion, provides the support needed to help survivors cope with a suicide death, addresses the social stigma associated with suicide, and disseminates factual information after the death of a member of the school community. Often a community or school's healthy postvention effort can lead to readiness to engage further with suicide prevention efforts and save lives.

Upstream strategies build protective factors that can mitigate risk, such as creating a sense of belonging, eliminating stigmatized language and discriminating actions, building resilience through life skills and mental hardiness, and enhancing mental health literacy.[1]

Midstream approaches help identify people in emerging risk and then link them to appropriate support before the issues develop into a suicidal crisis.

Midstream strategies include screening for mental health conditions and suicidal thoughts, promoting and normalizing many types of help-seeking/help-giving behavior, and training populations on how to have difficult suicide-specific conversations.[2]

Downstream tactics are needed to guide the response when a suicide crisis has happened, including when people have acute thoughts of suicide, attempt suicide, or die by suicide. Current thinking about effective downstream tactics is that they are not so much about constraint (e.g. involuntary hospitalization, restraints, and isolation) but rather focus on an attempt to answer the question "How can we approach these crises in a way that offers connection, dignity, and empowerment instead of fear?"[3]

DEFINITIONS IN ALPHABETICAL ORDER

At-risk Suicide risk is not a dichotomous concern, but rather exists on a continuum with various levels of risk. Each level of risk requires a different level of response and intervention by the school and the district. A student who is defined as high-risk for suicide is one who has made a suicide attempt, has the intent to die by suicide, or has displayed a significant change in behavior suggesting the onset of potential mental health conditions or a deterioration of mental health. The student may have thoughts about suicide, including potential means of death, and may have a plan. In addition, the student may exhibit behaviors or feelings of isolation, hopelessness, helplessness, and the inability to tolerate any more pain. This situation would necessitate a referral, as documented in the following procedures. The type of referral, and its level of urgency, shall be determined by the student's level of risk—according to local district policy.

BIPOC Acronym that stands for Black, Indigenous, and People of Color. It's usually used for people of color in general when compared to the white experience.

Colonialism Colonialism is a practice of domination, which involves the subjugation of one people to another. It is the policy or practice of a wealthy or powerful nation's maintaining or extending its control over other countries, especially in establishing settlements or exploiting resources. The practice of colonialism usually involved the transfer of an Indigenous population to a new territory, where the arrivals lived as permanent settlers while maintaining political allegiance to their country of origin.

Crisis team   A crisis team is a multidisciplinary team of administrative staff, mental health professionals, safety professionals, and support staff whose primary focus is to address crisis preparedness, intervention, response, and recovery. Crisis team members often include someone from the administrative leadership, school psychologists, school counselors, school social workers, school nurses, resource police officer, and others, including support staff and/or teachers. These professionals have been specifically trained in areas of crisis preparedness and take a leadership role in developing crisis plans, ensuring school staff can effectively execute various crisis protocols, and may provide mental health services for effective crisis interventions and recovery supports. Crisis team members who are mental health professionals may provide crisis intervention and services.

Evidence-based program   Evidence-based programs, also referred to as "programs with evidence of effectiveness," are programs that have been rigorously tested in controlled settings, proven effective, and translated into practical models that are widely available to community-based organizations. There are five steps that must be completed and repeated continuously for the life of the program, practice, or policy. This research is continuous in order to stay relevant and best for the current situation. This process is what most people think of when thinking about research, as in creating an answerable question, searching for evidence, evaluating for validity, integrating what has been found, and then evaluating outcomes. It is also important that the evaluations themselves have been subjected to critical peer review. That is, experts in the field and not just the people who developed and evaluated the program have examined the evaluation's methods and agreed with its conclusions about the program's effectiveness. Ultimately, when you implement an evidence-based program, you can be confident you're delivering a program that works and is highly likely to improve the health of your audience. Funders, leaders, community members, and stakeholders want to invest limited resources in programs that are based on programming with solid evidence of efficacy and science, which facilitates buy-in and funding.

Evidence-informed program   While evidence-based means that research is conducted through validated extensive and complex scientific processes that may take years to complete, evidence-informed refers to a program that uses already available research that is tested, tried, and true. This evidence is then combined with the experiences and expertise of the organization to best fit the population served. Evidence-informed is great for problems that are difficult to track and research due to underreporting, transitional population, and other reasons. Using evidence-informed practice allows agencies to use the best practices possible without having to reinvent the wheel or spend thousands of dollars on research of their own. It is a valid approach in a scenario when the amount of time it would take to develop and implement evidence-based research may cost precious lives.

Historical trauma   Also known as multigenerational trauma, historical trauma refers to the cumulative emotional and psychological damage to an individual or group of individuals as the result of traumatic experiences or events. Examples are slavery, the Holocaust, forced migration, and the violent colonization of Native Americans.

Jason Flatt Act   Jason Flatt was a young man who died by suicide and the Jason Flatt Act is the nation's most inclusive and mandatory youth suicide awareness and prevention legislation pertaining to teacher in-service training. In states where it has passed, it requires all educators in the state to complete two hours of youth suicide awareness and prevention training each year in order to be able to be licensed to teach in that state. In all states where it has passed, the Jason Flatt Act has been supported by the state's Department of Education, which points to the value seen in such preventive training. When introduced under the Jason Flatt Act, a state can pass this important lifesaving/life-changing legislation without a fiscal note. Visit JasonFoundation.com for more information.

Lethal means   Lethal means refers to objects such as medications, firearms, sharp objects, poisons, or ropes that can be used to engage in suicidal self-directed violence, including suicide attempts. Facilitating lethal means safety is an essential component of effective suicide prevention.

LGBTQ   Lesbian, Gay, Bisexual, Transgender, Queer, or Questioning

Transgender   Transgender refers to people whose gender identity differs from the sex they were assigned at birth. Many transgender people will transition to align their gender expression with their gender identity; however, you do not have to transition in order to be transgender.

Nonbinary   Nonbinary refers to people who don't identify with the traditional male and female gender roles. Many other words for identities outside the traditional categories of man and woman may be used, such as genderfluid, genderqueer, polygender, bigender, demigender, or agender. These identities, while similar, are not necessarily interchangeable or synonymous.

Cisgender   Cisgender is a term used to describe a person whose gender identity aligns with those typically associated with the sex assigned to them at birth.[4]

Mental health   A state of mental, emotional, and cognitive health that can impact perceptions, choices, and actions affecting wellness and functioning. Some mental health conditions include depression, anxiety, post-traumatic stress disorder, and substance use disorders. Mental health can be impacted by the home and social environment, early childhood adversity or trauma, physical health, and genetics.

Precipitating factors   These are the stressful life events that can trigger a suicidal crisis in a vulnerable person. Note that it's not one factor but a cluster of several that happen all at once that usually triggers someone to suicide; these can include a romantic breakup, grief from loss of a loved one, family conflict, poor school or athletic performance, and bullying/humiliation.

Protective factors   These are characteristics or conditions that decrease risk and help protect people from suicide. Protective factors may encompass biological, psychological, and/or social factors in the individual, family, and environment and can vary among different cultures and ethnic groups, but universal factors include a sense of belonging and connectedness to individuals, family, community, and social institutions; a sense of purpose or meaning in life; ability to cope; positive self-esteem; cultural or religious beliefs that discourage suicide; access to behavioral healthcare; and positive relationships with caregivers.

Risk assessment   An evaluation of a student who may be at-risk for suicide, conducted by the appropriate designated school staff (e.g. school psychologist, school social worker, school counselor, or in some cases trained school administrator). This assessment is designed to elicit information regarding the student's intent to die by suicide, previous history of suicide attempts, presence of a suicide plan and its level of lethality and availability of means, presence of support systems, level of hopelessness and helplessness, mental status, and other relevant risk factors.

Risk factors for suicide   Characteristics or conditions that increase the chance that a person may attempt to take their life. Suicide risk is most often the result of multiple risk factors converging at a moment in time. Risk factors may encompass biological, psychological, and/or social factors in the individual, family, and environment. The likelihood of an attempt is highest when there are multiple factors that are present or escalating, when protective factors and healthy coping techniques have diminished, and when the individual has access to lethal means.

Self-harm (also known as NSSI or non-suicidal self-injury)   Behavior that is self-directed and deliberately results in injury or the potential for injury to oneself. Self-harm behaviors can be either non-suicidal or suicidal. Although non-suicidal self-injury (NSSI) lacks suicidal intent, youth who engage in any type of self-harm should receive mental health care. Treatment can improve coping strategies to lower the urge to self-harm, and reduce the long-term risk of a future suicide attempt.

Suicidal behavior   Suicide attempts, injury to oneself associated with at least some level of intent, developing a plan or strategy for suicide, gathering the means for a suicide plan, or any other overt action or thought indicating intent to end one's life.

Suicidal ideation   Thinking about, considering, or planning for self-injurious behavior that may result in death. A desire to be dead without a plan or the intent to end one's life is still considered suicidal ideation and shall be taken seriously.

Suicide   Death caused by self-directed injurious behavior with any intent to die as a result of the behavior.
NOTE: The coroner's or medical examiner's office must first confirm that the death was a suicide before any school official may state this as the cause of death. Additionally, parent or guardian preference shall be considered in determining how the death is communicated to the larger community.

Suicide attempt   A self-injurious behavior for which there is evidence that the person had at least some intent to die. A suicide attempt may result in death, injuries, or no injuries. A mixture of ambivalent feelings, such as a wish to die and a desire to live, is a common experience with most suicide attempts. Therefore, ambivalence is not a reliable indicator of the seriousness or level of danger of a suicide attempt or the person's overall risk.

Suicide contagion   The process by which suicidal behavior or a suicide death influences an increase in the suicide risk of others. Glorification of the death or the deceased, identification with the deceased, modeling, and guilt are each thought to play a role in contagion. Although rare, suicide contagion can result in a cluster of suicides within a community.

NOTES

1.   Workplace Suicide Prevention, workplacesuicideprevention.com
2.   Ibid.
3.   Ibid.
4.   https://www.hrc.org/

Index

A

Ackley, Melissa K., 57
Action Alliance for Suicide
    Prevention, 265
Active Minds Mental Wellness Club
    (Wulff), 149–150, 157
ACT Steps Signs of Suicide, 101f
ADHD, 11, 114, 142
Adolescence, characteristics, 20
Adolescent precipitating events,
    examples, 34
Adolescent suicide
    attempt, 193
    grief, responses, 237–238
    protective factors, 19
    risk factors, 19, 22–23
    warning signs, 19, 46–48
Adverse childhood experiences
    (ACEs), 10, 31
Advice column activity (suicide
    prevention activity), 136
Affinity group, 147
After a Suicide: A Toolkit for
    Schools (AFSP/SPRC), 213,
    220–221, 231, 255
Aggression, 23, 50
Alaska, suicide ranking,
    225–226
Alcohol/drugs, usage (increase), 50
Alliance of Hope for Suicide Loss
    Survivors, 281

American Foundation of Suicide
    Prevention (AFSP), 71, 110–111,
    150, 160, 265, 309
    loss support group, 281
    training/programs, 97
American Indian Life Skills
    (AILS), 263
    life-skills training program,
        108–109
American Indians/Alaskan Native
    (AI/AN) youth, suicide rate/
    behaviors, 26–27, 108
American School Counselor
    Association (ASCA), 71, 309
Anorexia nervosa, 143
Anxiety, 10, 50, 142
    disorders, 1, 23, 45
    reduction, 173
Applied Suicide Intervention Skills
    Training (ASIST) (LivingWorks)
    training, usage, 99
Apps, resources, 282, 286
Ask Suicide-Screening Questions
    (ASQ), usage, 117–118
ASK Suicide Screening tool
    (ASQ), 63
At-risk, definition, 311
At-risk student populations, 23–38
Attention problems, reduction, 114
Autism Spectrum Disorder, 142
Autism, youth (involvement), 34

B

Belonging, culture (creation), 85–91
Bereaved student
    school return (planning
      checklist), 279–280
    struggle, 204
Biela, James, 96, 128, 211, 225–227
Bipolar disorder, 9, 11, 23, 130, 143
Black adolescents/children, suicide
    rates, 28
Black, Indigenous, and People of
    Color (BIPOC)
    definition, 311
    suicidal thoughts, 28
Black Lives Matter, 156
Born This Way Foundation, 111
Box breathing (mindfulness
    activity), 134
Breathing exercises, 236
Bring Change 2 Mind
    (BringChange2Mind), 158, 159
Brinton, Sam, 25, 69, 86
Bulimia/binge eating, 143
Bullying, 10, 34, 220
    complaints, 216
    impact, 66–67
    mitigation, 114
    worksheet, 302–303

C

Call to Action, 162
Calm/happiness, warning sign, 248
CASEL. *See* Collaborative
    for Academic, Social, and
    Emotional Learning
CAST. *See* Coping and
    Support Training
Child Mind Institute, 159, 266
Children, silent suffering, 228
*Children, Teens and Suicide
    Loss* (Dougy Center/AFSP),
    202, 205, 279

Children, suicide
    adopted children, risk, 33
    post-suicide family visit, 216
    screening, nonnecessity
      (myth), 62–63
    talking, desire, 173–181
Chock-Goldman, Jessica, 9, 87–88, 91,
    92, 118, 169
    hospitalization risk analysis, 199
    Korean Parent Group, 147
    student suicide, 180–181
    student thank you note, 254
Chronic illness/disabilities, impact, 33
Cinco de Mayo (suicide prevention
    activity), 137
Cisgender, definition, 314
Clark, Jim, 114
Classmate, death, 232
Classroom
    conversation (facilitation), scripts
      (usage), 233–238
    culture (building), collaboration
      (usage), 92–93
    teachers, student reentry (study
      load), 201
Coaches, three-step suicide
    prevention intervention, 191–192
Collaboration, usage, 92–93, 124, 179
Collaborative for Academic,
    Social, and Emotional Learning
    (CASEL), 112, 264
Colonialism, 28, 311–312
Columbia-Suicide Severity Rating
    Scale (C-SSRS), 118
Community Support Resource
    (CSR), 164
Comprehensive Approach to Mental
    Health Promotion and Suicide
    Prevention for High Schools, 107
Conduct disorder, 9, 10–11, 23
Confidentiality/discretion, 192
Confidentiality policy, 79
    sample (worksheet), 278–279
    template, 79, 80

Connect/Disconnect (suicide prevention activity), 140
Connectedness, culture (creation), 85–91
Connection, promotion (activities), 151
Co-occurring disorders, 9
Coping
   conversation starters, 288
   healthy exercises/strategies, 124, 288–289
   positive coping strategies, 287
   skills (worksheet), 292–293
   strategies, 191, 251
   tools, brainstorming, 281
   unhealthy strategies, 7
      student identification, 288–289
Coping and Support Training (CAST), 263
   evidence-based program, 108
Coping Strategies and Resilience Building Game (worksheet), 287–292
   problem-posting, talking points, 291
Copycat suicide, 37–38, 228, 238, 316
Counselors
   student contact, 188–189
   suicide inquiry, questioning, 193
Crisis
   experience, sharing, 300
   protocol, structure maintenance, 221–227
   response, 121
   suicidal crisis, 59, 247
   team, definition, 312
   text line, example, 174
   training programs, resources, 264
   USA hotlines/crisis lines, 282
   warnings signs, recognition, 191
Crying rooms, school setup, 223

D

DBT in Schools: Skills Training for Emotional Problem Solving for Adolescents (DBT STEPS-A) (Mazza/Dexter-Mazza/Murphy/Rathus), 112–114, 129, 264, 267
Death
   family, communication, 215–221
   occurrence, crisis team (activation), 213–214
   post-suicide death email, sample, 217–218
   suicide death (death by suicide), 29
      aspects, addressing, 214
      treatment, 75
Deceased
   memorialization, 75, 214
   script, stories (sharing), 234
Demographic region, suicidal thoughts, 28–29
Depression, 1, 23, 47, 50, 123, 142
   teenagers, 8
Derr, Billy (overdose), 148
Dexter-Mazza, Elizabeth T., 112, 267
Dia de los Muertos (Day of the Dead celebration) (suicide prevention activity), 137
Digital learning environment, creation, 93–94
   worksheet, 272–273
Discrimination, 28
Distance learning, student wellness survey, 273–274
Diversity, website resources, 260–262
"Dogs and Donuts," 241
Don't Balk, Do Talk (worksheet), 307–308
Dougy Center, 202, 279, 281
Drowning, drawing, 171f
Dunavant, Leigh, 148

E

Ears for Your Peers (worksheet), 304–305
Eating disorder, 9, 12
Education plan, parent battle, 216
Educators
    postvention, summary, 245
    suicide talking points, 227–231, 227f
    training programs, resources, 262
    youth bereavement, educator assistance (worksheet), 279–282
Emerson Model (OneHeartProject), 114–115, 264
Emotionally Naked blog, note (example), 43f
Emotional pain, communication, 62
Emotional wellness
    finding, 251
    mindfulness, contribution, 114
Empathy, usage, 204, 284
Empty desk syndrome
    class discussion, 231
    self-care, 241–245
Erbacher, Terri A., 268
Erika's Lighthouse (ErikasLighthouse), 159
Ethnicity, youth suicide factor, 26–28
Ethnic populations, risk/protective factors, 45
Evidence-based program, 95, 101, 312
Evidence-based universal school-based suicide prevention programs, curriculums, 100
Evidence-informed program, 95, 107, 313
Extracurricular stress, impact, 36–37

F

Faith, embracing, 236
Family
    cultural needs, sensitivity, 238
    death, communication, 215–221
    dysfunction/trauma, 45
    help, 191
    loss, school student reintegration, 197
    memorials, consultation, 214
    rejection, fear, 65
Fears, 270–272
    fear factor, impact, 123
Feelings, check-in script, 235
Firearms, access, 29–30, 190
Fishbowl game, student involvement, 153–154, 153f
Folder fear, 197
"For the Teen Contemplating Suicide and Looking for the Strength to Reach Out" (Rogers), 176
Fortunado-Kewin, Michelle, 24, 88
Framework for Successful Messaging, 162–164
Friend 2 Friend training, usage, 98
Friends, death (response), 232

G

Gaggle Safety Management, usage, 93
Gaggle, usage, 94, 273
Gag orders, issuance, 238
Gatekeeper training, 96–100
    programs, resources, 262
Gay Straight Alliance (GSANetwork), 159–160
Gender
    minorities, suicide vulnerability, 25–26
    suicide risk, relationship, 24
Genders & Sexualities Alliance (GSANetwork), 159–160

Gender Support Plan, 90
Generalized anxiety disorder, 9, 13
Goal setting, 128
Godwin Real Talk, goal, 156–157
Google for Educators, usage, 93
Government agencies,
    resources, 265–267
Grief, 6, 73, 223
    coping, 241
    journey, honoring, 231
    script, workthrough, 236–237
    teacher discussion, 230
    website resources, 259
GriefShare Group Locator, 281
GSA. See Genders & Sexual-
    ities Alliance

H

Habits, change, 252–253
Hamilton, Jennifer, 1, 122, 209,
    222–223, 278
    Nobles (mental health
        facility), 147
    thank you note, 217
Hardship, help, healing, hope (4 Hs),
    161–164, 301
HEARD Alliance Toolkit for Mental
    Health Promotion and Suicide,
    198, 256
Herzfelder, Desmond, 147, 151, 248,
    252–253, 297
High school age kids, suicidal
    thoughts, 20
High school students, suicide loss
    (worksheet), 283–287
Hines, Kevin (suicide attempt), 64
Hippocampus/amygdala,
    development, 5–6
Historical trauma (multigenerational
    trauma), definition, 313
Hope and Care video (suicide
    prevention activity), 138
Hopelessness, feeling, 50

Hope Squad, 263
    evidence-informed peer-to-
        peer suicide prevention
        program, 107
Hope versus Fear (suicide prevention
    activity), 141
Hospital
    post-stay, peer connections/
        support, 201–202
    psychiatric hospital, student
        reentry meeting, 200–201
    setting, student transition,
        199–202
Hospitalization risk, analysis, 199
"How to Tell a Parent You
    Are Thinking of Suicide"
    (Rogers), 175, 177
How to Use Social Media for
    Suicide Prevention User
    Guide (EmmResourceCenter),
    257
Hudnall, Gregory A., 107
Humiliation, 34, 50

I

Imposter syndrome, overcoming, 49
I'm Rooting for You (worksheet),
    306–307
Inclusion, website resources,
    260–262
Indian Health Service (IHS),
    27, 261, 267
Indicated prevention programs,
    95, 310
In-person learning, student wellness
    survey, 274
International Survivors of Suicide
    Loss Day (AFSP), 226
Irritability, 50
Issues and Options Surrounding
    a Student's Return to School
    Following a Suicide-Related
    Absence (SPRC), 198, 256

J

Jason Flatt Act, 266, 313
Jason Foundation, Inc. (JFI), 266
JED Foundation (JEDFoundation),
    160, 263, 266
JED High School (JEDFoundation),
    107–108
Johnny's Ambassadors, 7, 160

K

Karnath, Lea, 102, 120, 123
Kognito At-Risk for High School
    Educators (Kognito), 262
    gatekeeper training,
        usage, 98, 99f

L

Leadership, usage, 179
Lesbian, Gay, Bisexual, Transgender,
    and Questioning (LGBTQ)
    definition, 313–314
    family rejection, fear, 65
    students, parent communication/
        disconnection problems,
        88–89
    themes, incorporation, 86
Lesbian, Gay, Bisexual, Transgender,
    and Questioning (LGBTQ) youth
    suicide risk, 25, 70, 99
    support, 89
Lethal means, 45, 313
    removal, 191
License Plate Project (suicide
    prevention activity), 144–146
    designs, examples, 144f–145f
    requirements, 145–146
    specialty plate creation, student
        directions, 145
Life, 128
    skills, 45
    transitions, impact, 35–36

Lifelines: Prevention (evidence-based
    student curriculum) (Hazelden
    Publishing), 106
Listening, empathy (usage), 204, 284
LivingWorks, 262
Lock & Talk, 160
LoMurray, Scott, 44, 95, 104,
    120, 124, 197
Loss, impact, 73, 215
Louder than a Bomb, 267

M

Major depressive disorder
    (depression), 9, 10
Making Sounds (mindfulness
    activity), 134
Marijuana, impact, 7
Marijuana/suicide (relationship),
    education (website
    resources), 259
Mazza, James J., 83, 112–113,
    129–130, 167, 190, 267
McCauley, Jim, 186, 210–219, 299
McElwee, Sheila, 138–139, 243–244
Means safety, 182, 190
Memorial rooms, school setup, 223
Mental health, 23, 314
    check-in, 241
    disorders, 9–14
    improvement, 114
    problems, increase, 2–9
    student-driven mental
        health education website
        resources, 260
    student-led mental wellness
        clubs, 147–168
    student presentations
        (suicide prevention
        activity), 142–144
        steps/guidelines, 143
    training programs, 110–111
        resources, 264
    treatment, barriers, 3

Mental Health Awareness Month,
activities, 150
Mental Health Monday (suicide
prevention activity), 138–140
Mental wellness, 241
storytelling guidelines, 161–166
student events/ideas schedule,
sample (worksheet),
295–297
student-led mental wellness
clubs, 147–168
Mental wellness club
funding, 166–168
initiatives, organizational
support, 158–160
themes, 149
Middle school, NHT seniors
(visit), 155
Middle school students
mental health survey, 274
suicide loss, management
(worksheet), 283–287
Miller, Alec L., 267
Miller, Keygan, 72, 88
Mindful Jenga (mindfulness
activity), 134–135
Mindfulness, 113–114, 236
activities, 134–135
Minding Your Mind (MYM),
159, 266
Model School District Policy on
Suicide Prevention (AFSP),
255, 71–72
Mood
changes, 23
disorders, 45
display, suicide warning
sign, 50–51
More Than Sad (AFSP), 96,
110–111, 264
versions, usage, 111
Multi-Tiered Systems of
Support (MTSS) framework,
acceptance, 107

Murphy, Heather E., 267
Music, listening/playing (coping
strategies), 251

N

National Action Alliance for Suicide
Prevention, 265
National Alliance of Mental Illness
(NAMI), 97, 130, 159–160
Family Support Group/Family-to-
Family Class, 199
National Association of School
Psychologists (NASP),
70, 309
National Council for Behavioral
Health, 110
National Health Education
Standards, 108
National Survey on LGBTQ Mental
Health, 257
Native Americans
behavioral health resources, 27
SPRC resources, 211
Negativity, improvement, 252
NELB. See No Eagle Left Behind
Noble & Greenough School,
84, 148, 243
Nobles Heads Together (NHT),
148–149, 151
seniors, school visit, 155
video project, 152–154
No Eagle Left Behind (NELB), 148,
155–156, 155f
Nonbinary, definition, 314
Nonprofit agencies,
resources, 265–267
Non-suicidal self-injury
(NSSI), 30–31, 60
definition, 315
No-suicide contract
safety plans, contrast, 191
usage (myth), 59–60
NSSI. See Non-suicidal self-injury

O

Objects in a Bag (mindfulness activity), 134
O'Brien, Kim, 21
Obsessive Compulsive Disorder, 142
Online memorial pages, usage, 77
Our Minds Matter (Minding YourMind), 159
"Out of the Darkness Walks" (American Foundation of Suicide Prevention), 148, 150–151
Ozolins, Tammy, 130–131, 141, 224, 274
    mental health topic podcast guidelines/requirements, 146

P

Pain, solving, 212
Parents
    parenting strategy, 173
    student suicide
        information (myth), 65
        thoughts, website resources, 258
Passion, identification (worksheet), 294–295
Peer-to-Peer Depression Awareness Campaign (DepressionCenter), 160
Peyton Riekhof Foundation (ThePeytonRiekhof Foundation), 160
Phobias, 142
Photography (coping strategy), 251
Plemmons, Gregory, 4
Podcasts (suicide prevention activity), 146
    guidelines/requirements, 146
Poland, Scott, 268
Positive behavioral interventions and support (PBIS), 83–84
Positive coping strategies, 287

Positive narrative (messaging issue), 163–164
Post-suicide attempt, school student reintegration, 197
Post-traumatic stress disorder (PTSD), 1, 14
Postvention, 209
    goals, 210
    recommendations, 216
    teachers
        action/words, avoidance, 231–232
        talking tips, 229–231
Precipitating events, 34–35
    examples, 34
Precipitating factors, definition, 314
PREPaRE School Crisis Prevention and Intervention Training Curriculum (NASPonline), 70–71, 109, 264
Preteens, bereavement, 204
Prevent/prepare Reaffirm Evaluate Provide and Respond Examine (PREPaRE), 109, 221
Prince, Phoebe (suicide), 220
Protective factors (suicide), 44–45
    definition, 314
"Protect Your Space and Well-Being on Social Media" (Trevor Project), 152
Psychiatric hospital, student reentry meeting, 200–201

Q

Question, Persuade, Refer (QPR)
    programs, 262
    usage, 97

R

Race, youth suicide factor, 26–28
Racial populations, risk/protective factors, 45

Racial prejudice, 28
Ramsey, Shirley, 111
Rathus, Jill H., 267
Recommended Guidelines on
    Commemoration of Students at
    Time of Graduation, 256
Recovery, experience
    (sharing), 300
Reentry process, 198, 200–201
Reilly, Sean, 105, 114–115, 173
Reporting on Suicide, 258
Riekhof, Mike, 159
Risk. *See* Suicide risk
    assessment, definition,
        314–315
    at-risk youth, protec-
        tive factors (bolstering
        programs), 264–265
    factors, AFSP categories, 22
    risk factors for suicide,
        definition, 315
Risk and Protective Factors in Racial/
    Ethnic Populations in the U.S.
    (SPRC), 257
Riverside Trauma Center,
    98–99
Riverside Trauma Center
    Postvention Guidelines
    (SPRC), 257
Robot and Rag Doll (mindfulness
    activity), 135
Rock painting, student wellness
    activity, 154
Rogers, Anne Moss, 39–43
    social media comment, 74
    suicide comments, 174–175
    teachers
        message, example, 41f
        student trust, 176–177
    young person, interaction,
        187–188
Rowe, Shelby, 28, 90, 211
Rysko, Leigh, 122, 127, 136,
    171, 173

S

safeTALK (LivingWorks), usage, 97–98
Safety
    messaging issue, 162–163
    planning, 191
Safety plans, no-suicide contracts
    (contrast), 191
Schizophrenia, 9, 12–13, 23
Schools
    affinity groups, 147
    community, email (sample), 231
    confidentiality policy, 79–80
    culture
        building, collaboration,
            92–93
        health, 124
    extracurricular stress,
        impact, 36–37
    grief, website resources, 259
    mental wellness club
        initiatives, organizational
        support, 158–160
    staff, three-step suicide
        prevention intervention,
        191–192
    stressors, impact, 37
    student, reentry meeting,
        200–201
    suicide-related books, recommen-
        dations, 267–268
    suicide-related school-based
        models/toolkits, 255–257
    universal school-based suicide
        prevention programs,
        100–109
Schools, suicide
    class conversations/gatherings/
        support groups, elements,
        77–78
    commemoration/
        memorialization, 72–79
    commemoration policy, planning
        (student inclusion), 73–77
    counselors, questioning, 193

Schools, suicide (*Continued*)
crisis
plan, preparation, 70–71
protocol, structure
maintenance, 221–227
loss, student return, 202–207
memorial assemblies,
avoidance, 78
memorial events
family consultation, 78
parent approach, 75–76
occurrence, 70–79
on-campus erected physical
memorials funeral-type
events, avoidance, 75
online memorial pages, usage, 77
prevention, 70–79
activities, 127
efforts, barriers, 120–121
policy, 71–72
spontaneous materials, plan
(creation), 76–77
suicide-related school policies, 69
Schwartz, Victor, 3, 19, 20, 36, 47,
49, 84, 183
Screen time, increase (impact), 8–9
SEL. *See* Social and emotional learning
Selective prevention programs, 310
Self-esteem
building, 113
feelings, 11
Self-harm, 1, 6
definition, 315
reasons, 62
Self-hatred, change (pro-
cess), 250–251
Self-punishment, 62
Self-worth, positive sense, 45
Service projects, student
engagement (encouragement),
214
Sexual minorities (suicide
vulnerability), 25–26

Shadowing, 201–202
Simulated conversations, usage, 99f
Singer, Jonathan B., 70, 116, 120,
129, 182, 215, 268
whiteness, defaulting, 79
Social and emotional learning (SEL),
84, 95, 124
emphasis/source, 111, 112
Social justice movies (suicide
prevention activity), 136–137
Social media, impact, 4, 38–44
Social skills, improvement, 114
Social supports, contact, 191
SOS Signs of Suicide (MindWise
Innovations), evidence-
based program, 96, 101–102,
120, 123, 200
SOS Signs of Suicide Second ACT
(MindWise), 103
Sources of Strength, 263
evidence-based program,
103–106, 104f
Speaking Out About Suicide
(AFSP), 258
Special populations, risk factors
(example), 45
Stack, Johnny/Laura, 7
Stage, Dese'Rae L., 35, 62, 251
Standardized testing, usage, 4
Stanley H. King Institute, 84, 267
Start (LivingWorks), usage, 97
STEPS-A. *See* DBT in Schools: Skills
Training for Emotional Problem
Solving for Adolescents
Storytelling, 161–166, 236
guidelines (worksheet),
300–301
hardship, help, healing, hope
(4 Hs), 301
practices, 257–258
stories, sharing (script), 234
Storytelling for Suicide
Prevention Checklist, 257–258
Strategy (messaging issue), 162

Stress
    extracurricular stress,
        impact, 36–37
    reduction, promotion (activities),
        151
Students
    apps, resources, 282, 286
    assessment/support, need
        (identification), 229
    bereaved student, school
        return (planning checklist),
        279–280
    confidentiality policy sample
        (worksheet), 278–279
    coping, teacher awareness, 230
    cultural needs, sensitivity, 238
    digital devices, avoidance, 232
    drowning, drawing, 171f
    emotions, expression, 201
    fears, 270–272
    grief, website resources, 259
    handouts, 269
    information withholding
        suspicions, script response
        (worksheet), 297–298
    life transition
        impact, 35–36
        website resources, 259
    memorializing ideas,
        sharing, 230–231
    mental health
        presentations (suicide
          prevention activity),
          142–144
        topic podcast guidelines/
          requirements, 146
    mental wellness events/ideas
        schedule, sample (worksheet),
        295–297
    news, framework/guidelines,
        160–166
    pain, support, 204
    passion, identification
        (worksheet), 294–295

peers, support, 151
post-hospital stay, peer
    connections/support,
    201–202
protective factors (bolstering),
    programs (usage), 111–115
quizzes, 269
referral, 310
risk factors, teacher
    awareness, 230
school reentry
    meeting, 200–201
    parental involvement, 201
scripts, 269
self-acceptance, process,
    250–251
speaker panels, framework/
    guidelines, 160–166
storytelling, guidelines, 161
student-driven mental
    health education website
    resources, 260
student-led mental wellness
    clubs, 147–168
suicidal thoughts, website
    resources, 258
talking
    content, 280–281
    decision/person
      identification,
      270–271
    process, 271
    reactions, 271–272
    teacher listening, 229
triggers, 58, 181
videos, framework/guide-
    lines, 160–166
wellness clubs, initiatives/
    ideas, 150–151
Wellness Surveys, 142
    worksheet, 10, 273–274
worksheets, 269
Students (mental health problems),
    appearance (increase), 1

Student suicide
    bullying, impact/prevalence
        (myth), 66–67
    commemoration/memorialization,
        school policy, 72–79
    conversation (facilitation), scripts
        (usage), 233–238
    counselor, contact, 188–189
    deaths, treatment, 75
    family visitation
        recommendations, 78
    feelings check-in script, 235
    loss
        management (worksheet),
            283–287
        school return, process,
            202–207
    memorial activities/
        support, 238–241
    memorial assemblies,
        avoidance, 78
    memorial events
        family consultation, 78
        parental approval, 75–76
        student ideas,
            sharing, 230–231
    myths, debunking, 57–67
    on-campus erected physical
        memorials funeral-type
        events, avoidance, 75
    online memorial pages, usage, 77
    pain (expression),
        memorialization (usage), 77
    parental contact, results, 178
    parents, informing value
        (myth), 65
    perception, 48–51
    plan (absence), risk (myth), 65–66
    post-suicide attempt/family loss
        reintegration, 197
    postvention, 209
    presentation, guidelines, 162–164
    questions, educator talking
        points, 227–231, 227f

    safety
        educator engagement,
            184–185
        planning, 191
    school confidentiality
        policy, 79–80
    spontaneous memorials, plan
        (creation), 76–77
    struggles, words/
        actions, 182–189
    talking, desire, 173–181
    talking, parental contact
        (example), 176
Substance misuse, 6, 7, 11–12, 34
Substance use disorder, 9, 11–12, 23
Suicidal behavior, definition, 315
Suicidal crisis, 59
    student progress, 247
Suicidal despair, signal (phrases), 51
Suicidal ideation, definition, 315
Suicidal thoughts, 20, 86
    demographic region,
        relationship, 28–29
    episode, example, 21
    high school age kids, 20
    website resources, 258
Suicide
    ACT Steps Signs of Suicide, 101
    adolescent suicide, 19, 22–23
    apps, 282
    assessment, 310
    at-risk student populations,
        23–38
    attempts, 29, 35, 45
        definition, 315–316
        scenario, example, 193–194
        survival/knowledge, myth, 60
        survivor speaker, speech/
            presentation, 163
    behavior, warning sign, 50
    CDC definition, 19
    children, talking (desire), 173–181
    child screening, nonnecessity
        (myth), 62–63

consideration, signs
    (worksheet), 269–272
contagion (copycat suicide),
    37–38, 228, 238, 316
conversation, 219
counseling team, student
    interview, 164
deaths
    aspects, addressing, 214
    disclosure (parent
        permission), asking
        script (worksheet),
        298–300
    post-death email,
        sample, 217–218
    trauma, 210
    treatment, 75
definition, 315
discussion
    impact/myth, 58
    warning sign, 50
downstream tactics, 311
environmental risk factor, 22–23
family
    history, 30
    visitation recommendations,
        78
firearms, access, 29–30
grief, teacher discussion, 230
health risk factor, 23
help-seeking behavior/awareness,
    resources (handouts), 164
historical risk factor, 22
idea, talking (impact), 58
intervention, 169, 310
life transitions, impact, 35–36
loss
    grief support, resources, 281
    student return, 202–207
male/female deaths, 24
means, removal, 181–182
message, Seuss-like scripts
    (worksheet), 301–302
messaging, issues, 162–164

midstream approaches, 310–311
mood, display (warning
    sign), 50–51
non-suicidal self-injury
    (NSSI), 30–31, 60
no-suicide contract, usage
    (myth), 59–60
on-campus erected physical
    memorials funeral-type
    events, avoidance, 75
online memorial pages,
    usage, 77
plan (absence), risk nonexistence
    (myth), 65–66
postvention, 229–232, 310
preventability, absence
    (myth), 64–65
prior attempt, 29
protective factors, 44–45
psychological factors, 29
race/ethnicity factor (youth
    suicide), 26–28
reporting, resources, 257–258
resources, 255
safety
    educator engagement,
        184–185
    planning, 191
school-based class conversations/
    gatherings/support groups,
    elements, 77–78
school confidentiality
    policy, 79–80
    template, 80
screeners, usage, 118
screening questions,
    asking, 117–118
self-injury, relationship, 60–61
selfishness, myth, 59
sexual/gender minority
    vulnerability, 25–26
signs of suicide wallet card, 101f
spontaneous memorials, plan
    (creation), 76–77

Suicide (*Continued*)
  storytelling
    guidelines, 161–164, 165–166
    language, usage, 165
    support, 164–165
    timing, 164
  struggles, words/
    actions, 182–189
  suicide-related books,
    recommendations, 267–268
  suicide-related fact sheets, 257
  suicide-related school-based
    models/toolkits, 255–257
  suicide-related school policies, 69
  teachers, tips (resource), 256
  teenagers
    attention-getting,
      myth, 58–59
    holidays (peak
      time), myth, 66
  text message, example, 39f
  thoughts, coping strategies, 251
  trauma, impact, 31
  upstream strategies, 310
  USA hotlines/crisis lines, 282
  warning signs, 19, 46–48
  whole class-time discussion, focus
    (avoidance), 232
  youth bereavement, educator
    assistance (worksheet),
    279–282
Suicide in Schools (Erbacher/Singer/
  Poland), 268
Suicide in Schools (Singer), 70, 116
Suicide prevention
  artwork, display, 132f
  definition/focus, 309–310
  education, leadership buy-in
    (getting), 119–124
  evidence-based universal school-
    based suicide prevention
    programs, 100

  ideas/concepts, integration,
    129–135
  programs
    categories, 309–310
    customization/adaptation,
      115–116
  protective factors, bolstering
    (creative activities),
    135–146
  school
    activities, 127, 135–146
    policy, 71–72
  three-step suicide prevention
    intervention, 191–192
  true or false quiz (worksheet),
    275–278
  universal school-based suicide
    prevention programs,
    100–109
Suicide Prevention: A Gatekeeper
  Training for School Personnel
  training (Riverside Trauma
  Center), usage, 98–99
Suicide prevention culture
  collaboration, importance,
    92–93
  creation, educator role, 83
  digital learning environment,
    creation, 93–94
  educator/gatekeeper
    training, 96–100
  evidence-based universal school-
    based suicide prevention
    programs, 100
  program/training, selec-
    tion, 94–96
  protocol, example, 118–119
  trainings/program, offer-
    ings, 97–100
Suicide Prevention Month and
  Recovery Month, activities, 150
Suicide Prevention Resource
  Center (SPRC) resources,
  211, 265

Suicide Reporting Recommendations
  (AAS), 258
Suicide risk
  assessment, 190–191
  factors, 19, 22–23, 29, 45, 315
    variation, 44
  gender, relationship, 24
  increase
    chronic illness/disabilities,
      relationship, 33
    grief/loss, impact, 73
    psychosocial factors, 33
Suicide Risk Screening Tool,
  usage, 117–118
Suicidology, website
  recommendations, 258–262
Support for Suicidal Individuals
  on Social and Digital Media
  (National Suicide Prevention
  Lifeline), 209, 257

T

Talk Saves Lives, 96
Teachers
  empathy, display, 229–230
  message, example, 41f
  postvention talking tips,
    229–231
  routine, maintenance, 230
  student trust, example, 176–177
  suicide, postvention, 209
  three-step suicide prevention
    intervention, 191–192
Technology, impact, 2
Teenagers (teens)
  bereavement, 204
  connectedness, 6
  co-occurring disorders, 9
  coping strategies, pursuits, 251
  depression, 8
  family dynamics, challenges,
    32–33

habits, change, 252–253
mental health problems,
  increase, 2–9
mental health treatment,
  barriers, 3
no-suicide contract, usage
  (myth), 59–60
self-defeating cycle, escape
  (process), 249–254
self-harm, reasons, 62
self-injury, suicide relationship
  (myth), 60–62
suicide, 38–44
  attempt, survival/knowledge
    (myth), 60
  attention-getting,
    myth, 58–59
  holidays, peak times
    (myth), 66
  talk, content, 205–207
triggers, 58, 181
worries, list, 5
Teen Mental Health First Aid
  (TMHFA), 110
Texting
  impact, 38–44
  message, example, 39f
TMHFA. See Teen Mental
  Health First Aid
Toodle-oo To Taboo (worksheet),
  303–304
Transgender, definition,
  313–314
Trauma, 1
  historical trauma
    (multigenerational trauma),
    definition, 313
  impact, 31
Traumatic brain injury, 23
Trevor Project, 25, 72, 186, 309
  Connect, Accept, Respond,
    Empower (Trevor Project
    CARE) training, usage,
    99–100

Trevor Project (*Continued*)
  Crisis Line, 26
  LGBTQ youth support,
    90, 152
  resources, 262
Trusted adult, student
  identification, 200
Twitter, posts (example),
  39f–40f

U

Understanding and Addressing
  the Mental Health of
  High School Students
  (JEDFoundation), 256
Universal prevention programs,
  95, 309
Universal school-based suicide
  prevention programs,
  100–109
  resources, 263
US National Suicide Prevention
  Lifeline, 269

V

Virtual learning, student
  struggles/ghosting, 244
Visitation postvention
  recommendations, 216, 298–299
Volunteer day, implementation,
  214

W

Well-being, improvement, 114
Wellness. *See* Mental wellness;
  Mental wellness club
  culture (promotion),
    organizations (impact),
      159–160
  student wellness surveys
    (worksheet), 273–274
Withdrawal/isolation, suicide
  sign, 48, 50
Writing (coping strategy), 236, 251
Wulff, Aurora, 148, 157–158, 251, 297

Y

Youth
  at-risk youth, protective factors
    (bolstering programs), 264–265
  autism, 34–35
  bereavement, educator
    assistance (worksheet),
      279–282
  race/ethnicity suicide factor, 26–28
Youth Behavior Risk Survey
  (YRBSS), 23–24
Youth Mental Health First Aid
  (YMHFA), 110
Youth Motivating Others through
  Voices of Experience (Youth
  MOVE), 160
Youth Wellness Council (YWC)
  (WCClubs), 159